IMPERIALISM

Key Concepts in Critical Theory

Series Editor
Roger S. Gottlieb

Key Concepts in Critical Theory

IMPERIALISM

Theoretical Directions

EDITED BY

Ronald H. Chilcote

Humanity Books

an imprint of Prometheus Books
59 John Glenn Drive, Amherst, New York 14228-2197

Published 2000 by Humanity Books, an imprint of Prometheus Books

Imperialism: Theoretical Directions. Copyright © 2000 Ronald H. Chilcote. All rights reserved. No part of this publication may be reproduced, stored in a retrieval system, or trans- mitted in any form or by any means, digital, electronic, mechanical, photocopying, recording, or otherwise, or conveyed via the Internet or a website without prior written permission of the publisher, except in the case of brief quotations embodied in critical articles and reviews.

Inquiries should be addressed to
Humanity Books
59 John Glenn Drive
Amherst, New York 14228—2197
VOICE: 716—691—0133, ext. 207
FAX: 716—564—2711

04 03 02 01 00   5 4 3 2 1

Library of Congress Cataloging-in-Publication Data

Imperialism : theoretical directions / edited by Ronald Chilcote.
      p. cm. — (Key concepts in critical theory)
   Includes bibliographical references and index.
   ISBN 1—57392—821—6 (alk. paper)
   1. Imperialism. 2. Capitalism. I. Chilcote, Ronald H. II. Series.

JC359 .I474 2000
325'.32'01—dc21   00-022941
                                                                                                    CIP

Printed in the United States of America on acid-free paper

CONTENTS

{5}

PART TWO: IMPERIALISM IN CAPITALIST DEVELOPMENT AND UNDERDEVELOPMENT

The Legacy of Marx

The Legacy of Lenin

PART FOUR: IMPACTS OF IMPERIALISM

Retrospect and Prospect

ACKNOWLEDGMENTS

THIS BOOK HAS EVOLVED THROUGH my years of teaching in both economics and political science. For many years I taught two political science courses on development and underdevelopment, but I was unable to convince my colleagues of the usefulness of a course on imperialism that linked historical issues and debates with the more recent developmental literature. When in 1990 I was welcomed into economics, my colleagues endorsed a graduate seminar on the political economy of imperialism, and in this course the general framework and the selections for this book evolved. It complements an anthology of original essays I have edited for the "Economic Thought Series" by Kluwer Academic Publishers (*The Political Economy of Imperialism: Critical Appraisals* [Boston: Kluwer, 1999]), and it relates to a lengthy chapter in my book, *Theories of Comparative Political Economy* (Boulder: Westview Press, 2000). I am appreciative of the support of colleagues who understood the usefulness of this approach and especially to the students who confronted the material and became sensitive to the issues and debates through weekly discussion and position papers and whose comprehension in turn led to some modest theoretical breakthroughs. I also would like to thank Elvia Ramirez, a graduate student in sociology at the University of California, Riverside, for her assistance in the initial phase of organizing this volume, scanning material on computer, and contacts to obtain reprint permissions. It was the dedicated efforts of Krista Eissfeldt, a graduating senior at UCR and presently a graduate student at Indiana University, who ultimately brought this project to rest. Her contribution was impressive and included scanning and editing material on computer, reducing the length of various selections to manageable size, contacting publishers, and pulling the disparate selections together into the final draft. I should also like to thank Keith Ashfield for his encouragement of this project and ensuring it through publication. Finally, I acknowledge the modest financial support of the Research Committee of the UCR Academic Senate.

Ronald H. Chilcote

INTRODUCTION

Ronald H. Chilcote

A FUNDAMENTAL PREMISE UNDERLIES THIS volume and helps us to understand its purpose: capitalism, and its evolving forms and consolidation, is at the root of, and indeed links theories with, questions of imperialism and development. Theories and ideas about imperialism emerged largely during the late nineteenth and early twentieth centuries and focused critically on the impact of imperialism as a manifestation of advanced capitalism or monopoly as a high stage of the capitalist order. Theories and ideas about development emanating from the advanced capitalist centers traditionally tended to promote the prospects for growth and progress, together with the assumption that these positive trends could be diffused to the less developed and poorer nations of the world. After the Second World War and with the fall of empires and the imperial schemes of England, France, Portugal, and other European countries, the newly emerging nations of Africa, Asia, and Latin America began to question diffusionist and capitalist development. Their criticism drew from the literature of imperialism in the search for understanding about their poverty, exploitation, and lack of development. The links between explanations of imperialism and underdevelopment were not always clear, and indeed after 1945, intellectuals worked hard at promoting new alternative ideas and theories.

In his analysis of capitalism, Karl Marx focused on the logic of the capitalist system, drawing largely upon the European experience, especially in England. He worked out the conceptualization of capitalism in terms of accumulation, commodification, circulation and production, maximization of profit, and so on. In the *Communist Manifesto*, Marx, along with Friedrich Engels, also envisaged capitalism as permeating throughout the world, and they devoted some attention to the possibilities and consequences of capitalism spreading beyond Europe.

Their successors often looked at situations where capitalism scarcely existed. In making the point that capitalism is not uniquely universal throughout history and even today, Ellen Meiksins Wood reminds us that "every major development of Marxism in the twentieth century has been less about capitalism than about what is *not* capitalist" (see p. 122 in this volume). The classical writers of imperialism wrote about the exploitation of the noncapitalist world. The contemporary writers of underdevelopment and dependency also dwell on social formations outside the capitalist world. For both classical and contemporary writers, their theories of capitalism are founded on the experience of the noncapitalist or precapitalist world. The former tend to emphasize external dimensions of international production and trade, the latter attempt to direct attention to internal aspects. Sometimes their offerings were polemical rather than substantive and theoretical, but the language of their discourse, whether worked around imperialism or developmental questions, became synonymous with capitalism. Once "imperialism" was perceived as polemical, political economists turned to "development," often obscuring attention to fundamental issues of capitalism.

During the 1990s the language assimilated the term "globalization" to express the pervasive and expansive world economy, but fundamentally the principal concern was with capitalism and its impact. Whether we examine transnational or multinational corporations, the international political economy, or finance capital, it is important to recognize that the world economy and the global system are inherently capitalist, and have been so at least since Marx's time. As William Tabb reminds us in the present volume: "It's capitalism, not globalization" (see p. 320 in this volume).

Even occasional enclaves or deviations from the evolving capitalism could not really be seriously considered as delinked from the capitalist world. For example, Samir Amin astutely emphasized in his *Accumulation on a World Scale* that the so-called socialisms (communisms) of the former Soviet Union and Eastern Europe were largely dependent upon and integrated in the capitalist world. Thus, while capitalism today appears more pervasive than ever, it continues as in the past to influence the international arena.

This mystification of language obscures real issues around capitalism and imperialism, another reason why this volume seeks to place various perspectives into a long-range historical context. Prabhat Patnaik (1990) herein questions whatever happened to imperialism since the 1960s and early 1970s when it was directly associated with Marxist debates around the Vietnam War. What is to explain the silence over imperialism in the invasions of Grenada or Panama or in the counterinsurgency wars in El Salvador and Nicaragua? All the more mysterious for Patnaik is the "deafening silence about imperialism in the current Marxist discourse, especially in the United States,...thus a reflection of the extraordinary strength and vigor it is displaying at present" (see p. 313 in this volume).

LINKS BETWEEN IMPERIALISM AND DEVELOPMENT THEORY

Historical considerations lend support to our initial premise linking ideas and theories of imperialism with those of development. In general, these ideas and theories emanate from the past, but they tend to be reiterated and recycled in contemporary times. Early on, Giovanni Arrighi (1977 and 1983) explored the limits and ambiguities of the imperialist paradigm in thought of J. A. Hobson and attempted to reconstruct the term through an examination of Lenin. Later (1994) he examined the rise and decline of dominant states over the past seven hundred years, drawing on the proposition that finance capital is not necessarily a particular stage of world capitalism, as Franz Hilferding, Lenin, and others had claimed, but that it is in fact an ever persistent and recurring phenomenon that has characterized capitalism from its beginnings in medieval times to its role in contemporary times. Rather than confining his analysis to the more traditional conceptualization of the twentieth century, Arrighi recasts his historical overview to incorporate an historical analysis of the strategies and successes and declines of Genoa, Holland, Britain, and the United States.

As a first historical consideration, the effort to identify historical stages is suggestive. Traditionally the "old" meaning of imperialism was related to mercantile capitalism and the early phase of industrial capitalism. Harry Magdoff (1969 and 1978) divided it into three periods: from the late 1400s to the mid 1600s, an era when Europe exploited the resources of newly discovered regions; 1650 to 1770, a period of slave labor and search for commodities on behalf of the leading European powers; and 1770 to about 1870 when England turned to Africa and Asia after losing its American colonies. The old meaning, however, was eclipsed by an understanding of the "new" imperialism at the time of intense rivalry among advanced European nations in the scramble for Africa at the end of the nineteenth century. The new imperialism signified a shift from dominance over trade to control of industrial transformation associated with the industrial revolution and the push of Europe toward manufacturing which necessitated extraction of raw materials in the periphery and expansion of the world market. The early phase of the new imperialism involved primarily Great Britain and eventually the United States as dominant powers. A later phase, at the end of the Second World War, was signified by the rise of transnational and multinational corporations whose influence extended beyond the national borders of the dominant nations.

This periodization of imperialism compares similarly to the historical forms of dependency outlined by Theotônio dos Santos in chapter 23 in this volume. The first was colonial dependency in which trade monopolies were established over the land, mines, and labor of colonial societies. The second was financial industrial dependency, which accompanied the period of imperialism at the end of the nineteenth century and allowed the domination of big capital in the hegemonic centers and its expansion abroad. Finally, a new type of dependency appeared after the Second World War when capital investment by multinational corporations and industry turned to the internal markets of underdeveloped countries. Dos Santos describes this new dependency as conditioned by the relationship of dominant to dependent countries so that the expansion of the dominant country could have a positive or negative impact on the development of the dependent one.

A second historical consideration is the structural similarity within imperialist and development theory. In both types of theory structure is apparent in dichotomies: geographical (core and periphery), political (metropole and satellite), and economic (development and underdevelopment). The characterization of metropole and satellite Is rampant in the early literature on colonialism and imperialism, with colony usually substituted for satellite as terminology. This language is in Hobson, Lenin, and most writers of imperialism, and it was picked up by André Gunder Frank in his thesis on capitalist development of underdevelopment (see chapter 14 in this volume). The thesis may have some connection with Rosa Luxemburg's attention to the impact of capital accumulation and imperialism on primitive and noncapitalist economies (see chapter 6 in this volume), but clearly it derived from Paul Baran who in turn influenced Latin American intellectuals and others to elaborate on what he called the "morphology" of backwardness (see chapter 18 in this volume). Baran concluded that "the colonial and dependent countries had no recourse to such sources of primary accumulation of capital as were available to the advanced capitalist countries" and that "development in the age of monopoly capitalism and imperialism faced obstacles that had little in common with those encountered two or three hundred years ago" (1957, p. 16). This was then explored extensively in a series of regional studies by Frank (1967, chapter 19), Malcolm Caldwell (1977, chapter 21), and Manning Marable (1983, chapter 22). Frank argued that the contradictions of capitalism led to the expropriation of economic surplus which generated development in the metropolitan centers and underdevelopment in the peripheral satellites.

These structural distinctions incorporated an external-internal dimension in the sense that emphasis among the Latin American intellectuals turned from the traditional preoccupation with imperialism to concern with capitalism upon internal development and underdevelopment and the relationship to class and state forces within nations (see my *Theories of Development and Underdevelopment*, 1984, for a full analysis of this trend). For example, the Mexican political sociologist Pablo González Casanova worked out a theory of internal colonialism (1969), viewed as a relationship similar to the colonial ties between nations and substituting the terms metropole and satellite for center and periphery. Internal colonialism involved dominant and marginal groups within a single society. His theory discounted external imperialism because Mexico had asserted its autonomy from foreign control with the nationalization of foreign oil interests in 1938. Domination of capital was evident internally, however, as represented by the monopoly of the ruling "metropole" in Mexico City over the marginalized Indian communities. The underdevelopment of the marginal "satellites" was the consequence of their exploitation by and dependence on the developing metropole. During the 1960s and 1970s this idea was also applied by U.S. scholars to backward conditions in North American ghettos and barrios.

Other examples of structural dichotomies evolved within Latin America. During the 1940s, three Argentine theorists set forth important thinking. The colonial historian Sergio Bagú developed his ideas lecturing in the United States from 1944 to 1946. He emphasized that Europe dominated international markets and shaped the structure of colonial economics in a dependent relationship. In 1947, law professor Silvio Frondizi began to focus on dependency and underdevelopment in elaborating the impact on Argentina of two imperialisms, British commercial imperialism and U.S. industrial imperialism. Around 1949, economist Raúl Prebisch was one of the first to turn attention from the advanced capitalist nations and to divide the world into a center and periphery. His approach is usually referred to as inward-directed development, suggesting the possibility of autonomous or domestic capitalist development through the imposition of tariff barriers, building of an infrastructure for the local economy, and import substitution to stimulate production.

A third historical consideration arises from the plethora of literature concerned with unequal or uneven development. Samir Amin, who had envisaged (1974) the world as comprised of developed and underdeveloped societies, some of which were capitalist and others socialist, lumped all of them into a commercial and financial capitalist network on a worldscale. Later (1976) he analyzed unequal development in terms of disarticulation of different sectors of an economy, domination from the outside, and dependence caused by large foreign industrial business. Other writers included Arghiri Emmanuel (1972), whose theory of unequal exchange portrays capitalist production relations as penetrating a world economy whose units are distinguished by differences in specialization in the international division of labor and by unequal wage levels (see chapter 6 in this volume). Followers of Leon Trotsky delineated a theory of combined and uneven development, arguing that the most backward and the most modern forms of economic activity and exploitation are found in variable forms in different countries, but that they may also be linked or combined in their development, especially under the impact of imperialism. A combined and uneven social formation is evident in the period of transition from a precapitalist to a full capitalist economy so that elements of feudalism and capitalism might coexist. Ernest Mandel, for example, presented a theory of late capitalism based on the consequence of an integrated international system necessitating the transfer of surplus from underdeveloped to industrialized regions, thereby delaying the development of the former.

Finally, all these currents incorporate some form of center and periphery in their theoretical formulations. All of them stress the impact of market and relations of exchange rather than production, and most of them assume that capitalism rather than feudalism or other precapitalist social formations have predominated in the periphery since the colonial period. Some like Prebisch advocate a reformist approach along the capitalist road, while others like Frank favor a revolutionary path and eventual implantation of socialism. Usually they were distinguishable by their allegiances, either to a peaceful path through reformist capitalism or to a revolutionary path toward socialism. Another difference appeared in writings arguing that lack of development was attributable to underconsumptionism, an idea emanating early on in Hobson and emulated in many writings focused on market and commercial considerations, for example Frank in his reliance upon mercantile capitalism to demonstrate its underdevelopment of peripheral areas. Baran and Sweezy, among other thinkers, often have been accused of assimilating underconsumption into their argument (Brenner, 1977). Those advocating a revolutionary path also tended to replicate past debates based on idealistic assumptions that projected the possibility of skipping the capitalist stage altogether en route to socialism (for example, the Russian Narodniks during the late nineteenth century—see the critique of Carlos Johnson, 1981).

ORGANIZATION AND OBJECTIVES

The central thesis that capitalism is at the root of imperialism and development theory serves as the basis for the selections in this volume. Part One, Capitalism and Imperialism, is divided into two sections. The first section provides a conceptualization of imperialism in the context

of capitalism, initially through a typology of understandings, drawn
from George Lichtheim and definition and limits of imperialism elaborated by Paul Sweezy (the reader may wish to consult Brown, 1974;
Cohen, 1973; and Fieldhouse, 1967 for attempts at conceptualization). The
second section draws on a variety of perspectives, including the now-
classical early formulations of the English liberal J. A. Hobson, who
emphasizes underconsumptionism as an explanation; the Austrian
Marxist Rudolf Hilferding, who elaborates on finance capital; the
Russian Marxist theorist, Nikolai Bukharin, who links accumulation to
world capitalism; the Russian Marxist, V. I. Lenin, who stresses monopoly
capital; Rosa Luxemburg, who analyzes accumulation in the hinterland;
and Joseph Schumpeter, who envisages the withering away of imperialism with the advance of industrial capitalism. All these thinkers were
anti-imperialist, but they differed in their views of capitalism and
socialism. Both Hobson and Schumpeter envisage the containment and
eventual eroding of imperialism through either a reform of or the natural evolution of the capitalist system, whereas the others employ an
analysis critical of capitalism and favoring a socialist outcome as a means
of eradicating imperialism altogether. Excerpts from the extensive writings of all these thinkers serve to show the reader different lines of
political thinking around imperialism and the affinity of imperialism to
capitalism itself. Returning to these early and traditional understandings, the reader can adequately cope with contemporary understandings
of imperialism and further begin to note how the early debates on
imperialism frequently reflect contemporary debates on developmental
questions and issues.

Part Two, Imperialism in Capitalist Development and Underdevelopment, focuses on the relationship of imperialist theory to contemporary views of development and underdevelopment. The first section in
Part Two begins with Marx's insights and comprehension of capitalism
in its progressive manifestations in the European experience and in its
negative consequences in the form of primitive accumulation in the
non-European world. Ellen Meiksins Wood and Enrique Dussel appeal
for a return to Marx, both as a means of comprehending his approach
and also as a method of analysis and for examining how he viewed capitalist society.

What is considered Marxism today, of course, is in large measure premised on the thought of Marx. The scope of his thought was extensive and has been synthesized into five fundamental proponents: a philosophical approach based on dialectical, materialist, and humanistic reality; a theory of history based on the evolution of society, interdisciplinary inquiry, with a centrality on class struggle in human experience; analysis of capitalism; a political program for the working class; and a vision of a socialist future (Le Blanc, 1996, pp. 6–9). Of particular concern to our focus on imperialism would be the analysis of capitalism, especially a definition based on capitalism as an economy that is privately owned by a minority of owners of the means of production who make use of the labor power of the working class and accumulate through the extraction of surplus labor. Shlomo Avineri has extended this analysis to the world outside Europe in an effort to understand how Marx appears to provide us with an early understanding of imperialism through primitive accumulation, as capitalism diffuses into less developed areas. This theme is reinforced by Bill Warren who advocates an aggressive imperialism as the means of destroying precapitalist social formations and ushering in a progressive capitalism. In contrast, Kenzo Mohri compares this progressive capitalism in Marx (using India as an example of how British imperialism sweeps away the old social formations) with how the negative impact can be confronted by autonomy and self-sufficiency (for example, Ireland achieved autonomy through tariffs and protection in resistance to British capitalist domination and penetration).

The second section of Part Two examines the early roots of a theory in Lenin to uncover his comprehension of uneven development in a backward country. Lenin's elaboration of a theory of imperialism, for example, is seen by Terrence McDonough as a way out of a theoretical crisis in Marxism early in the twentieth century. Here imperialism arises as a new stage in a series of stages in capitalist development (see Willoughby, 1995, for a critical appraisal). In general, contemporary development specialists do not go back to Marx and Lenin to link contemporary theory with classical foundations, an exception being the work of Gabriel Palma who returned to Lenin's analysis of a delayed Russian development at the turn of the century and noted his contribution to an understanding of varying modes of production in the transition to capitalism.

The selections in Part Three build on the earlier theoretical contri-

butions of the classical thinkers, link imperialism to the underdevelop-
mental literature, and identify and trace the evolution of development-
underdevelopment theory after the Second World War. In an overview,
Anthony Brewer effectively illustrates these themes through a look at
the ideas and contributions of particular Marxist thinkers, including
Marx, Luxemburg, Hobson, Hilferding, Bukharin, and Lenin, among the
classical thinkers, and Baran, Frank, Amin, Wallerstein, Emmanuel, and
Rey, among contemporary thinkers. Jorge Larraín (1989) connects this
theory to colonialism. A selection from Paul Baran reflects one of the
very early conceptualizations of backwardness which also links to earlier ideas on imperialism and serves as a foundation for critical assess-
ments of capitalist development and its negative consequences for the
Third World. André Gunder Frank elaborated on this thesis of capitalist
development of underdevelopment, applied it to case studies in Latin
America, and influenced Manning Marable's analysis of its implications
for Black America. This part also includes selections on this theme by
Amílcar Cabral and by Malcolm Caldwell on the Third World in general and Asia in particular.

These writings are a backdrop for an array of theoretical selections
about the dependency of less developed or backward situations in the
Third World: conceptualization of the new dependency by Theotônio
dos Santos, the idea of subimperialism by Ruy Mauro Marini, the advo-
cacy of associated dependent capitalist development by Fernando Henrique Cardoso, unequal exchange by Arghiri Emmanuel, and combined
and uneven development by Ernest Mandel.

Part Four reminds us that some of these presumably dated theories
and concerns remain current and relevant today. Theories and concepts
may be cloaked in new terminology or even obscured to confuse readers
with the new discourses that distract from the real problems of the contemporary world. Whatever our concern about imperialism, it must be
understood as a manifestation of capitalism.

Among the many contributions of past theory, first, is the tendency
to focus on conditions of backwardness, inequality, exploitation, and
underdevelopment in early studies and to challenge traditional conservative and radical interpretations by emphasizing the role of capitalism
rather than relying upon and interpretation of feudalism and dual
society (Stern, 1988). Second, theory benefited from innovative ques-

tioning of late capitalism and the problems of development and under-development, examples being Baran and the question of surplus and backwardness, Frank and the thesis of capitalist underdevelopment, Dos Santos and the new dependency, Cardoso and dependent development, and Marini and subimperialism. Third, the concern with imperialism and attention on capital accumulation, international capital, and the hegemony of the international capitalist system has revealed different paths to capitalism and socialism and has led to empirical studies based on a theory of capitalism in the periphery. Fourth, rather than any single unified theory, a variety of theoretical trends is discernible. Fifth, the dependency idea can be understood as a reflection of competitive capitalism and its idealistic projection of outcome based on utopian socialism, seen as a recycling of nineteenth century; ideas drawn from import substitution and development conditioned on capitalist autonomy (Prebisch); and revolutionary assumptions that lead to a socialist stage (Baran, Frank, Marini). Finally, the developmental litera-ture has tended to neglect traditional relevant Marxist theory on Ire-land and India, on Marxist method, on Lenin and Russia, and on Trotsky and the theory of combined and uneven development.

THE DIVERSITY OF THEORY AND DICHOTOMIES

Thus far the discussion has emphasized links between imperialism and development theories, at the same time noting similarity in their struc-tural approach and incorporation of center (metropole) and periphery (satellite) in their formulation. Although this center-periphery dichoto-my permeates all the theories, no unified theory prevails, but significant advances in theory are clearly evident. The sketch below identifies some of the more prominent contributions and shows their tendency to assimilate into structural dichotomies and to work dialectically in con-testing ways.

Domestic Context	*International Context*
State Theory (state versus civil society)	World System Theory (core, semi-periphery, periphery)
Modes of Production Theory (agrarian question and transition to capitalism)	Internationalization of Capital Theory (national versus international)
Market Theory (market versus central planning)	Imperialism Theory (imperialist versus autonomous)
Class Struggle Theory (ruling versus exploited)	
Democracy Theory (representative versus participatory)	

These theoretical currents appear to stand in contrasting relationships (international and domestic) familiar to center and periphery theory. Although it might be useful to employ them in juxtaposition, a close look reveals their complexity and the difficulty of combining, for example, the internal peripheral thrust of modes of production theory and the external orientations of imperialism or internationalization of capital theory. A closer examination of these two theories may be helpful.

Development is largely determined by the level of the forces of production—the capital and technology, labor skill, and efficiency attained by society. Capital accumulation and reproduction are essential for the maintenance and expansion of capitalism (Rey, 1973). Crucial in promoting the forces of production, especially in the Third World, is whether capitalism itself must be strengthened en route to socialism or the capitalist stage skipped altogether. Amin (1976) identified precapitalist modes, including the communal mode, the tribute-paying mode, the feudal mode, and the slave-owning mode of production. This approach sometimes is deterministic in its reliance upon successive stages of development or limited by its reliance on predetermined modes that may not appear in some societies at particular historical periods (see Foster-Carter, 1978).

Theories of imperialism were posited by J. A. Hobson (who utilized an underconsumption theory), Rudolf Hilferding (finance capital), and N. Bukharin and Lenin (monopoly capital). Contemporary analyses by Baran and Sweezy (1966) emphasize the advanced character of capitalism, especially in its monopoly form and its impact on colonial and less developed areas, while Palma (1978) carefully examined Lenin's thought for the roots of a theory of underdevelopment. These writers showed the negative consequences of the imperialist advance, yet some on the left, for example Warren (1980), have attempted to demonstrate that imperialism tends to destroy precapitalist social formations and provides for capitalist development everywhere.

In an effort to move beyond imperialist and dependency explanations of capitalist underdevelopment or associated capitalist development, Becker et al. (1987) argued that global institutions tend to promote the integration of diverse national interests on a new international basis by offering access to capital resources and technologies; this necessitates the location of both foreign labor and management in the dependent country as well as local participation in the ownership of the corporation. In such a situation two segments of a new social class appear: privileged nationals or a managerial bourgeoisie and the foreign nationals who manage the businesses and transnational organizations. This coalescing of dominant class elements across national boundaries suggests the rise of an international oligarchy. A theory of postimperialism serves as an alternative to a determinist Leninist understanding of imperialism and to dependency orthodoxy, according to Becker. However, international capital has dominated Third World situations, and there is little evidence to affirm that a managerial national bourgeoisie will emerge as hegemonic and other classes will decline nor that the national bourgeoisie will favor democracy or authoritarianism.

A theory of internationalization of capital, however, may permit an analysis of the movement of capital and class struggle on an international level, particularly the foreign investments and capital accumulation by capitalist enterprises of the center which operate in the developing countries and the rapid growth in the internationalization of other forms of capital such as private and public export credits, bank loans, and commodity exports (elaborated by Hymer, 1972, and Palloix, 1977).

Both modes of production and internationalization of capital theories intend to transcend the traditional imperialist and development literature. The developmental writings in particular have tended to look at conditions of exploitation, poverty, and inequality; stress exchange, circulation, and trade rather than production and relations of production; ignore past relevant Marxist theory; usually overlook issues around the role of the state and class and planned economy or market mechanisms; emphasize capitalist accumulation and its consequences; sometimes provide concrete analysis of the socialist transition; and project idealistic and inevitable outcomes without concrete analysis.

Some of these problems are due to conceptual difficulties. First, there is the inclination to cast aside old conceptualizations without recognizing their potential utility. Political scientists emphasize the "political" dimension and usually focus on policy rather than theory, economists tend to ignore the political side and also lean toward policy considerations in the direction of capitalism. Second, the term Third World has been used to refer to a geographical area, to the nonaligned nations, or to the less developed part of the world. It has been given differing connotations by leaders such as Mao and Nkrumah. Its most important connotation implies a condition related to exploitation and oppression and backwardness, a condition appearing not only in backward parts of the world but even in advanced areas in the industrial world. Thus, assumptions that the less developed nations have been assimilated into the capitalist world or that the socialist world has disappeared may be misleading. Third, dependency was a term used by Latin Americans to lead them to a more concrete analysis of internal structural conditions that were a reflection of external circumstances. They moved away from polemics on imperialism. Brewer (1990), however, turns this discourse on its head and looks at these old theories and ideas of underdevelopment and dependency in terms of theories of imperialism. Dependency ideas were aimed against diffusion theory and the stereotyped stage theory of the right (Rostow) and of the Stalinist Communist parties. Dependency was viewed, however, in terms of its negative (Frank) and positive (Cardoso) oriented theory.

Further, in the industrialized nations, development has been miscast as political or representative democracy with an emphasis on Western-styled government institutions and political parties, thereby diverting attention from capital accumulation and capitalism and the consequences (negative and progressive) for people (see Moore, 1995). This problem could be corrected by shifting analysis from parties to the structure of the state and its institutional forces as well as class forces. Democracy also is used in its formal sense, implying representative and indirect forms of political involvement, yet there is need to transcend this conception and to examine participatory democracy in its political, social, and economic implications.

Finally, the new international order needs to be cast aside as a nomenclature for the old order (which is really the advancing, consolidating international capitalist order). Theories of imperialism and the internationalization of capital may be helpful and can be combined with analysis of internal structure to look at the international capitalist system and its consolidation, globalization and global markets, international capital investment in productive activities, and labor which can be examined in an international context.

All these concepts, once qualified in these ways, may continue to be useful in our analyses, but they should not be projected as correct or definitive or unified theories. They could constitute the elements of an approach toward a study of imperialism and the international capitalist order or system, its reorganization and consolidation, its negative and positive consequences, and the prospects for advance to transcend capitalism in its political, social, economic, and ecological dimensions. There is need at this level to combine analysis of the international capitalist system with analysis of internal aspects, including state and class as well as examination of the mode of production in city and countryside.

The policy implications of the early theory of imperialism as well as dependency and underdevelopment usually suggested revolution and socialism as responses to capitalism and autonomy. With counter insurgency by the United States during the sixties as a means of confronting the influences of the Cuban Revolution in Latin America and the Third World and the death of Che Guevara in 1967, policy considerations in the West turned to other strategies under the authoritarian regimes, and the idea of associated dependent capitalism emerged. The cooptation implied in the combination of state, domestic bourgeoisie, and international capital undermined the possibilities for broad coalition movements.

We need to focus on capital accumulation and its impact on city and countryside. Discourse on current policy lacks debate and revolves around capitalism as an economic outcome and parliamentary democracy as a political form. This tends to obscure attention on real social and economic problems and to avoid a critique of capitalism itself and its weaknesses. It also interferes with the advance toward socialism; thus the discourse turns to postforms of society in order to reach idealistically toward some form of society that will not have to confront the realities of the capitalist world. This suggests that there will also be rethinking around questions of socialism and Marxism, and that analysis will evolve …that deals more directly with these problems both theoretically and in terms of strategies designed to change the world order.

Finally, the structural dichotomy which underlies themes of dependency, underdevelopment, and development will serve future analysis as they have benefited past understanding dating to the nineteenth century. Voices of the Third World continue to focus on this fact, as Brazilian journalist Moacir Werneck de Castro reminded us recently:

> In our periphery, it is sometimes difficult to accompany what takes place in the strategy laboratories of the countries of the center....Cruelty is part of the strategic concepts elaborated by the "philosophy" of the rich countries. Our President [Cardoso] can articulate such concepts in the public arena, but it is unacceptable for a great country like Brazil to adopt them uncritically as legal guidelines just because they are formulated in supersophisticated laboratories....Must we permit a holocaust of the divinities of modernization simply because we live in an era of computer technology? (Castro, 1995)

Although they will not stand as polished unified theory, the imperialism and dependency ideas may help in understanding unequal development in an evolving consolidation of international capital on the world order; they may stimulate awareness of problems associated with delayed capitalist development and lead to theoretical and practical thinking on ways for deprived peoples to relate to and resist oppressive manifestations of capitalism and search for transitions to democracy and socialism.

REFERENCES

Amin, Samir. 1974. *Accumulation on a World Scale: A Critique of the Theory of Underdevelopment.* 2 vols. New York: Monthly Review Press.

———. 1976. *Unequal Development.* New York: Monthly Review Press.

Arrighi, Giovanni. 1978 and 1983. *The Geometry of Imperialism: The Limits of Hobson's Paradigm.* London: Verso.

———. 1994. *The Long Twentieth Century: Money, Power, and the Origins of Our Times.* London and New York. Verso.

Avineri, Shlomo. 1969. *Karl Marx on Colonialism and Modernization.* New York: Anchor Books.

Baran, Paul A. 1957. *The Political Economy of Growth.* New York: Monthly Review Press.

Baran, Paul A., and Paul W. Sweezy. 1996. *Monopoly Capital: An Essay on the American Economic and Social Order.* New York: Monthly Review Press.

Becker, David G., et al. 1987. *Postimperialism, International Capitalism, and Development in the Twentieth Century.* Boulder: Lynne Rienner.

Brenner, Robert. 1977. "The Origins of Capitalist Development: A Critique of Neo-Smithian Marxism," *New Left Review* 104 (July–August): 25–92

Brewer, Brewer. 1990. *Marxist Theories of Imperialism: A Critical Survey.* 2d ed. London and New York: Routledge.

Brown, Michael Barratt. 1974. *The Economics of Imperialism.* Baltimore: Penguin.

Bukharin, Nikolai. 1973. *Imperialism and World Economy.* New York: Monthly Review Press.

Cabral, Amílcar. 1979. "The Weapon of Theory." In *Unity and Struggle: Speeches and Writings of Amílcar Cabral.* New York: Monthly Review Press, pp 130–34.

Caldwell, Malcolm. *The Wealth of Some Nations.* London: Zed Press.

Cardoso, Fernando Henrique. 1792. "Dependency and Development in Latin America," *New Left Review* 74 (July–August): 83–95. See also his "Associated-Dependent Development: Theoretical and Practical Implications." In *Authoritarian Brazil: Origins, Policies, and Future,* edited by Alfred Stepan. New Haven: Yale University Press, 1973, pp. 142–76.

Castro, Moacir Werneck de. 1995. "'Sorry', Periferia," *Jornal do Brasil* (July 8).

Chilcote, Ronald H. 1984. *Theories of Development and Underdevelopment.* Boulder: Westview Press.

———. 1991. *Amílcar Cabral's Revolutionary Theory and Practice.* Boulder: Lynne Rienner Publishers.

Cohen, Banjamin J. 1973. *The Question of Imperialism: The Political Economy of Dominance and Dependence.* New York: Basic Books.

Dussel, Enrique. 1990. "Marx's Economic Manuscripts of 1861–63 and the 'Concept' of Dependency." *Latin American Perspectives* 17 (spring): 62–101.

Emmanuel, Arghiri. 1972. *Unequal Exchange: A Study of the Imperialism of Trade.* New York: Monthly Review Press, 1972.

Fieldhouse, D.K. 1961. "Imperialism: An Historiograpahical Revision." *The Economic History Review*, Second Series 14, no. 2.

Foster-Carter, Alden. 1978. "The Modes of Production Controversy." *New Left Review* 107 (January–February): 47–77.

Frank, André Gunder. 1966. "The Development of Underdevelopment." *Monthly Review* (September): 17–31. Also published in Robert I. Rhodes, *Imperialism and Underdevelopment: A Reader.* New York: Monthly Review Press, 1970, pp. 4–17.

–––––. 1967. *Capitalism and Underdevelopment in Latin America.* New York: Monthly Review Press.

González Casanova, Pablo. 1961. "Internal Colonialism and National Development." In *Latin American Radicalism*, edited by Irving Louis Horowitz et al. New York: Vintage Books, pp. 118–39.

Griffin, Keith, and John Gurley. 1985. "Radical Analyses of Imperialism, the Third World, and the Transition to Socialism: A Survey Article." *Journal of Economic Literature* 23 (September): 1089–1143.

Hilferding, Rudolf. 1981. *Finance Capital: A Study of the Latest Phase of Capitalist Development.* London: Routledge & Kegan Paul.

Hobson, J.A. 1965. *Imperialism: A Study.* Ann Arbor: University of Michigan Press.

Johnson, Carl. 1981. "Dependency Theory and Processes of Capitalism and Socialism." *Latin American Perspectives* 8 (summer–fall): 55–81.

Hymer, Stephen. 1972. "The Internationalization of Capital." *Journal of Economic Issues* 6, no. 1: 91–110.

Larraín, Jorge. 1989. *Theories of Development: Capitalism, Colonialism, and Dependency.* London: Polity Press.

Le Blanc, Paul, ed. 1996. *From Marx to Gramsci: A Reader in Revolutionary Marxist Politics.* Amherst, N.Y.: Humanity Books.

Lenin, V.I. 1899. *History of Capitalism in Russia.* Moscow: Foreign Languages Publishing House, 1956.

–––––. 1967. *Imperialism, the Highest Stage of Capitalism: A Popular Outline.* From V.I. Lenin, *Selected Works.* Vol. I. Originally published in 1917.

Lichtheim, George. 1971. *Imperialism.* New York: Praeger Publishers, 1971.

Luxemburg, Rosa. 1964. *The Accumulation of Capital.* New York: Monthly Review Press.

Magdoff, Harry. 1969. *The Age of Imperialism: The Economics of U.S. Foreign Policy.* Monthly Review Press.

Mandel, Ernest. 1970. "The Laws of Uneven Development." *New Left Review* 59 (January–February): 19–38.

———. 1975. *Late Capitalism.* London: NLB.

Marable, Manning. 1983. *How Capitalism Underdeveloped Black America.* Boston: South End Press.

Marini, Ruy Mauro. 1978. "World Capitalist Accumulation and Sub-Imperialism." *Two Thirds* 1 (fall): 29–39.

Marx, Karl. 1967. *Capital.* Vol. 1. New York: International Publishers.

McDonough, Terrence. 1995. "Lenin, Imperialism, and the Stages of Capitalist Development." *Science and Society* 59 (fall): 339–40, 346–67.

Mohri, Kenzo. 1989. "Marx an Underdevelopment." *Monthly Review* 41 (October): 1–17.

Moore, David B., and Gerald J. Schmitz, eds. 1995. *Debating Development Discourse: Institutional and Popular Perspectives.* New York and London: St. Martin's Press and Macmillan Press. See particularly, the essay by Moore, "Developmental Discourse as Hegemony: Towards an Ideological History, 1945–1995," pp. 1–53.

Palma, Gabriel. 1978. "Dependency: a Formal Theory of Underdevelopment or a Methodology for the Analysis of Concrete Situations of Underdevelopment?" *World Development* 6: 881–924.

Palloix, Christian. 1977. "The Self-Expansion of Capital on a World Scale." *Review of Radical Political Economy* 9 (summer): 1–28.

Patnaik, Prabhat. 1995. *Whatever Happened to Imperialism and Other Essays.* New Delhi: Tolika, pp. 102–104. Originally published in *Monthly Review* 42 (1990).

Rey, Pierre-Philippe. 1973. *Les alliances de classes.* Paris: Maspero.

Santos, Theotônio dos. 1970. "The Structure of Dependence," *American Economic Review* 60 (May): 231–36.

Schumpeter, Joseph. *Social Classes: Imperialism.* Cleveland and New York: Meridian Press, 1955,

Stern, Steve J. 1988. "Feudalism, Capitalism, and the World-System in the Perspective of Latin America and the Caribbean," *American Historical Review* 93 (October): 211–22.

Sweezy, Paul. 1942. *The Theory of Capitalist Development: The Principles of Marxian Political Economy.* New York: Monthly Review Press.

Tabb, William K. 1997. "Globalization Is an Issue, the Power of Capital Is the Issue," *Monthly Review* 49 (June): 20–30.

Warren, Bill. 1980. *Imperialism: Pioneer of Capitalism.* London: NLB.

Willoughby, John. 1995. "Evaluating the Leninist Theory of Imperialism," *Science and Society* 59 (fall), 320–33.

Wood, Ellen Meiksins. 1997. "Back to Marx." *Monthly Review* 49 (June): 1–9.

PART ONE

CAPITALISM AND IMPERIALISM

CONCEPTUALIZATION
AND
OVERVIEW

1

THE LIMITS OF IMPERIALISM

Paul Sweezy

In his now classic The Theory of Capitalist Development *(1942), Paul M. Sweezy included a chapter on imperialism which is reproduced in part below. He draws a definition from Lenin, relates imperialism to classes and the state, and identifies the limits to imperialism.*

IMPERIALISM MAY BE DEFINED AS a stage in the development of world economy in which (a) several advanced capitalist countries stand on a competitive footing with respect to the world market for industrial products, (b) monopoly capital is the dominant form of capital, and (c) the contradictions of the accumulation process have reached such maturity that capital export is an outstanding feature of world economic relations. As a consequence of these basic economic conditions, we have two further characteristics: (d) severe rivalry in the world market leading alternately to cutthroat competition and international monopoly combines, and (e) the territorial division of "unoccupied" parts of the world among the major capitalist powers (and their satellites). With minor qualifications, this is the definition of imperialism proposed by Lenin. Lenin's book on imperialism, it should be remembered, was brief and much of it was devoted to summarizing supporting

From Paul M. Sweezy, *The Theory of Capitalist Development: The Principles of Marxian Political Economy* (New York: Monthly Review Press, 1942), pp. 307–308, 311–20, 324–28. Copyright © 1942 by Monthly Review Press. Reprinted with permission of Monthly Review Foundation.

facts and figures. The more detailed theoretical analysis…may help to demonstrate the consistency and appropriateness of Lenin's conception of imperialism.

The international antagonisms of imperialism are fundamentally the antagonisms of rival national capitalist classes. Since in the international sphere the interests of capital are directly and quickly translated into terms of state policy, it follows that these antagonisms assume the form of conflicts between states and thus, indirectly, between whole nations. The resultant profound effects upon the internal economic and social structure of the capitalist countries must now be examined.…

IMPERIALISM AND THE CLASSES

In order to analyze the impact of imperialism on the internal social conflicts of capitalist society, it is necessary to digress briefly to call attention to certain characteristics of advanced capitalism which have so far remained largely unremarked.

In the first place, there is a marked tendency for the interests of large property-owners to merge under the leadership of monopoly capital. Under a regime of corporations, the ancient conflict between industrialists and big landowners tends to disappear; all sorts of physical assets are merged in the corporate balance sheet, and corporate securities are a common medium for the investment of surplus value whether its source be one type of property or another. Moreover with the development of monopoly in industry on the one hand, and the opening up of new agricultural countries on the other, the old dispute over tariff policy loses its meaning; all sections of the propertied class unite in demanding protective duties. This is not to say that conflicts of interest among large property owners can ever be eliminated; their severity, however, is reduced and has a diminishing significance for the formation of ruling-class policy. Hilferding gives an acute analysis of this trend for the case of Germany (Hilferding, 1931, chapter 33); in spite of differences in national conditions, which may assume great importance in times of crisis, the trend goes forward *pari passu* with the accumulation process all over the capitalist world.

Secondly, along with the unification of propertied interests goes the unification of the interests of the workers. In their struggle for higher wages, shorter hours, and better working conditions the workers in one industry after another discover that their strength lies in organization and cooperation. Consequently trade unionism grows up and spreads to ever wider sections of the working class. On the basis of experience in cooperation for the attainment of common ends the workers form their own political parties to win concessions which lie outside the reach of the economic struggle alone. On these foundations there arises a class consciousness and solidarity among the workers which fosters common action and common policies in all fields and makes possible the achievement of economic gains and political concessions which would otherwise be unattainable. This process was already well under way in England by the middle of the nineteenth century, but in the capitalist world at large it develops fully only during the imperialist epoch. Thus so far as capitalists and workers are concerned, imperialism is characterized by a tightening of class lines and an intensification of class struggle. This occurs independently of the special international characteristics of imperialism.

Thirdly, between capitalists and workers there stands an array of middle groups belonging to neither of the basic classes of capitalist society. Some of these are declining in importance, for example the independent farmers who are gradually succumbing to the spread of capitalist agriculture and hence tend to become (in a very few cases) capitalists or (in the vast majority of cases) wage workers or propertyless tenants; handicraftsmen and genuinely independent tradesmen also decline in numbers and importance: these are, in short, the groups which Marx and Engels had in mind when they spoke in the *Communist Manifesto* of the disappearance of "the lower strata of the middle class— the small tradespeople, shopkeepers, and retired tradesmen generally, the handicraftsmen and peasants." Alongside these declining sections of the middle class, however, there are the "new middle classes" which are brought into being by rising living standards, centralization of capital, and the growth of monopoly. The new middle classes include such diverse groups as industrial and governmental bureaucrats, salesmen, publicists, dealers who are in fact if not in form employees of big capital, professionals, teachers, and so forth. In the period of imperialism, particularly because of the expansionary effect of monopoly on the distributive machinery, these groups grow not only absolutely but also as a proportion of the total population. The numerical importance of the middle classes, old and new, should not, however, lead us to evaluate their role as we do that of the capitalists and workers. Instead of a growing solidarity of interests expressed in closer organizational unity and more conscious and effective political action, we find among the middle classes the utmost confusion and diversity of interests and aims. An objective basis for organizational unity and consciously oriented policy is lacking except in the case of relatively small groups which are too weak to be effective and often work at cross purposes into the bargain. Hence it is the fate of the middle classes in the period of ripening capitalist contradictions to be squeezed between the extortions of monopoly capital on the one hand and the demands of the working class for better conditions and greater security on the other hand; this much, at any rate, they all have in common, and it is this which determines the basic attitude characteristic of nearly all sectors of the middle classes. The attitude in question is hostility to both organized capital and organized labor which can manifest itself in seemingly contradictory ways. On the one hand the middle classes are the source of various degrees of nonproletarian anticapitalism; on the other hand of Utopias in which all organized class power is dissolved and the individual (i.e., the unattached member of a middle-class group) becomes the basic social unit as in the lost days of simple commodity production....

Let us now attempt to assess the impact of the special features of imperialism on the various social classes.

As far as the propertied class, under the leadership of monopoly capital, is concerned, little needs to be added....Monopoly capital needs to expand abroad, and for this purpose it requires the assistance and protection of the state. It is, therefore, here that we find the roots of imperialist policy with all its manifold implications.

The interests of the working class in an aggressive and expansionist foreign policy are more complex. Insofar as foreign trade and capital export make possible the importation of cheap wage goods and enlarge the profits of the capitalist class, it is clear that opportunities are opened up for the workers to improve their standard of living without necessarily arousing the bitter hostility of their employers. In this sense the workers gain. Moreover if, in the absence of capital export and the military expenditures incident to an imperialist policy, an advanced capitalist country would suffer from the effects of a low rate of profit and underconsumption, then it may be said that the working class benefits from a higher level of employment than would otherwise obtain. Against this, however, is to be set the loss in real wages which the workers bear if military expenditures go beyond a certain point and especially if interimperialist rivalries lead to actual armed conflict. It appears from these considerations that the working class of any country can gain most from an extension of foreign trade and capital export if the profits of the capitalists are enhanced, cheap imports of wage goods are fostered, and there is little danger of a collision with rival countries. This was precisely the peculiar situation in which the English working class found itself throughout the greater part of the nineteenth century, a fact which amply accounts for the complacent and even favorable attitude which the British working-class movement adopted toward the extension of British interests abroad in the years before the First World War.

Even in England conditions gradually changed in this respect. As Kautsky pointed out as early as 1902:

> So long as English industry ruled the world market the English workers could agree with their capitalists that live and let live is the best policy. That came to an end as soon as equal, frequently even superior, competitors appeared on the world market in the shape of Germany and America. Now begins again in England too the struggle against the trade unions which becomes the more intensive in proportion to the sharpness of the competition among these great industrial powers. (Kautsky, 1902, p. 142)

As soon, in other words, as international rivalry becomes acute, each capitalist class attempts to hold its position without sacrificing its profits by depressing wages and lengthening hours in its own country. Moreover, it must not be forgotten, as Dobb has stressed, that capital export keeps wages from rising at home as they would if the capital were invested domestically: Dobb even regards this as "the reason why, fundamentally, the interest of capital and of labor in this matter are opposed" (Dobb, 1939, p. 235). And finally, with the intensification of imperialist rivalries it becomes increasingly clear to the working class that the end of the process can only be war, from which it stands to lose much and gain little. While, therefore, there may be times when the economic interests of the working class are benefited by an imperialist policy, this cannot last long and ultimately the more fundamental and lasting opposition of the workers must come to the surface. On this, as on other issues, the interests and policies of capital and labor are fundamentally antagonistic.

Few worthwhile generalizations about the economic interests of the middle classes can be made, and this holds true of their relations to imperialism. Some groups no doubt stand to gain, others to lose; in still other cases the balance depends upon particular circumstances or is altogether indeterminate. Lacking common interests and a common organizational base, the middle classes are peculiarly unstable and become easily attached to vague ideals of national greatness or racial superiority, a propensity which is magnified by the difficult position which they occupy between organized capital and organized labor in advanced capitalist society. The nation or the race becomes the substitute for the solidarity of class interests which their isolated position in society denies to the middle classes, and at the same time it offers to them a kind of psychological escape from the frustrations of their everyday life. Objectively, therefore, wide sectors of the middle classes are ripe for enlistment in the cause of foreign expansion. Monopoly capital appreciates these susceptibilities of the middle classes and, moreover, knows how to take advantage of them for its own ends. In this connection it is a fact of great importance that the vast sums which monopoly causes to be spent on advertising and publicity bring all the channels of public opinion under the direct influence of the top oligarchy of the ruling class. By playing on the susceptibilities of the middle classes, and to a less extent of the unorganized sections of the working class, it is possible to build up formidable mass support for an aggressive imperialist policy. It is in this connection that the nationalist and racist ideologies, which were analyzed in the preceding section, acquire their greatest importance. The advantages to the propertied interests are even greater than this would indicate. Since, as we have seen, the working class tends to be hostile to imperialist expansion, its organizations and policies can be made to appear "unpatriotic" and "selfish." In this fashion the hostility of the middle classes to the working class, which is present in any case, can be intensified. Thus the net result of imperialism is to bind the middle classes closer to big capital and to widen the gulf between the middle classes and the working class.

IMPERIALISM AND THE STATE

It goes without saying that the renewed rise of empires and the growth of militarism imply an augmentation in the power of the state and an extension of the scope of its functions. The maturing contradictions of the accumulation process in the epoch of imperialism provide additional grounds for increased state activity, particularly in the economic sphere.

From the standpoint of the capitalist class there are two basic methods of countering the growing power and unity of the working class: repression and concession. Though these two methods may appear to be contradictory they are in fact complementary, being mixed together in varying proportions at different times. Both necessitate an expansion in the power and functions of the state. Thus we observe simultaneously the growth of the instruments of force designed to guarantee internal "law and order" and the extension of social legislation in the form of workmen's compensation, unemployment insurance, old-age benefit payments, and so forth.

An additional factor impelling the state to interference in the economic process is the centralization of capital and the growth of monopoly. The revisionists believed that monopoly would have the effect of regulating the anarchy of capitalist production, an opinion which, like so much of revisionist theorizing, has the remarkable quality of being the precise opposite of the truth. Actually monopoly intensifies the anarchy of capitalist production: the various monopolized industries attempt to go their own way in defiance of the requirements of the system as a whole. In this way disproportionalities are multiplied and the equilibrating force of the market is prevented from exercising its influence. The state is obliged to step in and attempt to substitute its own action for the "law of supply and demand." Moreover the strategic position of the so-called natural monopolies (railroads and public utilities) is so strong that the state finds it necessary to curb their exercise of monopoly power. This is frequently interpreted as state action in the

interests of consumers, and to a degree of course it is; but a more important consideration is the protection of the vast majority of capitalist
enterprises, which are absolutely dependent on electric power and
transportation, from the exactions of a small number of very powerful
monopolists. The history of railroad regulation in the United States, for
example, would be quite unintelligible in any other terms. It is interesting to note that Marx recognized the connection between monopoly
and state intervention; the growth of joint-stock companies, he
remarked, "establishes a monopoly in certain spheres and thereby challenges the interference of the state" (Marx, 1933, p. 519).

Finally, we may note in this connection that the contradictions of
the accumulation process and the uneven development as between
branches of industry bring it about that now one line of production,
now another, ceases to expand and becomes actually unprofitable. In
the days of competitive capitalism the result was a disappearance of
numerous firms, the bankruptcy and ruin of many capitalists. When a
declining industry, however, is the home of great monopolistic combines with ramifications throughout the economic system, failures and
bankruptcies are a much more serious matter; it becomes necessary for
the state to take a hand by way of loans of public funds, subsidies, and
even in some cases government ownership of the no-longer profitable
enterprises. In this fashion capitalist states are forced to go in for an ever
greater degree of "socialism." What is socialized is almost invariably the
losses of the capitalists involved. "A state monopoly in capitalist society,"
Lenin dryly remarked, "is nothing more than a means of increasing and
guaranteeing the income of millionaires in one branch of industry or
another who are on the verge of bankruptcy" (Lenin, 1933, p. 37).

Along with the expansion of the power of the state and the scope
of its economic functions goes a decline in the effectiveness of parliamentary institutions. In the words of Otto Bauer, "Imperialism reduces
the power of the legislature [Gesetzgebung] as against the executive [Ver-
waltung]" (Bauer, 1907, p. 488). The reasons for this are not far to seek. Parliament grew out of the struggle of the capitalist class against the arbitrary exercise of power by the centralized monarchies which characterized the early modern period; its function has always been to check and
control the exercise of governmental power. Consequently parliamentary institutions flourished and reached the peak of their prestige in the

period of competitive capitalism when the functions of the state, particularly in the economic sphere, were reduced to a minimum. At that time it was possible to look forward to a day when all the nations of the world would be under parliamentary governments on the English or American model. In the period of imperialism, however, a sharp change occurs. With the tightening of class lines and the increasing severity of social conflict, parliament becomes more and more a battle ground for contending parties representing divergent class and group interests. While on the one hand parliament's capacity for positive action declines, on the other hand there emerges an increasing need for a strong centralized state ready and able to rule over distant territories, to direct the activities of fleets and armies, and to solve difficult and complex economic problems. Under the circumstances, parliament is forced to give up one after another of its cherished prerogatives and to see built up under its very eyes the kind of centralized and uncontrolled authority against which, in its youth, it had fought so hard and so well.

So far as the effect of imperialism on the capitalist state is concerned, we observe on the one hand a vast expansion in the power and functions of the state, on the other hand the decline of parliamentarism. These are not two separate movements but rather two aspects of one and the same development which is connected in the closest way with the economic and social characteristics of imperialism in general.

THE LIMITS OF IMPERIALISM

If we consider the system of imperialism as a whole, rather than single imperialist nations, it is apparent that it raises up against itself two types of opponents and that its expansion enhances their potential power of opposition. It is here that we must seek for the factors which will ultimately set the limits of imperialism and prepare the way for its downfall as a system of world economy.

The first opposition force arises, as we have already seen, from the internal development of the imperialist countries. Class lines are drawn ever more tightly and class conflict grows in intensity. Eventually the working class is forced to adopt an anticapitalist position and to set as its goal the attainment of socialism. But in the era of imperialism, anticapitalism necessarily means also anti-imperialism. The special features of imperialist policy, which make for increased internal exploitation and international war, serve to enhance the opposition of workers, though the roots of this working-class attitude are to be found in the structure of capitalist society in general. We may speak in this connection of socialist opposition to imperialism. Such opposition is in itself not capable of preventing the expansion of imperialism. Its real significance emerges only in the closing stages of a war of redivision when the economic and social structure of the imperialist powers is seriously weakened and revolutionary situations mature in the most severely affected areas. Successful socialist revolutions then become possible; the chain of world imperialism tends to break in its weakest links. This is what took place in Russia in 1917. The Bolshevik revolution established new socialist relations of production in Russia with the result that a large part of the earth's surface was withdrawn at one stroke from the world system of imperialism and formed the nucleus for a future world economy on a socialist basis. It seems safe to predict that this process will be repeated, perhaps on an even larger scale, before the present international conflict has exhausted itself. Thus we see that the first limit to imperialism is the result of the interaction of its national and international aspects. The crucial opposition force originates within the imperialist nations but the conditions for its triumph are established by the wars of redivision which are a recurring feature of imperialism considered as an international system. This is the dialectic, so to speak, of the birth and growth of socialism. Moreover, the limit to imperialism implicit in the rise of socialism is in the long run a contracting limit....

The second fundamental limit to imperialism arises from the relations between metropolis and colony. The introduction of cheap manufactured commodities and the import of capital into the colonial economy revolutionize the preexisting mode of production. Handicraft industries are dealt a crippling blow; modern means of transport and communication break down the local separatism inherent in precapitalist production; old social relations are dissolved; a native bourgeoisie arises and takes the lead in promoting a spirit of nationalism such as that which characterized the early development of capitalism in the now advanced industrial nations. At the same time, however, the development of colonial economy is not well balanced. Under the domination of imperialism, industrialization advances very slowly, too slowly to absorb the steady flow of handicraft producers who are ruined by the competition of machine-made products from the factories of the advanced regions. The consequence is a swelling of the ranks of the peasantry, increased pressure on the land, and a deterioration of the productivity and living standards of the agricultural masses who constitute by far the largest section of the colonial populations. Imperialism thus creates economic problems in the colonies which it is unable to solve. The essential conditions for improvement are fundamental changes in the land system, reduction of the numbers dependent upon agriculture, and increase in the productivity of agriculture, all objectives which can be attained only in conjunction with a relatively high rate of industrialization. Imperialism is unwilling to reform the land system because its rule typically depends upon the support of the colonial landlord class, both native and foreign; the interests of producers, and especially monopolistically organized producers, in the metropolis prevent the erection of colonial protective-tariff barriers and in other ways inhibit the growth of industrialism in the backward areas. The inevitable consequence is that colonial economy stagnates, and living conditions for the great majority of the people tend to become worse rather than better. All classes of the colonial populations, with the exception of the landlords and a few relatively small groups which are in effect agents of imperialist rule, are therefore thrown into the struggle for national independence. Alongside the socialist opposition to imperialism within the advanced countries we have here the nationalist opposition in the backward countries.

The relation between the two major forces opposing imperialism is a complex one which cannot be fully analyzed here. We must be content with a few brief suggestions. There obviously exists a firm foundation for an alliance between the socialist opposition to imperialism in the advanced countries and the nationalist opposition in the colonial countries. The rise and spread of an independent socialist section of the world, however, introduces certain complications. It was pointed out above that the colonial bourgeoisie takes the lead in organizing and promoting movements of national independence, but the ultimate objective of the colonial bourgeoisie is the establishment of independent capitalist nations. Consequently it sees enemies in both imperialism and socialism. The colonial working class on the other hand, though numer-

ically small, adopts a socialist goal almost from the outset; while the
oppressed agricultural masses are not unreceptive to socialist ideas and
tend to follow the leadership of those who demonstrate most clearly by
their actions that they mean to win a genuine improvement in conditions. The position of the colonial bourgeoisie tends more and more to
unfit it for the role of leadership which it assumes in the early stages of
the national movement. It wavers between accepting the support of the
forces of socialism, both external and internal, against imperialism, and
temporizing with imperialism in order to keep in check the socialist
menace. The result is a policy which always stops short of decisive action,
reverses itself and backtracks, then once again moves hesitantly forward.
Since this is not the kind of policy which can make a strong appeal to
the mass of the peasantry, and since without such support the national
independence movement is impotent, it follows that leadership gradually tends to slip out of the hands of bourgeois elements and into the
hands of the working class in alliance with the more advanced sections
of the peasantry, which, though not necessarily socialist in their convic-
tions, nevertheless have no stake in the maintenance of capitalist relations of production after independence is achieved. Eventually, therefore,
it falls to the lot of the working class to lead the nationalist opposition
to imperialism in the colonial countries just as it stands at the head of
the socialist opposition to imperialism in the advanced countries. When
this stage has been reached the two great opposition forces are united
not only in their immediate objectives but also in their ultimate resolve
to work for a socialist world economy as a way out of the growing contradictions of imperialist world economy. In the long run the colonial
bourgeoisie is unable to play an independent historical role and must
split up into two opposing factions, one of which attempts to save its
own precarious privileges by means of an open alliance with imperialism, while the other remains true to the cause of national independence even though the price is the acceptance of socialism.

Hence we see, finally, that what started as two independent forces
opposed to imperialism tend to merge into one great movement. Just as
in the advanced capitalist countries themselves, so also on a world scale
the issue becomes ever more clearly defined as Imperialism versus
Socialism, with the mounting contradictions of imperialism ensuring its
own decline and the concomitant spread of socialism.

REFERENCES

Bauer, Otto. 1907. *Die Nationalitatenfrage und die Sozialdemokratie.* Vienna: Verlad der Wiener Volksbuchhandlung Ignaz Brand.

Dobb, Maurice. 1939. *Political Economy and Capitalism.* New York: International Publishers.

Hilferding, Rudolf. 1931. "Die Eigengesetzlichkeit der kapitalistischen Entwicklung," in *Kapital und Kapitalismus.* Vol. 1. Edited by Bernhard Harms, R. Hobbing, Berlin.

Kautsky, Karl. 1910–11. "Finanzkapital und Krisen," *Die Neue Zeit,* Jhrg.XXIX, Bd. 1.

Lenin, V.I. 1933. *Imperialism.* New York: International Publishers Company, Inc.

Marx, Karl. 1933. *Capital III.* Chicago: Charles Kerr & Company.

CLASSICAL
THEORIES
OF
IMPERIALISM

2

UNDERCONSUMPTION AND IMPERIALISM

J. A. Hobson

John Atkinson Hobson saw British imperialism as a reflection of domestic prob-
lems caused by overproduction and an excess of commodities that necessitated export
abroad. In short, capitalist underconsumption at home was a driving force in the
imperialist expansion. Imperialism also required excessive investments abroad
which could better benefit the domestic economy. In the introduction to the edition
from which the following segment is drawn, Philip Siegelman refers to the criti-
cism of Hobson as reductionist and reliant on a discontinuous view of the nine-
teenth century (see D. K. Fieldhouse, "Imperialism: An Historiographical Revi-
sion," The Economic History Review, Second Series 14, no. 2 [1961]).

NO MERE ARRAY OF FACTS and figures adduced to illustrate the economic
nature of the new imperialism will suffice to dispel the popular delusion that the use of national force to secure new markets by annexing
fresh tracts of territory is a sound and a necessary policy for an advanced
industrial country like Great Britain. It has indeed been proved that
recent annexations of tropical countries, procured at great expense, have
furnished poor and precarious markets, that our aggregate trade with
our colonial possessions is virtually stationary, and that our most profitable and progressive trade is with rival industrial nations, whose territories we have no desire to annex, whose markets we cannot force, and
whose active antagonism we are provoking by our expansive policy.

From J. A. Hobson, *Imperialism: A Study* (Ann Arbor: University of Michigan Press, 1965), pp.
71–93.

But these arguments are not conclusive. It is open to imperialists to argue thus: We must have markets for our growing manufactures, we must have new outlets for the investment of our surplus capital and for the energies of the adventurous surplus of our population: such expansion is a necessity of life to a nation with our great and growing powers of production. An ever larger share of our population is devoted to the manufactures and commerce of towns, and is thus dependent for life and work upon food and raw materials from foreign lands. In order to buy and pay for these things we must sell our goods abroad. During the first three-quarters of the nineteenth century we could do so without difficulty by a natural expansion of commerce with continental nations and our colonies, all of which were far behind us in the main arts of manufacture and the carrying trades. So long as England held a virtual monopoly of the world markets for certain important classes of manufactured goods, imperialism was unnecessary. After 1870 this manufacturing and trading supremacy was greatly impaired: other nations, especially Germany, the United States, and Belgium, advanced with great rapidity, and while they have not crushed or even stayed the increase of our external trade, their competition made it more and more difficult to dispose of the full surplus of our manufactures at a profit. The encroachments made by these nations upon our old markets, even in our own possessions, made it most urgent that we should take energetic means to secure new markets. These new markets had to lie in hitherto undeveloped countries, chiefly in the tropics, where vast populations lived capable of growing economic needs which our manufacturers and merchants could supply. Our rivals were seizing and annexing territories for similar purposes, and when they had annexed them closed them to our trade. The diplomacy and the arms of Great Britain had to be used in order to compel the owners of the new markets to deal with us: and experience showed that the safest means of securing and developing such markets is by establishing 'protectorates' or by annexation. The value in 1905 of these markets must not be taken as a final test of the economy of such a policy; the process of educating civilized needs which we can supply is of necessity a gradual one, and the cost of such imperialism must be regarded as a capital outlay, the fruits of which posterity would reap. The new markets might not be large, but they formed serviceable outlets for the overflow of our great textile and metal industries, and, when the vast Asiatic and African populations of the interior were reached, a rapid expansion of trade was expected to result.

Far larger and more important is the pressure of capital for external fields of investment. Moreover, while the manufacturer and trader are well content to trade with foreign nations, the tendency for investors to work toward the political annexation of countries which contain their more speculative investments is very powerful. Of the fact of this pressure of capital there can be no question. Large savings are made which cannot find any profitable investment in this country; they must find employment elsewhere, and it is to the advantage of the nation that they should be employed as largely as possible in lands where they can be utilized in opening up markets for British trade and employment for British enterprise.

However costly, however perilous, this process of imperial expansion may be, it is necessary to the continued existence and progress of our nation; if we abandoned it we must be content to leave the development of the world to other nations, who will everywhere cut into our trade, and even impair our means of securing the food and raw materials we require to support our population. Imperialism is thus seen to be, not a choice, but a necessity.

The practical force of this economic argument in politics strikingly illustrated by the later history of the United States. Here is a country which suddenly broke through a conservative policy, strongly held by both political parties, bound up with every popular instinct and tradition, and flung itself into a rapid imperial career for which it possessed neither the material nor the moral equipment, risking the principles and practices of liberty and equality by the establishment of militarism and the forcible subjugation of peoples which it could not safely admit to the condition of American citizenship.

Was this a mere wild freak of spread-eaglism, a burst of political ambition on the part of a nation coming to a sudden realization of its destiny? Not at all. The spirit of adventure, the American "mission of civilization," were as forces making for imperialism, clearly subordinate to the driving force of the economic factor. The dramatic character of the change is due to the unprecedented rapidity of the industrial revolution in the United States from the eighties onward. During that period the United States, with her unrivaled natural resources, her immense resources of skilled and unskilled labor, and her genius for invention and organization, developed the best equipped and most productive manufacturing economy the world has yet seen. Fostered by rigid protective tariffs, her metal, textile, tool, clothing, furniture, and other manufactures shot up in a single generation from infancy to full maturity, and, having passed through a period of intense competition, attained, under the able control of great trust-makers, a power of production greater than has been attained in the most advanced industrial countries of Europe.

An era of cutthroat competition, followed by a rapid process of amalgamation, threw an enormous quantity of wealth into the hands of a small number of captains of industry. No luxury of living to which this class could attain kept pace with its rise of income, and a process of automatic saving set in upon an unprecedented scale. The investment of these savings in other industries helped to bring these under the same concentrative forces. Thus a great increase of savings seeking profitable investment is synchronous with a stricter economy of the use of existing capital. No doubt the rapid growth of a population, accustomed to a high and an always ascending standard of comfort, absorbs in the satisfaction of its wants a large quantity of new capital. But the actual rate of saving, conjoined with a more economical application of forms of existing capital, exceeded considerably the rise of the national consumption of manufactures. The power of production far outstripped the actual rate of consumption, and, contrary to the older economic theory, was unable to force a corresponding increase of consumption by lowering prices.

This is no mere theory. The history of any of the numerous trusts or combinations in the United States sets out the facts with complete distinctness. In the free competition of manufactures preceding combination, the chronic condition is one of "overproduction," in the sense that all the mills or factories can only be kept at work by cutting prices down towards a point where the weaker competitors are forced to close down, because they cannot sell their goods at a price which covers the true cost of production. The first result of the successful formation of a trust or combine is to close down the worse equipped or worse placed mills, and supply the entire market from the better equipped and better placed ones. This course may or may not be attended by a rise of price and some restriction of consumption: in some cases trusts take most of their profits by raising prices, in other cases by reducing the costs of production through employing only the best mills and stopping the waste of competition.

For the present argument it matters not which course is taken; the point is that this concentration of industry in "trusts," "combines," etc., at once limits the quantity of capital which can be effectively employed and increases the share of profits out of which fresh savings and fresh capital will spring. It is quite evident that a trust which is motivated by cutthroat competition, due to an excess of capital, cannot normally find inside the "trusted" industry employment for that portion of the profits which the trust-makers desire to save and to invest. New inventions and other economies of production or distribution within the trade may absorb some of the new capital, but there are rigid limits to this absorption. The trust-maker in oil or sugar must find other investments for his savings: if he is early in the application of the combination principles to his trade, he will naturally apply his surplus capital to establish similar combinations in other industries, economizing capital still further, and rendering it even harder for ordinary saving men to find investments for their savings.

Indeed, the conditions alike of cutthroat competition and of combination attest the congestion of capital in the manufacturing industries which have entered the machine economy. We are not here concerned with any theoretic question as to the possibility of producing by modern machine methods more goods than can find a market. It is sufficient to point out that the manufacturing power of a country like the United States would grow so fast as to exceed the demands of the home market. No one acquainted with trade will deny a fact which all American economists assert, that this is the condition which the United States reached at the end of the century, so far, as the more developed industries are concerned. Her manufacture were saturated with capital and could absorb no more. One after another they sought refuge from the waste of competition in "combines" which secure a measure of profitable peace by restricting the quantity of operative capital. Industrial and financial princes in oil, steel, sugar, railroads, banning, etc., were faced with the dilemma of either spending more than they knew how to spend, or forcing markets outside the home area. Two economic

courses were open to them, both leading toward the abandonment of
the political isolation of the past and the adoption of imperialist
methods in the future. Instead of shutting down inferior mills and
rigidly restricting output to correspond with profitable sales in the
home markets, they might employ their full productive power, applying
their savings to increase their business capital, and, while still regulating
output and prices for the home market, may "hustle" for foreign markets, dumping down their surplus goods at prices which would not be
possible save for the profitable nature of their home market. So likewise
they might employ their savings in seeking investments outside their
country, first repaying the capital borrowed from Great Britain and
other countries for the early development of their railroads, mines, and
manufactures, and afterward becoming themselves a creditor class to
foreign countries.

It was this sudden demand for foreign markets for manufactures
and for investments which was avowedly responsible for the adoption
of imperialism as a political policy and practice by the Republican party
to which the great industrial and financial chiefs belonged, and which
belonged to them. The adventurous enthusiasm of President Theodore
Roosevelt and his "manifest destiny" and "mission of civilization" party
must not deceive us. It was Messrs. Rockefeller, Pierpont Morgan, and
their associates who needed imperialism and who fastened it upon the
shoulders of the great Republic of the West. They needed imperialism
because they desired to use the public resources of their country to find
profitable employment for their capital which otherwise would be
superfluous.

It is not indeed necessary to own a country in order to do trade
with it or to invest capital in it, and doubtless the United States could
find some vent for their surplus goods, and capital in European countries. But these countries were for the most part able to make provision
for themselves: most of them erected tariffs against manufacturing
imports, and even Great Britain was urged to defend herself by reverting
to protection. The big American manufacturers and financiers were
compelled to look to China and the Pacific and to South America for
their most profitable chances; protectionists by principle and practice,
they would insist upon getting as close a monopoly of these markets as
they can secure, and the competition of Germany, England, and other

trading nations would drive them to the establishment of special political relations with the markets they most prize. Cuba, the Philippines, and Hawaii were but the *hors d'oeuvre* to whet an appetite for an ampler banquet. Moreover, the powerful hold upon politics which these industrial and financial magnates possessed formed a separate stimulus, which, as we have shown, was operative in Great Britain and elsewhere; the public expenditure in pursuit of an imperial career would be a separate immense source of profit to these men, as financiers negotiating loans, shipbuilders and owners handling subsidies, contractors and manufacturers of armaments and other imperialist appliances.

The suddenness of this political revolution is due to the rapid manifestation of the need. In the last years of the nineteenth century the United States nearly trebled the value of its manufacturing export trade, and it was to be expected that, if the rate of progress of those years continued, within a decade it would overtake our more slowly advancing export trade, and stand first in the list of manufacture-exporting nations.

This was the avowed ambition, and no idle one, of the keenest business men of America; and with the natural resources, the labor and the administrative talents at their disposal, it was quite likely they would achieve their object. The stronger and more direct control over politics exercised in America by business men enabled them to drive more quickly and more straightly along the line of their economic interests than in Great Britain. American imperialism was the natural product of the economic pressure of a sudden advance of capitalism which could not find occupation at home and needed foreign markets for goods and for investments.

The same needs existed in European countries, and, as is admitted, drove governments along the same path. Overproduction in the sense of an excessive manufacturing plant, and surplus capital which could not find sound investments within the country, forced Great Britain, Germany, Holland, France to place larger and larger portions of their economic resources outside the area of their present political domain, and then stimulate a policy of political expansion so as to take in the new areas. The economic sources of this movement are laid bare by periodic trade-depressions due to an inability of producers to find adequate and profitable markets for what they can produce. The Majority Report of the Commission upon the Depression of Trade in 1885 put the matter in a nutshell. "That, owing to the nature of the times, the demand for our commodities does not increase at the same rate as formerly; that our capacity for production is consequently in excess of our requirements, and could be considerably increased at short notice; that this is due partly to the competition of the capital which is being steadily accumulated in the country." The Minority Report straightly imputed the condition of affairs to "over-production." Germany was in the early 1900s suffering severely from what is called a glut of capital and of manufacturing power: she had to have new markets; her Consuls all over the world were "hustling" for trade; trading settlements were forced upon Asia Minor; in East and West Africa, in China and elsewhere the German Empire was impaled to a policy of colonization and protectorates as outlets for German commercial energy.

Every improvement of methods of production, every concentration of ownership and control, seems to accentuate the tendency. As one nation after another enters the machine economy and adopts advanced industrial methods, it becomes more difficult for its manufacturers, merchants, and financiers to dispose profitably of their economic resources, and they are tempted more and more to use their governments in order to secure for their particular use some distant undeveloped country by annexation and protection.

The process, we may be told, is inevitable, and so it seems upon a superficial inspection. Everywhere appear excessive powers of production, excessive capital in search of investment. It is admitted by all business men that the growth of the powers of production in their country exceeds the growth in consumption, that more goods can be produced than can be sold at a profit, and that more capital exists than can find remunerative investment.

It is this economic condition of affairs that forms the taproot of imperialism. If the consuming public in this country raised its standard of consumption to keep pace with every rise of productive powers, there could be no excess of goods or capital clamorous to use imperialism in order to find markets: foreign trade would indeed exist, but there would be no difficulty in exchanging a small surplus of our manufactures for the food and raw material we annually absorbed, and all the savings that we made could find employment, if we chose, in home industries.

There is nothing inherently irrational in such a supposition. Whatever is, or can be, produced, can be consumed, for a claim upon it, as rent, profit, or wages, forms part of the real income of some member of the community, and he can consume it, or else exchange it for some other consumable with some one else who will consume it. With everything that is produced a consuming power is born. If, then, there are goods which cannot get consumed, or which cannot even get produced because it is evident they cannot get consumed, and if there is a quantity of capital and labor which cannot get full employment because its products cannot get consumed, the only possible explanation of this paradox is the refusal of owners of consuming power to apply that power in effective demand for commodities.

It is, of course, possible that an excess of producing power might exist in particular industries by misdirection, being engaged in certain manufactures, whereas it ought to have been engaged in agriculture or some other use. But no one can seriously contend that such misdirection explains the recurrent gluts and consequent depressions of modern industry, or that, when overproduction is manifest in the leading manufactures, ample avenues are open for the surplus capital and labor in other industries. The general character of the excess of producing power is proved by the existence at such times of large bank stocks of idle money seeking any sort of profitable investment and finding none.

The root questions underlying the phenomena are clearly these: "Why is it that consumption fails to keep pace automatically in a community with power of production?" "Why does underconsumption or oversaving occur?" For it is evident that the consuming power, which, if exercised, would keep tense the reins of production, is in part withheld, or in other words is "saved" and stored up for investment. All saving for investment does not imply slackness of production; quite the contrary. Saving is economically justified, from the social standpoint, when the capital in which it takes material shape finds full employment in helping to produce commodities which, when produced, will be consumed. It is saving in excess of this amount that causes mischief, taking shape in surplus capital which is not needed to assist current consumption, and which either lies idle, or tries to oust existing capital from its employment, or else seeks speculative use abroad under the protection of the government.

But it may be asked, "Why should there be any tendency to over-saving? Why should the owners of consuming power withhold a larger quantity for savings than can be serviceably employed?" Another way of putting the same question is this: "Why should not the pressure of present wants keep pace with every possibility of satisfying them?" The answer to these pertinent questions carries us to the broadest issue of the distribution of wealth. If a tendency to distribute income or consuming power according to needs were operative, it is evident that consumption would rise with every rise of producing power, for human needs are illimitable, and there could be no excess of saving. But it is quite otherwise in a state of economic society where distribution has no fixed relation to needs, but is determined by other conditions which assign to some people a consuming power vastly in excess of needs or possible uses, while others are destitute of consuming power enough to satisfy even the full demand of physical efficiency. The following illustration may serve to make the issue clear. "The volume of production has been constantly rising owing to the development of modern machinery. There are two main channels to carry off these products—one channel carrying off the product destined to be consumed by the workers, and the other channel carrying off the remainder to the rich. The workers' channel is in rock-bound banks that cannot enlarge, owing to the competitive wage system preventing wages rising *pro rata* with increased efficiency. Wages are based upon cost of living, and not upon efficiency of labor. The miner in the poor mine gets the same wages per day as the miner in the adjoining rich mine. The owner of the rich mine gets the advantage—not his laborer. The channel which conveys the goods destined to supply the rich is itself divided into two streams. One stream carries off what the rich 'spend' on themselves for the necessities and luxuries of life. The other is simply an 'overflow' stream carrying off their 'savings.' The channel for spending, i.e., the amount wasted by the rich in luxuries, may broaden somewhat, but owing to the small number of those rich enough to indulge in whims it can never be greatly enlarged, and at any rate it bears such a small proportion to the other channel that in no event can much hope of avoiding a flood of capital be hoped for from this division. The rich will never be so ingenious as to spend enough to prevent overproduction. The great safety overflow channel which has been continuously more and more widened and deepened to carry off the ever-increasing flood of new capital is that division of the stream which carried the savings of the rich, and this is not only suddenly found to be incapable of further enlargement, but actually seems to be in the process of being dammed up."

Though this presentation overaccentuates the cleavage between rich and poor and overstates the weakness of the workers, it gives forcible and sound expression to a most important and ill-recognized economic truth. The "overflow" stream of savings is of course fed not exclusively from the surplus income of "the rich"; the professional and industrial middle classes, and to some slight extent the workers, contribute. But the "flooding" is distinctly due to the automatic saving of the surplus income of rich men. This is of course particularly true of America, where multi-millionaires rise quickly and find themselves in possession of incomes far exceeding the demands of any craving that is known to them. To make the metaphor complete, the overflow stream must be represented as reentering the stream of production and seeking to empty there all the "savings" that it carries. Where competition remains free, the result is a chronic congestion of productive power and of production, forcing down home prices, wasting large sums in advertising and in pushing for orders, and periodically causing a crisis followed by a collapse, during which quantities of capital and labor lie unemployed and unremunerated. The prime object of the trust or other combine is to remedy this waste and loss by substituting regulation of output for reckless overproduction. In achieving this it actually narrows or even dams up the old channels of investment, limiting the overflow stream to the exact amount required to maintain the normal current of output. But this rigid limitation of trade, though required for the separate economy of each trust, does not suit the trust-maker, who is driven to compensate for strictly regulated industry at home by cutting new foreign channels as outlets for his productive power and his excessive savings. Thus we reach the conclusion that imperialism is the endeavor of the great controllers of industry to broaden the channel for the flow of their surplus wealth by seeking foreign markets and foreign investments to take off the goods and capital they cannot sell or use at home.

The fallacy of the supposed inevitability of imperial expansion as a necessary outlet for progressive industry is now manifest. It is not industrial progress that demands the opening up of new markets and areas of investment, but maldistribution of consuming power which prevents the absorption of commodities and capital within the country. The over-saving which is the economic root of imperialism is found by analysis to consist of rents, monopoly profits, and other unearned or excessive elements of incomes which, not being earned by labor of head or hand, have no legitimate *raison d'etre*. Having no natural relation to effort of production, they impel their recipients to no corresponding satisfaction of consumption: they form a surplus wealth, which, having no proper place in the normal economy of production and consumption, tends to accumulate as excessive savings. Let any turn in the tide of politico-economic forces divert from these owners their excess of income and make it flow, either to the workers in higher wages, or to the community in taxes, so that it will be spent instead of being saved, serving in either of these ways to swell the tide of consumption—there will be no need to fight for foreign markets or foreign areas of investment.

Many have carried their analysis so far as to realize the absurdity of spending half our financial resources in fighting to secure foreign markets at time when hungry mouths, ill-clad backs, ill-furnished houses indicate countless unsatisfied material wants among our own population. If we may take the careful statistics of Mr. Rowntree for our guide, we shall be aware that more than one-fourth of the population of our towns is living at a standard which is below bare physical efficiency. If, by some economic readjustment, the products which flow from the surplus saving of the rich to swell the overflow streams could be diverted so as to raise the incomes and the standard of consumption of this inefficient fourth, there would be no need for pushful imperialism, and the cause of social reform would have won its greatest victory.

It is not inherent in the nature of things that we should spend our natural resources on militarism, war, and risky, unscrupulous diplomacy, in order to find markets for our goods and surplus capital. An intelligent progressive community, based upon substantial equality of economic and educational opportunities, will raise its standard of consumption to correspond with every increased power of production, and can find full employment for an unlimited quantity of capital and labor within the limits of the country which it occupies. Where the distribution of incomes is such as to enable all classes of the nation to convert their felt wants into an effective demand for commodities, there can be no overproduction, no underemployment of capital and labor, and no necessity to fight for foreign markets.

The most convincing condemnation of the current economy is conveyed in the difficulty which producers everywhere experience in finding consumers for their products: a fact attested by the prodigious growth of classes of agents and middlemen, the multiplication of every sort of advertising, and the general increase of the distributive classes. Under a sound economy the pressure would be reversed: the growing wants of progressive societies would be a constant stimulus to the inventive and operative energies of producers, and would form a constant strain upon the powers of production. The simultaneous excess of all the factors of production, attested by frequency recurring periods of trade depression, is a most dramatic exhibition of the false economy of distribution. It does not imply a mere miscalculation in the application of productive power, or a brief temporary excess of that power; it manifests in an acute form an economic waste which is chronic and general throughout the advanced industrial nations, a waste contained in the divorcement of the desire to consume and the power to consume.

If the apportionment of income were such as to evolve no excessive saving, full constant employment for capital and labor would be furnished at home. This, of course, does not imply that there would be no foreign trade. Goods that could not be produced at home, or produced as well or as cheaply, would still be purchased by ordinary process of international exchange, but here again the pressure would be the wholesome pressure of the consumer anxious to buy abroad what he could not buy at home, not the blind eagerness of the producer to use every force or trick of trade or politics to find markets for his "surplus" goods.

The struggle for markets, the greater eagerness of producers to sell than of consumers to buy, is the crowning proof of a false economy of distribution. Imperialism is the fruit of this false economy; "social reform" is its remedy. The primary purpose of "social reform," using the term in its economic signification, is to raise the wholesome standard of private and public consumption for a nation, so as to enable the nation to live up to its highest standard of production. Even those social reformers who aim directly at abolishing or reducing some bad form of consumption, as in the Temperance movement, generally recognize the necessity of substituting some better form of current consumption which is more educative and stimulative of other tastes, and will assist to raise the general standard of consumption.

There is no necessity to open up new foreign markets; the home markets are capable of indefinite expansion. Whatever is produced in England can be consumed in England, provided that the "income" or power to demand commodities, is properly distributed. This only appears untrue because of the unnatural and unwholesome specialization to which this country has been subjected, based upon a bad distribution of economic resources, which has induced an overgrowth of certain manufacturing trades for the express purpose of effecting foreign sales. If the industrial revolution had taken place in an England founded upon equal access by all classes to land, education, and legislation, specialization in manufactures would not have gone so far (though more intelligent progress would have been made, by reason of a widening of the area of selection of inventive and organizing talents); foreign trade would have been less important, though more steady; the standard of life for all portions of the population would have been high, and the present rate of national consumption would probably have given full, constant, remunerative employment to a far larger quantity of private and public capital than is now employed. For the oversaving or wider consumption that is traced to excessive incomes of the rich is a suicidal economy, even from the exclusive standpoint of capital; for consumption alone vitalizes capital and makes it capable of yielding profits. An economy that assigns to the "possessing" classes an excess of consuming power which they cannot use, and cannot convert into really serviceable capital, is a dog-in-the-manger policy. The social reforms which deprive the possessing classes of their surplus will not, therefore, inflict upon them the real injury they dread; they can only use this surplus by forcing on their country a wrecking policy of imperialism. The only safety of nations lies in removing the unearned increments of income from the possessing classes, and adding them to the wage-income of the working classes or to the public income, in order that they may be spent in raising the standard of consumption.

Social reform bifurcates, according as reformers seek to achieve this end by raising wages or by increasing public taxation and expenditure. These courses are not essentially contradictory, but are rather complementary. Working-class movements aim, either by private cooperation or by political pressure on legislative and administrative government, at increasing the proportion of the national income which accrues to labor in the form of wages, pensions, compensation for injuries, etc. State socialism aims at getting for the direct use of the whole society an increased share of the "social values" which arise from the closely and essentially cooperative world: of an industrial society, taxing property and incomes so as to draw into the public exchequer for public expenditure the "unearned elements" of income, leaving to individual producers those incomes which are necessary to induce them to apply in the best way their economic energies, and to private enterprises those businesses which do not breed monopoly, and which the public need not or cannot undertake. These are not, indeed, the sole or perhaps the best avowed objects of social reform movements. But for the purposes of this analysis they form the kernel.

Trade unionism and socialism are thus the natural enemies of imperialism, for they take away from the "imperialist" classes the surplus incomes which form the economic stimulus of imperialism. This does not pretend to be a final statement of the full relations of these forces. When we come to political analysis we shall perceive that the tendency of imperialism is to crush trade unionism and to "nibble" at or parasitically exploit state socialism. But, confining ourselves for the present to the narrowly economic setting, trade unionism and state socialism may be regarded as complementary forces arrayed against imperialism, in as far as, by diverting to working-class or public expenditure elements of income which would otherwise be surplus savings, they raise the general standard of home consumption and abate the pressure for foreign markets. Of course, if the increase of working-class income were wholly or chiefly "saved," not spent, or if the taxation of unearned incomes were utilized for the relief of other taxes borne by the possessing classes, no such result as we have described would follow. There is, however, no reason to anticipate this result from trade-union or socialistic measures. Though no sufficient natural stimulus exists to force the well-to-do classes to spend in further luxuries the surplus incomes which they save, every working-class family is subject to powerful stimuli of economic needs, and a reasonably governed state would regard as its prime duty the relief of the present poverty of public life by new forms of socially useful expenditure.

But we are not here concerned with what belongs to the practical issues of political and economic policy. It is the economic theory for which we claim acceptance—a theory which, if accurate, dispels the delusion that expansion of foreign-trade, and therefore of empire, is a necessity of national life.

Regarded from the standpoint of economy of energy, the same "choice of life" confronts the nation as the individual. An individual may expend all his energy in acquiring external possessions, adding field to field, barn to barn, factory to factory—may "spread himself" over the widest area of property, amassing material wealth which is in some sense "himself" as containing the impress of his power and interest. He does this by specializing upon the lower acquisitive plane of interest at the cost of neglecting the cultivation of the higher qualities and interests of his nature. The antagonism is not indeed absolute. Aristotle has said, " We must first secure a livelihood and then practice virtue." Hence the pursuit of material property as a reasonable basis of physical comfort would be held true economy by the wisest men; but the absorption of time, energy, and interest upon such quantitative expansion at the necessary cost of starving the higher tastes and faculties is condemned as false economy. The same issue comes up in the business life of the individual: it is the question of intensive *versus* extensive cultivation. A rude or ignorant farmer, where land is plentiful, is apt to spread his capital and labor over a large area, taking in new tracts and cultivating them poorly. A skilled, scientific farmer will study a smaller patch of land, cultivate it thoroughly, and utilize its diverse properties, adapting it to the special needs of his most remunerative markets. The same is true of other businesses; even where the economy of large-scale production is greatest there exists some limit beyond which the wise business man will not go, aware that in doing so he will risk by enfeebled management what he seems to gain by mechanical economics of production and market.

Everywhere the issue of quantitative *versus* qualitative growth comes up. This is the entire issue of empire. A people limited in number and energy and in the land they occupy have the choice of improving to the utmost the political and economic management of their own land, confining themselves to such accessions of territory as are justified by the most economical disposition of a growing population; or they may proceed, like the slovenly farmer, to spread their power and energy over the whole earth, tempted by the speculative value or the quick profits of some new market, or else by mere greed of territorial acquisition, and ignoring the political and economic wastes and risks involved by this imperial career. It must be clearly understood that this is essentially a choice of alternatives; a full simultaneous application of intensive and extensive cultivation is impossible. A nation may either, following the example of Denmark or Switzerland, put brains into agriculture, develop a finely varied system of public education, general and technical, apply the ripest science to its special manufacturing industries, and so support in progressive comfort and character a considerable population upon a strictly limited area; or it may, like Great Britain, neglect its agriculture, allowing its lands to go out of cultivation and its population to grow up in towns, fall behind other nations in its methods of education and in the capacity of adapting to its uses the latest scientific knowledge, in order that it may squander its pecuniary and military resources in forcing bad markets and finding speculative fields of investment in distant corners of the earth, adding millions of square miles and of unassimilable population to the area of the Empire.

The driving forces of class interest which stimulate and support this false economy we have explained. No remedy will serve which permits the future operation of these forces. It is idle to attack imperialism or militarism as political expedients or policies unless the axe is laid at the economic root of the tree, and the classes for whose interest Imperialism works are shorn of the surplus revenues which seek this outlet.

3

FINANCE CAPITAL

Rudolf Hilferding

First published in 1910, Rudolf Hilferding's Finance Capital *set forth one of the cornerstones of imperialist theory. He argues that the development of capitalist industry leads to concentration of banking, that banking is important in capitalist concentration in the form of cartels and trusts, and that finance capital must follow an imperialist path.*

THE DEVELOPMENT OF CAPITALIST INDUSTRY produces concentration of banking, and this concentrated banking system is itself an important force in attaining the highest stage of capitalist concentration in cartels and trusts. How do the latter then react upon the banking system? The cartel or trust is an enterprise of very great financial capacity. In the relations of mutual dependence between capitalist enterprises it is the amount of capital that principally decides which enterprise shall become dependent upon the other. From the outset the effect of advanced cartelization is that the banks also amalgamate and expand in order not to become dependent upon the cartel or trust. In this way cartelization itself requires the amalgamation of the banks, and, conversely, amalgamation of the banks requires cartelization. For example, a number of banks have an interest in the amalgamation of steel concerns, and they work together to bring about this amalgamation even against the will of individual manufacturers.

From Rudolf Hilferding, Finance Capital: A Study of the Latest Phase of Capitalist Development (London: Routledge & Kegan Paul, 1981, 1985), pp. 223–26, 367–70.

Conversely, a consortium established in the first place by manufacturers can have the consequence that two previously competing banks develop common interests and proceed to act in concert in a particular sphere. In a similar fashion, industrial combinations may influence the expansion of the industrial activities of a bank, which was perhaps previously concerned only with the raw materials sector of an industry, and is now obliged to extend its activities to the processing sector as well.

The cartel itself presupposes a large bank which is in a position to provide, on a regular basis, the vast credits needed for current payments and productive investment in a whole industrial sector. But the cartel also brings about a still closer relationship between banking and industry. When competition in an industry is eliminated there is, first of all, an increase in the rate of profit, which plays an important role. When the elimination of competition is achieved by a merger, a new undertaking is created which can count upon higher profits, and these profits can be capitalized and constitute promoter's profit. With the development of trusts this process becomes important in two respects. First, its realization constitutes a very important motive for the banks to encourage monopolization; and second, a part of the promoter's profits can be used to induce reluctant but significant producers to sell their factories, by offering a higher purchase price, thus facilitating the establishment of the cartel. This can perhaps be expressed in the following way: the cartel exerts a demand on the enterprises in a particular branch of industry; this demand increases to a certain degree the price of the enterprises, and this higher price is then paid in part out of the promoter's profit.

Cartelization also means greater security and uniformity in the earnings of the cartelized enterprises. The dangers of competition, which often threatened the existence of the individual enterprise, are eliminated and this leads to an increase in the share prices of these enterprises, which involves further promoter's profit when new shares are issued. Furthermore, the security of the capital invested in these enterprises is significantly increased. This permits a further expansion of industrial credit by the banks, which can then acquire a larger share in industrial profits. As a result of cartelization, therefore, the relations between the banks and industry become still closer, and at the same time the banks acquire an increasing control over the capital invested in industry.

We have seen that in the early stages of capitalist production, the money available to the banks is derived from two sources: on one side, from the resources of the nonproductive classes, and on the other side, from the capital reserves of industrial and commercial capitalists. We have also seen how credit develops in such a way as to place at the disposal of industry not only the whole capital reserves of the capitalist class but also the major part of the funds of the nonproductive classes. In other words, present-day industry is carried on with an amount of capital far exceeding that which is owned by the industrial capitalists. With the development of capitalism there is also a continual increase in the amount of money which the nonproductive classes place at the disposal of the banks, who in turn convey it to the industrialists. The control of these funds which are indispensable to industry rests with the banks, and consequently, with the development of capitalism and of the machinery of credit, the dependence of industry upon the banks increases. On the other side, the banks can only attract the funds of the nonproductive classes, and retain their continually growing capital over the long term, by paying interest on them. They could do this in the past, so long as the volume of money was not too great, by employing it in the form of credit for speculation and circulation. With the increase in the available funds on one side, and the diminishing importance of speculation and trade on the other, they were bound to be transformed more and more into industrial capital. Without the continuous expansion of credit for production, the availability of funds for deposit would have declined long ago, as would the rate of interest on bank deposits. In fact, this is to some extent the case in England, where the deposit banks only furnish credit for commerce, and consequently the rate of interest on deposits is minimal.

Hence deposits are continually withdrawn for investment in industry by the purchase of shares, and in this case the public does directly what is done by the bank where industrial and deposit banks are closely linked. For the public the result is the same, because in neither case does it receive any of the promoter's profits from the merger, but so far as industry is concerned it involves less dependence on bank capital in England as compared with Germany.

The dependence of industry on the banks is therefore a consequence of property relationships. An ever-increasing part of the capital of industry does not belong to the industrialists who use it. They are able to dispose over capital only through the banks, which represent the owners. On the other side, the banks have to invest an ever-increasing part of their capital in industry, and in this way they become to a greater and greater extent industrial capitalists. I call bank capital, that is, capital in money form which is actually transformed in this way into industrial capital, finance capital. So far as its owners are concerned, it always retains the money form, it is invested by them in the form of money capital, interest-bearing capital, and can always be withdrawn by them as money capital. But in reality the greater part of the capital so invested with the banks is transformed into industrial, productive capital (means of production and labor power) and is invested in the productive process. An ever-increasing proportion of the capital used in industry is finance capital, capital at the disposition of the banks which is used by the industrialists.

Finance capital develops with the development of the joint-stock company and reaches its peak with the monopolization of industry. Industrial earnings acquire a more secure and regular character, and so the possibilities for investing bank capital in industry are extended. But the bank disposes of bank capital, and the owners of the majority of the shares in the bank dominate the bank. It is clear that with the increasing concentration of property, the owners of the fictitious capital which gives power over the banks, and the owners of the capital which gives power over industry, become increasingly the same people. As we have seen, this is all the more so as the large banks increasingly acquire the power to dispose over fictitious capital.

We have seen how industry becomes increasingly dependent upon bank capital, but this does not mean that the magnates of industry also become dependent on banking magnates. As capital itself at the highest stage of its development becomes finance capital, so the magnate of capital, the finance capitalist, increasingly concentrates his control over the whole national capital by means of his domination of bank capital. Personal connections also play an important role here.

With cartelization and trustification finance capital attains its greatest power while merchant capital experiences its deepest degradation. A cycle in the development of capitalism is completed. At the outset of capitalist production, money capital, in the form of usurers' and merchants' capital, plays a significant role in the accumulation of capital as well as in the transformation of handicraft production into capitalism. But there then arises a resistance of "productive" capital, i.e., of the profit-earning capitalists—that is, of commerce and industry—against the interest-earning capitalists. Usurer's capital becomes subordinated to industrial capital. As money-dealing capital it performs the functions of money which industry and commerce would otherwise have had to carry out themselves in the process of transformation of their commodities. As bank capital it arranges credit operations among the productive capitalists. The mobilization of capital and the continual expansion of credit gradually brings about a complete change in the position of the money capitalists. The power of the banks increases and they become founders and eventually rulers of industry, whose profits they seize for themselves as finance capital, just as formerly the old usurer seized, in the form of "interest," the produce of the peasants and the ground rent of the lord of the manor. The Hegelians spoke of the negation of the negation: bank capital was the negation of usurer's capital and is itself negated by finance capital. The latter is the synthesis of usurer's and bank capital, and it appropriates to itself the fruits of social production at an infinitely higher stage of economic development.

The development of commercial capital, however, is quite different. The development of industry gradually excluded it from the ruling position over production which it had occupied during the period of manufacture. This decline is definitive, and the development of finance capital reduces the significance of trade both absolutely and relatively, transforming the once proud merchant into a mere agent of industry which is monopolized by finance capital.

Finance capital puts control over social production increasingly into the hands of a small number of large capitalist associations, separates the management of production from ownership, and socializes production to the extent that this is possible under capitalism. The limits of capitalist socialization are constituted, in the first place, by the division of the world market into national economic territories of individual states, a division which can only be overcome partially and with great difficulty through international cartelization, and which also prolongs the duration of the competitive struggle which the cartels and trusts wage against one another with the aid of state power. Socialization is also limited by another factor which should be mentioned here for the sake of completeness, namely, the formation of ground rent, which is an obstacle to concentration in agriculture; and finally, by measures of economic policy intended to prolong the life of medium and small enterprises.

The tendency of finance capital is to establish social control of production, but it is an antagonistic form of socialization, since the control of social production remains vested in an oligarchy. The struggle to dispossess this oligarchy constitutes the ultimate phase of the class struggle between bourgeoisie and proletariat.

The socializing function of finance capital facilitates enormously the task of overcoming capitalism. Once finance capital has brought the most importance branches of production under its control, it is enough for society, through its conscious executive organ—the state conquered by the working class—to seize finance capital in order to gain immediate control of these branches of production. Since all other branches of production depend upon these, control of large-scale industry already provides the most effective form of social control even without any further socialization. A society which has control over coal mining, the iron and steel industry, the machine tool, electricity, and chemical industries, and runs the transport system, is able, by virtue of its control of these most important spheres of production, to determine the distribution of raw materials to other industries and the transport of their products. Even today, taking possession of six large Berlin banks would mean taking possession of the most important spheres of large-scale industry, and would greatly facilitate the initial phases of socialist policy during the transition period, when capitalist accounting might still prove useful. There is no need at all to extend the process of expropriation to the great bulk of peasant farms and small businesses, because as a result of the seizure of large-scale industry upon which they have long been dependent, they would be indirectly socialized just as industry is directly socialized. It is therefore possible to allow the process of expropriation to mature slowly, precisely in those spheres of decentralized production where it would be a long drawn out and politically dangerous process. In other words, since finance capital has already achieved expropriation to the extent required by socialism, it is possible to dispense with a sudden act of expropriation by the state, and to substitute a gradual process of socialization through the economic benefits which society will confer.

While thus creating the final organizational prerequisites for socialism, finance capital also makes the transition easier in a political sense. The action of the capitalist class itself as revealed in the policy of imperialism necessarily directs the proletariat into the path of independent class politics, which can only end in the final overthrow of capitalism. As long as the principles of *laissez-faire* were dominant, and state intervention in economic affairs, as well as the character of the state as an organization of class accumulation, were concealed, it required a comparatively mature level of understanding to appreciate the necessity for political struggle, and above all the necessity for the ultimate political goal, the conquest of state power. It is no accident, then, that in England, the classical country of nonintervention, the emergence of independent working-class political action was so difficult. But this is now changing. The capitalist class seizes possession of the state apparatus in a direct, undisguised, and palpable way and makes it the instrument of its exploitative interests in a manner which is apparent to every worker, who must now recognize that the conquest of political power by the proletariat is his own most immediate personal interest. The blatant seizure of the state by the capitalist class directly compels every proletarian to strive for the conquest of political power as the only means of putting an end to his own exploitation.

The struggle against imperialism intensifies all the class contradictions within bourgeois society. The proletariat, as the most decisive enemy of imperialism, gains support from other classes. Imperialism, which was initially supported by all other classes, eventually repels its followers. The more monopolization progresses the greater is the burden which extra profit imposes upon all other classes. The rise in the cost of living brought about by the trusts reduces living standards, and all the more so because the upward trend in food prices increases the cost of the most essential necessities of life. At the same time the tax burden increases, and this also hits the middle classes, who are increasingly in revolt. The white collar employees see their career-prospects fade, and begin to regard themselves more and more as exploited proletarians. Even the middle strata in commerce and industry become aware of their dependence upon the cartels, which transform them into mere agents working on commission. All these contradictions are bound to become unbearably acute at the moment when the expansion of capital enters a period of slower development. This is the case when the development of corporations and cartels no longer proceeds so rapidly, and when the emergence of new promoter's profits, together with the drive to export capital, slows down. And it is bound to slow down when the rapid opening up of foreign countries by the introduction of capitalism tapers off. The opening up of the Far East, and the rapid development of Canada, South Africa and South America, have made a major contribution to the dizzy pace of capitalist development, interrupted only by brief depressions, since 1895. Once this development begins to slow down, however, the domestic market is bound to feel the pressure of the cartels all the more acutely, for it is during periods of depression that concentration proceeds most rapidly. At the same time, as the expansion of the world market slows down, the conflicts between capitalist nations over their share in it will become more acute, and all the more so when large markets which were previously open to competition, such as England, for example, are closed to other countries by the spread of protective tariffs. The danger of war increases armaments and the tax burden, and finally drives the middle strata, whose living standards are increasingly threatened, into the ranks of the proletariat, which thus reaps the harvest of the decline in the power of the state, and of the collisions of war.

It is a historical law that in all forms of society based upon class antagonisms the great social upheavals only occur when the ruling class has already attained the highest possible level of concentration of its power. The economic power of the ruling class always involves at the same time power over people, disposal over human labor power. But that itself makes the economic ruler dependent upon the power of the ruled, and in augmenting his own power he simultaneously increases the power of those who stand opposed to him as class enemies. As subjects, however, the latter appear to be powerless. Their power is only potential, and can only materialize in the struggle to overthrow the power of the ruling class while the power of the ruler is self-evident. Only in a collision between the two powers, in revolutionary periods, does the power of the subjects prove to be a reality.

Economic power also means political power. Domination of the economy gives control of the instruments of state power. The greater the degree of concentration in the economic sphere, the more unbounded is the control of the state. The rigorous concentration of all the instruments of state power takes the form of an extreme deployment of the power of the state, which becomes the invincible instrument for maintaining economic domination; and at the same time the conquest of political power becomes a precondition of economic liberation. The bourgeois revolution only began when the absolutist state, having overcome the autonomous regional power of the large landowners, had concentrated in its own hands all the means of power; and the concentration of political power in the hands of a few of the largest landowners was itself a precondition for the victory of the absolute monarchy. In the same way the victory of the proletariat is bound up with the concentration of economic power in the hands of a few capitalist magnates, or associations of magnates, and with their domination of the state.

Finance capital, in its maturity, is the highest stage of the concentration of economic and political power in the hands of the capitalist oligarchy. It is the climax of the dictatorship of the magnates of capital. At the same time it makes the dictatorship of the capitalist lords of one country increasingly incompatible with the capitalist interests of other countries, and the internal domination of capital increasingly irreconcilable with the interests of the mass of the people, exploited by finance capital but also summoned into battle against it. In the violent clash of these hostile interests the dictatorship of the magnates of capital will finally be transformed into the dictatorship of the proletariat.

4

IMPERIALISM AND WORLD ECONOMY

Nikolai Bukharin

In his Imperialism and World Economy, Nikolai Bukharin, the Russian
Marxist theorist, followed the argument of Hilferding and envisaged imperialism
as an advanced stage of capitalism in the world economy. He emphasized that trusts
and cartels represented the highest form of capitalist organization at the international level. He believed that banking capital would transform industrial capital
to become finance capital. His view of the world economy as a system of production
and exchange relations on a worldscale complemented his emphasis on the contradiction of modern capitalism as operating simultaneously both to "nationalize" and
"internationalize" capital. His work on imperialism is coherent and clear in its
presentation of theory with evidence. Another relevant work, his Imperialism
and the Accumulation of Capital, was written in 1915 and published in
1921 as a critique of Rosa Luxemburg's Accumulation of Capital (1913).

FROM THE POINT OF VIEW of the ruling circles of society, frictions, and conflicts between "national" groups of the bourgeoisie, inevitably arising
inside of present-day society, lead in their further development to war
as the only solution of the problem. We have seen that those frictions
and conflicts are caused by the changes that have taken place in the conditions of reproducing world capital. Capitalist society, built on a number
of antagonistic elements, can maintain a relative equilibrium only at the

From Nikolai Bukharin, Imperialism and World Economy, with an introduction by V. I. Lenin
(New York: Monthly Review Press, 1973), pp. 104–109, 168–70. Copyright © 1973 by
Monthly Review Press. Reprinted with permission of Monthly Review Foundation.

price of painful crises; the adaptation of the various parts of the social organism to each other and to the whole can be achieved only with a colossal waste of energy, under tremendous *"faux frais"* of this adaptation, which flow from the character of capitalist society as such, i.e., from a definite historical formulation of the development in general.

We have laid bare three fundamental motives for the conquest policies of modern capitalist states: increased competition in the sales markets, in the markets of raw materials, and for the spheres of capital investment. This is what the modern development of capitalism and its transformation into finance capitalism has brought about.

Those three roots of the policy of finance capitalism, however, represent in substance only three facets of the same phenomenon, namely, of the conflict between the growth of productive forces on the one hand, and the "national" limits of the production organization on the other.

Indeed, overproduction of manufactured goods is at the same time underproduction of agricultural products. Underproduction of agricultural products is in this case important for us in so far as the demand on the part of industry is excessively large, i.e., in so far as there are large volumes of manufactured goods which cannot be exchanged for agricultural products; in so far as the ratio between those two branches of production has been (and is more and more) disturbed. This is why growing industry seeks for an agrarian "economic supplement" which, within the framework of capitalism, particularly its monopoly form, i.e., finance capital, inevitably expresses itself in the form of subjugating agrarian countries by force of arms.

We have just discussed the exchange of commodities. Capital export, however, does not represent an isolated phenomenon, either. Capital export, as we have seen, is due to a certain overproduction of capital. Overproduction of capital, however, is nothing but another formulation for overproduction of commodities:

> Overproduction of capital [says Marx] never signifies anything else but overproduction of means of production means of production and necessities of life—which may serve as capital, that is, serve for the exploitation of labor at a given degree of exploitation....Capital consists of commodities, and therefore the overproduction of capital implies an overproduction of commodities. (Marx, 1894, pp. 300–301)

Conversely, when the overproduction of capital decreases, there is also a decrease in the overproduction of commodities. This is why capital export, in decreasing overproduction of capital, aids also in decreasing the overproduction of commodities. (Let us note parenthetically that if, for instance, iron beams are exported into another country to be sold there, we have commodity export pure and simple; if, however, the beam-producing firm establishes an enterprise in another country and exports its commodities to equip the enterprise, we have capital export; obviously, the criterion is whether the transactions of purchase and sale take place or not.)

But even aside from simply "relieving the congestion" by exporting capital in commodity form, there is also a further connection between capital export and the decrease in the overproduction of commodities. Otto Bauer has very well formulated this connection.

> Thus [he says] the exploitation of economically backward countries by the capitalists of a European country has two series of consequences: directly, it creates new spheres of investment for capital in the colonial country, and at the same time more selling opportunities for the industry of the dominating power; indirectly, it creates new spheres for the application of capital also inside of the dominating country, and increases the sale of the products of all its industries. (Bauer, 1907, p. 464)

If we thus consider the problem in its entirety, and take thereby the objective point of view, i.e., the point of view of the adaptation of modern society to its conditions of existence, we find that there is here a growing discord between the basis of social economy which has become worldwide and the peculiar class structure of society, a structure where the ruling class (the bourgeoisie) itself is split into "national" groups with contradictory economic interests, groups which, being opposed to the world proletariat, are competing among themselves for the division of the surplus value created on a world scale. Production is of a social nature; international division of labor turns the private "national" economies into parts of a gigantic all-embracing labor process, which extends over almost the whole of humanity. Acquisition, however, assumes the character of "national" (state) acquisition where the beneficiaries are huge state companies of the bourgeoisie of finance capital. The development of productive forces moves within the narrow limits of state boundaries while it has already outgrown those limits. Under such conditions there inevitably arises a conflict, which, given the existence of capitalism, is settled through extending the state frontiers in bloody struggles, a settlement which holds the prospect of new and more grandiose conflicts.

The social representatives of this contradiction are the various groups of the bourgeoisie organized in the state, with their conflicting interests. The development of world capitalism leads, on the one hand, to an internationalization of the economic life and, on the other, to the leveling of economic differences,—and to an infinitely greater degree, the same process of economic development intensifies the tendency to "nationalize" capitalist interests, to form narrow "national" groups armed to the teeth and ready to hurl themselves at one another any moment. It is impossible to describe the fundamental aims of present-day politics better than was done by R. Hilferding. "The policy of finance capital," he says, "pursues a threefold aim: first, the creation of the largest possible economic territory which, secondly, must be protected against foreign competition by tariff walls, and thus, thirdly, must become an area of exploitation for the national monopoly companies" (Hilferding, 1910, p. 412). The increase in the economic territory opens agrarian regions to the national cartels and, consequently, markets for raw materials, increasing the safes markets and the sphere of capital investment; the tariff policy makes it possible to suppress foreign competition, to obtain surplus profit, and to put into operation the battering ram of dumping; the "system" as a whole facilitates the increase of the rate of profit for the monopoly organizations. This policy of finance capital is imperialism.

Such a policy implies violent methods, for the expansion of the state territory means war. The reverse, however, is not true, not every war or every increase in the state territory implies an imperialist policy. The determining factor is whether the war expresses the policy of finance capital, the latter term being taken in accordance with the above definition. Here, as everywhere, we find some intermediary forms, whose existence, however, by no means vitiates the main definition. This is why attempts like those made by the well-known Italian economist and sociologist Achille Loria are fundamentally incorrect.

Loria, namely, has attempted to construct two conceptions of imperialism which, he alleges, contain "entirely heterogeneous relations" (*des relations tout ~ fait Heterogenes*). Loria distinguishes (Loria, 1907, p. 459) between "economic" imperialism (*l'imperialisme economique, okonomischer Imperialismus*) and "commercial" or "trade" imperialism (*l'imperialisme commercial, Handelsimperialismus*). The object of the former, be says, are tropical countries, the object of the latter are countries whose conditions make them suitable also for European colonization; the method of the former is armed force, the method of the latter, peaceful treaties (*des accords pacifiques*); the former has no shadings or grades, in the latter they range from the maximum of full assimilation or a single tariff to incomplete forms, like preference tariffs between the colonies and the mother countries, etc.

This is Loria's theory. It is quite obvious that it is made out of whole cloth. Both the "commercial" and the "economic" imperialisms are in substance the expression of the same tendencies, as we have seen above. A closed ring of tariff duties, and the raising of the latter, may not result in an armed conflict immediately; they will, however, bring about such a conflict later. It is thus obvious that we cannot contrast "peaceful treaties" with "armed forces." (Peaceful treaties between England and its colonies mean a straining of the relations between England and other countries.) Neither can we assert that "economic" imperialism is merely of a "tropical" nature. The best proof is the fate of Belgium, Galicia, and the probable fate of South America, China, Turkey, and Persia.

To sum up: the development of the productive forces of world capitalism has made gigantic strides in the last decades. The upper hand in the competitive struggle has everywhere been gained by large-scale production; it has consolidated the "magnates of capital" into an ironclad organization, which has taken possession of the entire economic life. State power has become the domain of a financial oligarchy; the latter manages production which is tied up by the banks into one knot. This process of the organization of production has proceeded from below; it has fortified itself within the framework of modern states, which have become an exact expression of the interests of finance capital. Every one of the capitalistically advanced "national economies" has turned into some kind of a "national" trust. This process of the organization of the economically advanced sections of world economy, on the other hand, has been accompanied by an extraordinary sharpening of their mutual competition. The overproduction of commodities, which is connected with the growth of large enterprises; the export policy of the cartels, and the narrowing of the sales markets in connection with the colonial and tariff policy of the capitalist powers; the growing disproportion between tremendously developed industry and backward agriculture; the gigantic growth of capital export and the economic subjugation of entire regions by "national" banking combines—all this has thrown into the sharpest possible relief the clash of interests between the "national" groups of capital. Those groups find their final argument in the force and power of the state organization, first of all in its army and navy. A mighty state military power is the last trump in the struggle of the powers. The fighting force in the world market thus depends upon the power and consolidation of the "nation," upon its financial and military resources. A self-sufficient national state, and an economic unit limitlessly expending its great power until it becomes a world kingdom—a worldwide empire—such is the ideal built up by finance capital.

> With a steady and clear eye does it [finance capital] view the Babylonian confusion of peoples, and above all of them it sees its own nation. The latter is real; it lives in a powerful state, which keeps on increasing its power and grandeur, and which devotes all its forces to making them greater. In this way, the interests of the individual are subjugated to the interests of the whole—a condition without which no social ideology can live; a nation and a state that are hostile to the people are tied into one whole, and the national idea, as a motive power, is subjugated to politics. The class conflicts have disappeared; they have been annihilated, absorbed as they are in serving the interests of the whole. In place of the dangerous class struggle, fraught for the owners with unknown consequences, there appear the general actions of the nation which is united by one aim—the striving for national grandeur. (Hilferding, 1910, pp. 428–29)

Thus the interests of finance capital acquire a grandiose ideological formulation; every effort is made to inculcate it into the mass of workers, for, as a German imperialist has correctly remarked from his point of view: "We must gain power not only over the legs of the soldiers, but also over their minds and hearts."...

History moves in contradictions. The skeleton of historic existence, the economic structure of society, also develops in contradictions. Forms eternally follow forms. Everything has only a passing being. The dynamic force of life creates the new over and over again—such is the law inherent in reality. Hegel's dialectics, which Marx placed on its feet, is valuable for this very reason that it grasps the dialectics of life, that it fearlessly analyses the present without being disturbed by the fact that every existence hides within itself the germ of its own destruction.

In its mystified form, dialectic became the fashion in Germany because it seemed to transfigure and to glorify the existing state of things. In its rational form it is a scandal and abomination to bourgeoisdom and its doctrinaire professors, because it includes in its comprehension an affirmative recognition of the existing state of things, at the same time also, the recognition of the negation of that state, of its inevitable breaking up; because it regards every historically developed social form as in fluid movement, and therefore takes into account its transient nature not less than its momentary existence; because it lets nothing impose upon it, and is in its essence critical and revolutionary in spirit....

Many years have passed since; we already hear a new future knocking at history's door. Present-day society, which developing productive forces to a gigantic degree, while powerfully conquering ever new realms, while subjugating nature to man's domination on an unprecedented scale, begins to choke in the capitalist grip. Contradictions inherent in the very essence of capitalism, and appearing in an embryonic state at the beginning of its development, have grown, have widened their scope with every stage of capitalism; in the period of imperialism they have reached proportions that cry to heaven. Productive forces in their present volume insistently demand new production relations. The capitalist shell must inevitably burst.

The epoch of finance capital has made all the elements of maladjustment of the capitalist organization stand out in the boldest possible relief. In former times, when capitalism, as well as its class sponsor, the bourgeoisie, appeared as a progressive force, it was in a position partly to conceal its inner defects by comparing itself with the backwardness and maladaptation of precapitalist relations. Large-scale production, equipped with gigantic machines, ruthlessly crushed the handicrafts with their poor technique. This painful process was nothing but the collapse of pre-capitalist production forms. On the other hand, the very existence of those forms, of those various "third persons" in the capitalist production process, allowed capitalism to extend its power "peacefully," without exposing the limits put to economic evolution by its capitalist shell. This is why the general features of the contradictions inherent in capitalism as such, and forming its "*law*," appeared in the sharpest possible form only at a stage of economic development when capitalism had outgrown its swaddling clothes, when it had not only become the prevailing form of the socioeconomic life, but had even become the general form of economic relations, in other words, when it had appeared as world capitalism. It is only now that the inner contradictoriness of capitalism is expressed with dramatic force. The convulsions of the present-day capitalist world that is drenched in blood and is agonized in mortal pain, are the expression of those contradictions in the capitalist system, which in the long run will cause it to explode.

Capitalism has attempted to overcome its own anarchy by pressing it into the iron ring of state organization. But having eliminated competition within the state, it let loose all the devils of a world scuffle.

Capitalism has attempted to tame the working class and to subdue social contradictions by decreasing the steam pressure through the aid of a colonial valve. But having accomplished this task for a moment, it thus prepared the explosion of the whole capitalist boiler. Capitalism has attempted to adapt the development of productive forces to state limits of exploitation by resorting to imperialist conquests. But it proved unable to solve that problem even through its own methods.

Capitalism has increased the power of militarism enormously. It has brought to the historic arena millions of armed men. The arms, however, begin to turn against capitalism itself. The masses of the people, aroused to political life and originally tame and docile, raise their voices ever higher. Steeled in battles forced upon them from above, accustomed to look into the face of death every minute, they begin to break the front of the imperialist war with the same fearlessness by turning it into civil war against the bourgeoisie. Thus capitalism, driving the concentration of production to extraordinary heights, and having created a centralized production apparatus, has therewith prepared the immense ranks of its own grave-diggers. In the great clash of classes, the dictatorship of finance capital is being replaced by the dictatorship of the revolutionary proletariat. "The hour of capitalist property has struck. The expropriators are being expropriated."

REFERENCES

Bauer, Otto. 1907. *Die Nationalitatenfrage und die Sozialdemokratie.* Vienna.

Hilferding, Ruldolf. 1910. *Finanz Kapital: eine Studie uber die junste Entwicklung des Kapitalismus.* Vienna.

Loria, Achille. 1907. "Les deux notions de l'imperialisme." In *Revue economique internationale,* vol. 3.

Marx, Karl. 1894. *Capital.* Vol. 3. Edited by F. Engels. Moscow: Foreign Languages Publishing House, 1962.

5

IMPERIALISM
The Highest Stage of Capitalism

V. I. Lenin

Somewhat eclectically, Lenin, a Russian Marxist, drew his ideas on imperialism from Hobson and Hilferding, emphasizing the political and economic context into which the former placed his conceptualization and the form of finance capital which was the foundation for the latter's treatise on imperialism. Lenin focused on the highest stage of commodity production under which monopolies export capital and the economies reflect uneven development and the accumulation of a surplus in the advanced nations under the supreme control of a financial oligarchy of bankers. Lenin's political tract was a popularization of the earlier writing on imperialism. He characterized this high phase of capitalism in terms of the concentration of production in monopolies, the merging of bank and industrial capital under a financial oligarchy, the export of capital, and the division of the world into international monopoly blocs and territories.

DURING THE LAST FIFTEEN TO twenty years, especially since the Spanish-American War (1898) and the Anglo-Boer War (1899–1902), the economic and also the political literature of the two hemispheres has more and more often adopted the term "imperialism" in order to describe the present era. In 1902, a book by the English economist J. A. Hobson, *Imperialism*, was published in London and New York. This author, whose point of view is that of bourgeois social-reformism and pacifism which, in

Originally published in V. I. Lenin, *Imperialism, the Highest Stage of Capitalism: A Popular Outline* (1917). From V. I. Lenin, *Selected Works*, vol. 1 (Moscow: Progress Works, 1967), pp. 684, 710–11, 744–48, 772–79.

essence, is identical with the present point of view of the ex-Marxist, Karl Kautsky, gives a very good and comprehensive description of the principal specific economic and political features of imperialism. In 1910, there appeared in Vienna the work of the Austrian Marxist, Rudolf Hilferding, *Finance Capital* (Russian edition, Moscow, 1912). In spite of the mistake the author makes on the theory of money, and in spite of a certain inclination on his part to reconcile Marxism with opportunism, this work gives a very valuable theoretical analysis of "the latest phase of capitalist development," as the subtitle runs. Indeed, what has been said of imperialism during the last few years, especially in an enormous number of magazine and newspaper articles, and also in the resolutions, for example, of the Chemnitz and Basle congresses which took place in the autumn of 1912, has scarcely gone beyond the ideas expounded, or more exactly, summed up by the two writers mentioned above....

Later on, I shall try to show briefly, and as simply as possible, the connection and relationships between the *principal* economic features of imperialism. I shall not be able to deal with the noneconomic aspects of the question, however much they deserve to be dealt with. References to literature and other notes which, perhaps, would not interest all readers, are to be found at the end of this pamphlet....

FINANCE CAPITAL AND THE FINANCIAL OLIGARCHY

"A steadily increasing proportion of capital in industry," writes Hilferding, "ceases to belong to the industrialists who employ it. They obtain the use of it only through the medium of the banks which, in relation to them, represent the owners of the capital. On the other hand, the bank is forced to sink an increasing share of its funds in industry. Thus, to an ever greater degree the banker is being transformed into an industrial capitalist. This bank capital, i.e., capital in money form, which is thus actually transformed into industrial capital; I call 'finance capital'." "Finance capital is capital controlled by banks and employed by industrialists."

This definition is incomplete insofar as it is silent on one extremely important fact—on the increase of concentration of production and of capital to such an extent that concentration is leading, and has led, to monopoly. But throughout the whole of his work, and particularly in the two chapters preceding the one from which this definition is taken, Hilferding stresses the part played by *capitalist monopolies.*

The concentration of production, the monopolies arising therefrom, the merging or coalescence of the banks with industry—such is the history of the rise of finance capital and such is the content of that concept.

We now have to describe how, under the general conditions of commodity production and private property, the "business operations" of capitalist monopolies inevitably lead to the domination of a financial oligarchy. It should be noted that German—and not only German—bourgeois scholars, like Riesser, Schulze Gaevernitz, Liefmann, and others, are all apologists of imperialism and of finance capital. Instead of revealing the "mechanics" of the formation of an oligarchy, its methods, the size of its revenues "impeccable and peccable," its connections with parliaments, etc., etc., they obscure or gloss over them. They evade these "vexed questions" by pompous and vague phrases, appeals to the "sense of responsibility" of bank directors, by praising "the sense of duty" of Prussian officials, giving serious study to the petty details of absolutely ridiculous parliamentary bills for the "supervision" and "regulation" of monopolies, playing spillikins with theories, like, for example, the following "scholarly" definition, arrived at by Professor Liefmann: "*Commerce is an occupation having for its object the collection, storage and supply of goods*" (the professor's italics)…. From this it would follow that commerce existed in the time of primitive man, who knew nothing about exchange, and that it will exist under socialism!

But the monstrous facts concerning the monstrous rule of the financial oligarchy are so glaring that in all capitalist countries, in America, France, and Germany, a whole literature has sprung up, written from the *bourgeois* point of view, but which, nevertheless, gives a fairly truthful picture and criticism—petty-bourgeois, naturally—of this oligarchy.

IMPERIALISM AS A SPECIAL STAGE OF CAPITALISM

We must now try to sum up, to draw together the threads of, what has been said above on the subject of imperialism. Imperialism emerged as the development and direct continuation of the fundamental characteristics of capitalism in general. But capitalism only became capitalist imperialism at a definite and very high stage of its development, when certain of its fundamental characteristics began to change into their opposites, when the features of the epoch of transition from capitalism to a higher social and economic system had taken shape and revealed themselves in all spheres. Economically, the main thing in this process is the displacement of capitalist free competition by capitalist monopoly. Free competition is the basic feature of capitalism, and of commodity production generally; monopoly is the exact opposite of free competition, but we have seen the latter being transformed into monopoly before our eyes, creating large-scale industry and forcing out small industry, replacing large-scale by still larger-scale industry, and carrying concentration of production and capital to the point where out of it has grown and is growing monopoly: cartels, syndicates, and trusts, and merging with them, the capital of a dozen or so banks, which manipulate thousands of millions. At the same time the monopolies, which have grown out of free competition, do not eliminate the latter, but exist above it and alongside it, and thereby give rise to a number of very acute, intense antagonisms, frictions, and conflicts. Monopoly is the transition from capitalism to a higher system.

If it were necessary to give the briefest possible definition of imperialism we should have to say that imperialism is the monopoly stage of capitalism. Such a definition would include what is most important, for, on the one hand, finance capital is the bank capital of a few very big monopolist banks, merged with the capital of the monopolist associations of industrialists; and, on the other hand, the division of the world is the transition from a colonial policy which has extended without hindrance to territories unseized by any capitalist power, to a colonial policy of monopolist possession of the territory of the world, which has been completely divided up.

But very brief definitions, although convenient, for they sum up the main points, are nevertheless inadequate, since we have to deduce from them some especially important features of the phenomenon that has to be defined. And so, without forgetting the conditional and relative value of all definitions in general which can never embrace all the concatenations of a phenomenon in its full development, we must give a definition of imperialism that will include the following five of its basic features: (1) the concentration of production and capital has developed to such a high stage that it has created monopolies which play a decisive role in economic life; (2) the merging of bank capital with industrial capital, and the creation, on the basis of this "finance capital," of a financial oligarchy; (3) the export of capital as distinguished from the export of commodities acquires exceptional importance; (4) the formation of international monopolist capitalist associations which share the world among themselves; and (5) the territorial division of the whole world among the biggest capitalist powers is completed. Imperialism is capitalism at that stage of development at which the dominant of monopolies and finance capital is established; in which the export of capital has acquired pronounced importance, in which the division of the world among the international trusts has begun, in which the division of all territories of the globe among the biggest capitalist powers has been completed.

We shall see later that imperialism can and must be defined differently if we bear in mind not only the basic, purely economic concepts—to which the above definition is limited—but also the historical place of this stage of capitalism in relation to capitalism in general, or the relation between imperialism and the two main trends in the working-class movement. The thing to be noted at this point is that imperialism, as interpreted above, undoubtedly represents a special stage in the development of capitalism. To enable the reader to obtain the most well-grounded idea of imperialism, I deliberately tried to quote as extensively as possible *bourgeois* economists who have to admit the particularly incontrovertible facts concerning the latest stage of capitalist economy. With the same object in view, I have quoted detailed statistics which enable one to see to what degree bank capital, etc., has grown, in what precisely the transformation of quantity into quality, of developed capitalism into imperialism was expressed. Needless to say, of course, all boundaries in nature and in society are conventional and changeable, and it would be absurd to argue, for example, about the particular year or decade in which imperialism "definitely" became established.

In the matter of defining imperialism, however, we have to enter into controversy, primarily, with Karl Kautsky, the principal Marxist theoretician of the epoch of the so-called Second International—that is, of the twenty-five years between 1889 and 1914. The fundamental ideas expressed in our definition of imperialism were very resolutely attacked by Kautsky in 1915, and even in November 1914, when he said that imperialism must not be regarded as a "phase" or stage of economy, but as a policy, a definite policy "preferred" by finance capital; that imperialism must not be "identified" with "present-day capitalism," that if imperialism is to be understood to mean "all the phenomena of present-day capitalism"—cartels, protection, the domination of the financiers, and colonial policy—then the question as to whether imperialism is necessary to capitalism becomes reduced to the "flattest tautology," because, in that case, "imperialism is naturally a vital necessity for capitalism," and so on. The best way to present Kautsky's idea is to quote his own definition of imperialism, which is diametrically opposed to the substance of the ideas which I have set forth (for the objections coming from the camp of the German Marxists, who have been advocating similar ideas for many years already, have been long known to Kautsky as the objections of a definite trend in Marxism).

Kautsky's definition is as follows:

> Imperialism is a product of highly developed industrial capitalism. It consists in the striving of every industrial capitalist nation to bring under its control or to annex all large areas of *agrarian* territory, irrespective of what nations inhabit it. (Kautsky, 1914, Kautsky's italics)

This definition is of no use at all because it one-sidedly, i.e., arbitrarily, singles out only the national question (although the latter is extremely important in itself as well as in its relation to imperialism), it arbitrarily and *inaccurately* connects this question *only* with industrial capital in the countries which annex other nations, and in an equally arbitrary and inaccurate manner pushes into the forefront the annexation of agrarian regions.

Imperialism is a striving for annexations—this is what the *political* part of Kautsky's definition amounts to. It is correct, but very incomplete, for politically, imperialism is, in general, a striving toward violence and reaction. For the moment, however, we are interested in the *economic* aspect of the question, which Kautsky *himself* introduced into *his* definition. The inaccuracies in Kautsky's definition are glaring. The characteristic feature of imperialism is not industrial but finance capital. It is not an accident that in France it was precisely the extraordinarily rapid development of finance capital, and the weakening of industrial capital, that from the eighties onward, gave rise to the extreme intensification of annexationist (colonial) policy. The characteristic feature of imperialism is precisely that it strives to annex *not only* agrarian territories, but even most highly industrialized regions (German appetite for Belgium; French appetite for Lorraine), because (1) the fact that the world is already partitioned obliges those contemplating a *redivision* to reach out for *every kind* of territory, and (2) an essential feature of imperialism is the rivalry between several great powers in the striving for hegemony, i.e., for the conquest of territory, not so much directly for themselves as to weaken the adversary and undermine *his* hegemony. (Belgium is particularly important for Germany as a base for operations against Britain; Britain needs Baghdad as a base for operations against Germany, etc.)

Kautsky refers especially—and repeatedly—to English writers who, he alleges, have given a purely political meaning to the word "imperialism" in the sense that he, Kautsky, understands it. We take up the work by the English writer Hobson, *Imperialism*, which appeared in 1902, and there we read:

> The new imperialism differs from the older, first, in substituting for the ambition of a single growing empire the theory and the practice of competing empires, each motivated by similar lusts of political aggrandizement and commercial gain; secondly, in the dominance of financial or investing over mercantile interests. (Hobson, 1902)

We see that Kautsky is absolutely wrong in referring to English writers generally (unless he meant the vulgar English *imperialists*, or the avowed apologists for imperialism). We see that Kautsky, while claiming that he continues to advocate Marxism, as a master of fact takes a step backward compared with the *social-liberal* Hobson, who *more correctly* takes into account two "historically concrete" (Kautsky's definition is a mockery of historical concreteness!) features of modern imperialism: (1) the competition between *several* imperialisms, and (2) the predominance of the financier over the merchant. If it is chiefly a question of the annexation of agrarian countries by industrial countries, then the role of the merchant is put in the forefront.

THE PLACE OF IMPERIALISM IN HISTORY

We have seen that in its economic essence imperialism is monopoly capitalism. This in itself determines its place in history, for monopoly that grows out of the soil of free competition, and precisely out of free competition, is the transition from the capitalist system to a higher socioeconomic order. We must take special note of the four principal types of monopoly, or principal manifestations of monopoly capitalism, which are characteristic of the epoch we are examining.

Firstly, monopoly arose out of the concentration of production at a very high stage. This refers to the monopolist capitalist associations, cartels, syndicates, and trusts. We have seen the important part these play in present-day economic life. At the beginning of the twentieth century, monopolies had acquired complete supremacy in the advanced countries, and although the first steps toward the formation of the cartels were taken by countries enjoying the protection of high tariffs (Germany, America), Great Britain, with her system of free trade, revealed the same basic phenomenon, only a little later, namely, the birth of monopoly out of the concentration of production.

Secondly, monopolies have stimulated the seizure of the most important sources of raw materials, especially for the basic and most highly cartelized industries in capitalist society: the coal and iron industries. The monopoly of the most important sources of raw materials has enormously increased the power of big capital, and has sharpened the antagonism between cartelized and noncartelized industry.

Thirdly, monopoly has sprung from the banks. The banks have developed from modest middleman enterprises into the monopolists of finance capital. Some three to five of the biggest banks in each of the foremost capitalist countries have achieved the "personal link-up" between industrial and bank capital, and have concentrated in their hands the control of thousands upon thousands of millions which form the greater part of the capital and income of entire countries. A financial oligarchy, which throws a close network of dependence relationships over all the economic and political institutions of present-day bourgeois society without exception—such is the most striking manifestation of this monopoly.

Fourthly, monopoly has grown out of colonial policy. To the numerous "old" motives of colonial policy, finance capital has added the struggle for the sources of raw materials, for the export of capital, for spheres of influence, i.e., for spheres for profitable deals, concessions, monopoly profits, and so on, economic territory in general. When the colonies of the European powers, for instance, comprised only one-tenth of the territory of Africa (as was the case in 1876), colonial policy was able to develop by methods other than those of monopoly—by the "free grabbing" of territories, so to speak. But when nine-tenths of Africa had been seized (by 1900), when the whole world had been divided up, there was inevitably ushered in the era of monopoly possession of colonies and, consequently, of particularly intense struggle for the division and the redivision of the world.

The extent to which monopolist capital has intensified all the contradictions of capitalism is generally known. It is sufficient to mention the high cost of living and the tyranny of the cartels. This intensification of contradictions constitutes the most powerful driving force of the transitional period of history, which began from the time of the final victory of world finance capital.

Monopolies, oligarchy, the striving for domination and not for freedom, the exploitation of an increasing number of small or weak nations by a handful of the richest or most powerful nations—all these have given birth to those distinctive characteristics of imperialism which compel us to define it as parasitic or decaying capitalism. More and more prominently there emerges, as one of the tendencies of imperialism, the creation of the "rentier state," the usurer state, in which the bourgeoisie to an ever-increasing degree lives on the proceeds of capital exports and by "clipping coupons." It *would* be a mistake to believe that this tendency to decay precludes the rapid growth of capitalism. It does not. In the epoch of imperialism, certain branches of industry, certain strata of the bourgeoisie and certain countries betray, to a greater or lesser degree, now one and now another of these tendencies. On the whole, capitalism is growing far more rapidly than before; but this growth is not only becoming more and more uneven in general; its unevenness also manifests itself, in particular, in the decay of the countries which are richest in capital (Britain).

In regard to the rapidity of Germany's economic development,

Riesser, the author of the book on the big German banks, states: "The progress of the preceding period (1848—70), which had not been exactly slow, compares with the rapidity with which the whole of Germany's national economy, and with it German banking, progressed during this period (1870—1905) in about the same way as the speed of the mail coach in the good old days compares with the speed of the present-day automobile...which is whizzing past so fast that it endangers not only innocent pedestrians in its path, but also the occupants of the car." In its turn, this finance capital which has grown with such extraordinary rapidity is not unwilling, precisely because it has grown so quickly, to pass on to a more "tranquil" possession of colonies which have to be seized—and not only by peaceful methods—from richer nations. In the United States, economic development in the last decades has been even more rapid than in Germany, *and for this very reason*, the parasitic features of modern American capitalism have stood out with particular prominence. On the other hand, a comparison of, say, the republican American bourgeoisie with the monarchist Japanese or German bourgeoisie shows that the most pronounced political distinction diminishes to an extreme degree in the epoch of imperialism—not because it is unimportant in general, but because in all these cases we are talking about a bourgeoisie which has definite features of parasitism.

The receipt of high monopoly profits by the capitalists in one of the numerous branches of industry, in one of the numerous countries, etc., makes it economically possible for them to bribe certain sections of the workers, and for a time a fairly considerable minority of them, and win them to the side of the bourgeoisie of a given industry or given nation against all the others. The intensification of antagonisms between imperialist nations for the division of the world increases this urge. And so there is created that bond between imperialism and opportunism, which revealed itself first and most clearly in Great Britain, owing to the fact that certain features of imperialist development were observable there much earlier than in other countries. Some writers, L. Martov, for example, are prone to wave aside the connection between imperialism and opportunism in the working-class movement—a particularly glaring fact at the present time—by resorting to "official optimism" (à la Kautsky and Huysmans) like the following: the cause of the opponents of capitalism would be hopeless if it were progressive capitalism that led to the increase of opportunism, or, if it were the best-paid workers who were inclined toward opportunism, etc. We must have no illusions about "optimism" of this kind. It is optimism in respect of opportunism; it is optimism which serves to conceal opportunism. As a matter of fact the extraordinary rapidity and the particularly revolting character of the development of opportunism is by no means a guarantee that its victory will be durable: the rapid growth of a painful abscess on a healthy body can only cause it to burst more quickly and thus relieve the body of it. The most dangerous of all in this respect are those who do not wish to understand that the fight against imperialism is a sham and humbug unless it is inseparably bound up with the fight against opportunism.

From all that has been said...on the economic essence of imperialism, it follows that we must define it as capitalism in transition, or, more precisely, as moribund capitalism. It is very instructive in this respect to note that bourgeois economists, in describing modern capitalism, frequently employ catchwords and phrases like "interlocking," "absence of isolation," etc.; "in conformity with their functions and course of development," banks are "not purely private business enterprises; they are more and more outgrowing the sphere of purely private business regulation." And this very Riesser, whose words I have just quoted, declares with all seriousness that the "prophecy" of the Marxists concerning "socialization" has "not come true!

What then does this catchword "interlocking" express? It merely expresses the most striking feature of the process going on before our eyes. It shows that the observer counts the separate trees, but cannot see the wood. It slavishly copies the superficial, the fortuitous, the chaotic. It reveals the observer as one who is overwhelmed by the mass of raw material and is utterly incapable of appreciating its meaning and importance. Ownership of shares, the relations between owners of private property "interlock in a haphazard way." But underlying this interlocking, its very base, are the changing social relations of production. When a big enterprise assumes gigantic proportions, and on the basis of an exact computation of mass data, organizes according to plan the supply of primary raw materials to the extent of two-thirds, or three-fourths, of all that is necessary for tens of millions of people; when the raw materials are transported in a systematic and organized manner to the most suitable places of production, sometimes situated hundreds or thousands of miles from each other; when a single center directs all the consecutive stages of processing the material right up to the manufacture of numerous varieties of finished articles; when these products are distributed according to a single plan among tens and hundreds of millions of consumers (the marketing of oil in America and Germany by the American oil trust)—then it becomes evident that we have socialization of production, and not mere "interlocking"; that private economic and private property relations constitute a shell which no longer fits its contents, a shell which must inevitably decay if its removal is artificially delayed, a shell which may remain in a state of decay for a fairly long period (if, at the worst, the cure of the opportunist abscess is protracted), but which will inevitably be removed.

The enthusiastic admirer of German imperialism, Schulze-Gaevernitz, exclaims:

> Once the supreme management of the German banks has been entrusted to the hands of a dozen persons, their activity is even today more significant for the public good than that of the majority of the Ministers of State....[The "interlocking" of bankers, ministers, magnates of industry and rentiers is here conveniently forgotten.] If we imagine the development of those tendencies we have noted carried to their logical conclusion we will have: the money capital of the nation united in the banks; the banks themselves combined into cartels; the investment capital of the nation cast in the shape of securities. Then the forecast of that genius Saint-Simon will be fulfilled: "The present anarchy of production, which corresponds to the fact that economic relations are developing without uniform regulation, must make way for organization in production. Production will no longer be directed by isolated manufacturers, independent of each other and ignorant of man's economic needs; that will be done by a certain public institution. A central committee of management, being able to survey the large field of social economy from a more elevated point of view, will regulate it for the benefit of the whole of society, will put the means of production into suitable hands, and above all will take care that there be constant harmony between production and consumption. Institutions already exist which have assumed as part of their functions a certain organization of economic labor, the banks." We are still a long way from the fulfillment of Saint-Simon's

forecast, but we are on the way towards it: Marxism, different from what Marx imagined, but different only in form. (Marx, 1859)

A crushing "refutation" of Marx, indeed, which retreats a step from Marx's precise, scientific analysis to Saint-Simon's guess-work, the guess-work of a genius, but guess-work all the same.

REFERENCES

Hobson, J. A. 1902. *Imperialism.* London: George Allen & Unwin Ltd., 1938.

Kautsky, K. 1914. *Die Neue Zeit* (September 11).

Marx, K. 1859. *Grundrisse Foundations of the Critique of Political Economy.* Harmondsworth: Penguin, 1973.

6

ACCUMULATION

Rosa Luxemburg

In the following selection, Rosa Luxemburg explores the impact of capitalism on natural economy in its various forms as well as the thesis that imperialism is the manifestation of capitalist accumulation. She attempts to expand and refine Marx's early understanding of accumulation and relate this to imperialism. Her work is important for its examination of capital penetration into primitive and noncapitalist economies, and she expanded her analysis, first, to capitalist struggles with a commodity economy and, second, to imperialism. She understood the imperialist phase of capitalist accumulation as involving industrialization and capitalist development of the "hinterland" as well as a political expression of the struggle for control of the noncapitalist world.

CAPITALISM ARISES AND DEVELOPS HISTORICALLY amidst a noncapitalist society. In Western Europe it is found at first in a feudal environment from which it in fact sprang—the system of bondage in rural areas and the guild system in the towns—and later, after having swallowed up the feudal system, it exists mainly in an environment of peasants and artisans, that is to say in a system of simple commodity production both in agriculture and trade. European capitalism is further surrounded by vast

From Rosa Luxemburg, *The Accumulation of Capital*, trans. by Agnes Schwarzschild (New York: Monthly Review Press, 1964), pp. 368–70, 452–53; and *The Accumulation of Capital: An Anti-Critique* (New York: Monthly Review Press, 1972), pp. 61–62. Copyright © 1964, 1972, by Monthly Review Press. Reprinted with permission from Monthly Review Foundation. For a rebuttal, see Nikolai Bukharin, *Imperialism and the Accumulation of Capital* (New York: Monthly Review Press, 1972), pp. 238–57.

territories of non-European civilization ranging over all levels of development, from the primitive communist hordes of nomad herdsmen, hunters, and gatherers, to commodity production by peasants and artisans. This is the setting for the accumulation of capital.

We must distinguish three phases: the struggle of capital against natural economy, the struggle against commodity economy, and the competitive struggle of capital on the international stage for the remaining conditions of accumulation.

The existence and development of capitalism requires an environment of noncapitalist forms of production, but not every one of these forms will serve its ends. Capitalism needs noncapitalist social strata as a market for its surplus value, as a source of supply for its means of production and as a reservoir of labor power for its wage system. For all these purposes, forms of production based upon a natural economy are of no use to capital. In all social organizations where natural economy prevails, where there are primitive peasant communities with common ownership of the land, a feudal system of bondage or anything of this nature, economic organization is essentially in response to the internal demand; and therefore there is no demand, or very little, for foreign goods, and also, as a rule, no surplus production, or at least no urgent need to dispose of surplus products. What is most important, however, is that, in any natural economy, production only goes on because both means of production and labor power are bound in one form or another. The communist peasant community no less than the feudal *corvee* farm and similar institutions maintain their economic organization by subjecting the labor power, and the most important means of production, the land, to the rule of law and custom. A natural economy thus confronts the requirements of capitalism at every turn with rigid barriers. Capitalism must therefore always and everywhere fight a battle of annihilation against every historical form of natural economy that it encounters, whether this is slave economy, feudalism, primitive communism, or patriarchal peasant economy. The principal methods in this struggle are political force (revolution, war), oppressive taxation by the state, and cheap goods; they are partly applied simultaneously, and partly they succeed and complement one another. In Europe, force assumed revolutionary forms in the fight against feudalism (this is the ultimate explanation of the bourgeois revolutions in the seventeenth, eighteenth and nineteenth centuries); in the non-European countries, where it fights more primitive social organizations, it assumes the forms of colonial policy. These methods, together with the systems of taxation applied in such cases, and commercial relations also, particularly with primitive communities, form an alliance in which political power and economic factors go hand in hand.

In detail, capital in its struggle against societies with a natural economy pursues the following ends:

1. To gain immediate possession of important sources of productive forces such as land, game in primeval forests, minerals, precious stones and ores, products of exotic flora such as rubber, etc.
2. To "liberate" labor power and to coerce it into service.
3. To introduce a commodity economy.
4. To separate trade and agriculture.

At the time of primitive accumulation, i.e., at the end of the Middle Ages, when the history of capitalism in Europe began, and right into the nineteenth century, dispossessing the peasants in England and on the Continent was the most striking weapon in the large-scale transformation of means of production labor power into capital. Yet capital in power performs the same task even today, and on an even more important scale by modern colonial policy. It is an illusion to hope that capitalism will ever be content with the means of production which it can acquire by way of commodity exchange.

Thus capitalist accumulation as a whole, as an actual historical process, has two different aspects. One concerns the commodity market and the place where surplus value is produced—the factory, the mine, the agricultural estate. Regarded in this light, accumulation is a purely economic process, with its most important phase a transaction between the capitalist and wage laborer. In both its phases, however, it is confined to the exchange of equivalents and remains within the limits of commodity exchange. Here, in form at any rate, peace, property, and equality prevail, and the keen dialectics of scientific analysis were required to reveal how the right of ownership changes in the course of accumulation into appropriation of other people's property, how commodity exchange turns into exploitation and equality becomes class-rule.

The other aspect of the accumulation of capital concerns the relations between capitalism and the noncapitalist modes of production which start making their appearance on the international stage. Its predominant methods are colonial policy, an international loan system—a policy of spheres of interest—and war. Force, fraud, oppression, looting are openly displayed without any attempt at concealment, and it requires an effort to discover within this tangle of political violence and contests of power the stern laws of the economic process.

Bourgeois liberal theory takes into account only the former aspect: the realm of "peaceful competition," the marvels of technology and pure commodity exchange; it separates it strictly from the other aspect: the realm of capital's blustering violence which is regarded as more or less incidental to foreign policy and quite independent of the economic sphere of capital.

In reality, political power is nothing but a vehicle for the economic process. The conditions for the reproduction of capital provide the organic link between these two aspects of the accumulation of capital. The historical career of capitalism can only be appreciated by taking them together. "Sweating blood and filth with every pore from head to toe" characterizes not only the birth of capital but also its progress in the world at every step, and thus capitalism prepares its own downfall under ever more violent contortions and convulsions....

There is no doubt that the explanation for the economic roots of imperialism must be deduced from the laws of capital accumulation, since, according to common empirical knowledge, imperialism as a whole is nothing but a specific method of accumulation. But how is that possible, if one does not question Marx's assumptions in the second volume of Capital which are constructed for a society in which capitalist production is the only form, where the entire population consists solely of capitalists and wage laborers?

However one defines the inner economic mechanisms of imperialism, one thing is obvious and common knowledge: the expansion of the rule of capital from the old capitalist countries to new areas, and the economic and political competition of those countries for the new parts of the world. But Marx assumes, as we have seen in the second volume of Capital, that the whole world is one capitalist nation, that all other forms of economy and society have already disappeared. How can one explain imperialism in a society where there is no longer any space for it?

It was at this point that I believed I had to start my critique. The theoretical assumption of a society of capitalists and workers only—which is legitimate for certain aims of investigation (as in the first volume of *Capital*, the analysis of individual capital and its practice of exploitations in the factory)—no longer seems adequate when we deal with the accumulation of gross social capital. As this represents the real historical process of capitalist development, it seems impossible to me to understand it if one abstracts it from all conditions of historical reality. Capital accumulation as the historical process develops in an environment of various precapitalist formations, in a constant political struggle and in reciprocal economic relations. How can one capture this process in a bloodless theoretical fiction, which declares this whole context, the struggle and the relations, to be nonexistent?

Here especially it seems necessary, in the spirit of Marxist theory, to abandon the premise of the first volume, and to carry out the inquiry into accumulation as a total process, involving the metabolism of capital and its historical environment. If one does this, then the explanation of the process follows freely from Marx's basic theories, and is consistent with the other portions of his major works on economics.

Marx himself only posed the question of the accumulation of gross capital, but his answer went no further. As a basis for his analysis, he first selected that pure capitalist society; but not only did he not take this analysis to its conclusion, he also broke off at just this central question. In order to illustrate his conception he constructed some mathematical models, but hardly had he started on their significance for practical social possibilities and their verification from this standpoint when sickness and death forced him to stop writing. It was clearly left to his pupils to solve this problem (like many others), and my *Accumulation* was intended as an attempt in this direction.

The solution I proposed might have been judged as correct or incorrect; it could have been criticized, contested, supplemented; or another solution could have been produced. None of this happened. What followed was quite unexpected: the "experts" explained that there was no problem to be solved! Marx's illustrations in the second volume of *Capital* were a sufficient and exhaustive explanation of accumulation; the models there proved quite conclusively that capital could grow excellently, and production could expand, if there was no other mode of production in the world than the capitalist one; it was its own market, and only my complete inability to understand the ABC of Marx's models could persuade me to see a problem here.

7

IMPERIALISM AND CAPITALISM

Joseph Schumpeter

Joseph Schumpeter, a German-American economist, takes issue with Marx and also with Marxists who envisage negative consequences for imperialism. He analyzes examples of imperialism, from the empires of antiquity to modern times. He understood imperialism to be associated with irrational precapitalist conditions shaped by war, monopoly, and imperialism. The progressive development of capitalism, in contrast, is associated with the gradual disappearance of imperialism. He believed that eventually opposition to war, expansion, and armaments would increase and that no class would desire expansion if free trade were to prevail. Modern capitalism would thus destroy the irrational alliances of high finance and cartels so that imperialism would eventually "wither and die."

...MENTION OF KARL KAUTSKY'S PERSPECTIVE may be relevant and instructive. A renowned Marxist involved most of his life in Germany, Kautsky differed with Lenin and Bolsheviks whom he felt had undermined the democratic base of Marxism. He drew from Hobson the emphasis on imperialism as a manifestation of protectionism and militarism, but his "ultraimperialist" theory assumed that the major powers would reach consensus on their exploitation of the world rather than struggle to divide it. Thus, an internationally united finance capital might bring about a peaceful resolution of real and potential conflict generated by the rivalry of national finance capitals.

From Joseph Schumpeter, *Social Classes: Imperialism* (Cleveland and New York: Meridian Press, 1955), pp. 64–66, 81–83, 93–98.

IMPERIALISM AND CAPITALISM

Our analysis of the historical evidence has shown, first, the unquestionable fact that "objectless" tendencies toward forcible expansion, without definite, utilitarian limits—that is, nonrational and irrational, purely instinctual inclinations toward war and conquest—play a very large role in the history of mankind. It may sound paradoxical, but numberless wars—perhaps the majority of all wars—have been waged without adequate "reason"—not so much from the moral viewpoint as from that of reasoned and reasonable interest. The most herculean efforts of the nations, in other words, have faded into the empty air. Our analysis, in the second place, provides an explanation for this drive to action, this will to war—a theory by no means exhausted by mere references to an "urge" or an "instinct." The explanation lies, instead, in the vital needs of situations that molded peoples and classes into warriors—if they wanted to avoid extinction—and in the fact that psychological dispositions and social structures acquired in the dim past in such situations, once firmly established, tend to maintain themselves and to continue in effect long after they have lost their meaning and their life-preserving function. Our analysis, in the third place, has shown the existence of subsidiary factors that facilitate the survival of such dispositions and structures—factors that may be divided into two groups. The orientation toward war is mainly fostered by the domestic interests of ruling classes, but also by the influence of all those who stand to gain individually from a war policy, whether economically or socially. Both groups of factors are generally overgrown by elements of an altogether different character, not only in terms of political phraseology, but also of psychological motivation. Imperialisms differ greatly in detail, but they all have at least these traits in common, turning them into a single phenomenon in the field of sociology....

Imperialism thus is atavistic in character. It falls into that large group of surviving features from earlier ages that play such an important part in every concrete social situation. In other words, it is an element that stems from the living conditions, not of the present, but of the past—or, put in terms of the economic interpretation of history, from past rather than present relations of production. It is an atavism in the social structure, in individual, psychological habits of emotional reaction. Since the vital needs that created it have passed away for good, it, too, must gradually disappear, even though every warlike involvement, no matter how nonimperialist in character, tends to revive it. It tends to disappear as a structural element because the structure that brought it to the fore goes into a decline, giving way, in the course of social development, to other structures that have no room for it and eliminate the power factors that supported it. It tends to disappear as an element of habitual emotional reaction, because of the progressive rationalization of life and mind, a process in which old functional needs are absorbed by new tasks, in which heretofore military energies are functionally modified. If our theory is correct, cases of imperialism should decline in intensity the later they occur in the history of a people and of a culture.

Our most recent examples of unmistakable, clear-cut imperialism are absolute monarchies of the eighteenth century. They are unmistakably "more civilized" than their predecessors.

It is from absolute autocracy that the present age has taken over what imperialist tendencies it displays. And the imperialism of absolute autocracy flourished before the Industrial Revolution that created the modern world, or rather, before the consequences of that revolution began to be felt in all their aspects. These two statements are primarily meant in a historical sense, and as such they are no more than self-evident. We shall nevertheless try, within the framework of our theory, to define the significance of capitalism for our phenomenon and to examine the relationship between present-day imperialist tendencies and the autocratic imperialism of the eighteenth century....

It is necessary to keep two factors in mind. In the first place, everywhere except, significantly, in England, there has come into being a close alliance between high finance and the cartel magnates, often going as far as personal identity. Although the relation between capitalists and entrepreneurs is one of the typical and fundamental *conflicts* of the capitalist economy, monopoly capitalism has virtually fused the big banks and cartels into one. Leading bankers are often leaders of the national economy. Here capitalism has found a central organ that supplants its automatism by conscious decisions. In the second place, the interests of the big banks coincide with those of their depositors even less than do the interests of cartel leaders with those of the firms belonging to the cartel. The policies of high finance are based on control of a *large* proportion of the national capital, but they are in the actual interest of only a *small* proportion and, indeed, with respect to the alliance with big business, sometimes not even in the interest of capital as such at all. The ordinary "small" capitalist foots the bills for a policy of forced exports, rather than enjoying its profits. He is a tool; his interests do not really matter. This possibility of laying all the sacrifices connected with a monopoly policy on one part of capital, while removing them from another, makes capital exports far more lucrative for the favored part than they would otherwise be. Even capital that is independent of the banks is thus often forced abroad—forced into the role of a shock troop for the real leaders, because cartels successfully impede the founding of new enterprises. Thus the customs area of a trustified country generally pours a huge wave of capital into new countries. There it meets other, similar waves of capital, and a bitter, costly struggle begins but never ends.

In such a struggle among "dumped" products and capitals, it is no longer a matter of indifference who builds a given railroad, who owns a mine or a colony. Now that the law of costs is no longer operative, it becomes necessary to fight over such properties with desperate effort and with every available means, including those that are not economic in character, such as diplomacy. The concrete objects in question often become entirely subsidiary considerations; the anticipated profit may be trifling, because of the competitive struggle—a struggle that has very little to do with normal competition. What matters is to gain a foothold of some kind and then to exploit this foothold as a base for the conquest of new markets. This costs all the participants dear—often more than can be reasonably recovered, immediately or in the future. Fury lays hold of everyone concerned—and everyone sees to it that his fellow countrymen share his wrath. Each is constrained to resort to methods that he would regard as evidence of unprecedented moral depravity in the other. It is not true that the capitalist system as such must collapse from immanent necessity, that it necessarily makes its continued existence impossible by its own growth and development. Marx's line of reasoning on this point allows serious defects, and when these are corrected the proof vanishes. It is to the great credit of Hilferding that he abandoned this thesis of Marxist theory. Nevertheless, the situation that has just been described is really untenable both politically and economically. Economically, it amounts to a *reductio ad absurdum*. Politically, it unleashes storms of indignation among the exploited consumers at home and the threatened producers abroad. Thus the idea of military force readily suggests itself. Force may serve to break down foreign customs barriers and thus afford relief from the vicious circle of economic aggression. If that is not feasible, military conquest may at least secure control over markets in which heretofore one had to compete with the enemy. In this context, the conquest of colonies takes on an altogether different significance. Nonmonopolist countries, especially those adhering to free trade, reap little profit from such a policy. But it is a different matter with countries that function in a monopolist vis-à-vis their colonies. There being no competition, they can use cheap native labor without its ceasing to be cheap they can market their products, even in the colonies, at monopoly prices; they can, finally, invest capital that would only depress the profit rate at home and that could be placed in other civilized countries only at very low interest rates. And they can do all these things even though the consequence may be much slower colonial development. It would seem as though there could be no such interest in expansion at the expense of other advanced capitalist countries—in Europe, for example—because their industry would merely offer competition to the domestic cartels. But it is sufficient for the industry of the conquering state to be superior to that of the one to be subjugated—superior in capital power, organization, intelligence, and self-assertion—to make it possible to treat the subjugated state, perhaps not quite, but very much like a colony, even though it may become necessary to make a deal with individual groups of interests that are particularly powerful. A much more important fact is that the conqueror can face the subjugated nation with the hearing of the victor. He has countless means at his disposal for expropriating raw material resources and the like and placing them in the service of his cartels. He can seize them outright, nationalize them, impose a forced sale, or draft the proprietors into industrial groups of the victor nation under conditions that insure control by the domestic captains of industry. He can exploit them by a system of quotas or allotments. He can administer the conquered means of communication in the interests of his own cartels. Under the pretext of military and political security, he can deprive the foreign workers of the right to organize, thus not only making cheap labor in the annexed territory available to his cartels, but also holding a threat over the head of domestic labor....

The nobility entered the modern world in the form into which it had been shaped by the autocratic state—the same state that had also molded the bourgeoisie. It was the sovereign who disciplined the nobility, instilled loyalty into it, "statized" it, and, as we have shown, imperialized it. He turned its nationalist sentiments—as in the case of the bourgeoisie—into an aggressive nationalism, and then made it a pillar of his organization, particularly his war machine. It had not been that in the immediately preceding period. Rising absolutism had at first availed itself of much more dependent organs. For that very reason, in his position as leader of the feudal powers and as warlord, the sovereign survived the onset of the Industrial Revolution, and as a rule—except in France—won victory over political revolution. The bourgeoisie did not simply supplant the sovereign, nor did it make him its leader, as did the nobility. It merely wrested a portion of his power from him and for the rest submitted to him. It did not take over from the sovereign the state as an abstract form of organization. The state remained a special social power, confronting the bourgeoisie. In some countries it has continued to play that role to the present day. It is in the *state* that the bourgeoisie with its interests seeks refuge, protection against external and even domestic enemies. The bourgeoisie seeks to win over the state for itself and in return serves the state and state interests that are different from its own. Imbued with the spirit of the old autocracy, trained by it, the bourgeoisie often takes over its ideology, even where, as in France, the sovereign is eliminated and the official power of the nobility has been broken. Because the sovereign needed soldiers, the modern bourgeois— at least in his slogans—is an even more vehement advocate of an increasing population. Because the sovereign was in a position to exploit conquests, needed them to be a victorious warlord, the bourgeoisie thirsts for national glory—even in France, worshiping a headless body, as it were. Because the sovereign found a large gold hoard useful, the bourgeoisie even today cannot be swerved from its bullionist prejudices. Because the autocratic state paid attention to the trader and manufacturer chiefly as the most important sources of taxes and credits, today even the intellectual who has not a shred of property looks on international commerce, not from the viewpoint of the consumer, but from that of the trader and exporter. Because pugnacious sovereigns stood in constant fear of attack by their equally pugnacious neighbors, the modern bourgeois attributes aggressive designs to neighboring peoples. All such modes of thought are essentially noncapitalist. Indeed, they vanish most quickly wherever capitalism fully prevails. They are survivals of the autocratic alignment of interests, and they endure wherever the autocratic state endures on the old basis and with the old orientation, even though more and more democratized and otherwise transformed. They bear witness to the extent to which essentially imperialist absolutism has patterned not only the economy of the bourgeoisie but also its mind—in the interests of autocracy and against those of the bourgeoisie itself.

This significant dichotomy in the bourgeois mind—which in part explains its wretched weakness in politics, culture, and life generally; earns it the understandable contempt of the Left and the Right; and proves the accuracy of our diagnosis—is best exemplified by two phenomena that are very close to our subject: present-day nationalism and militarism. Nationalism is affirmative awareness of national character, together with an aggressive sense of superiority. It arose from the autocratic state. In conservatives, nationalism in general is understandable as an inherited orientation, as mutation of the a battle instincts of the medieval knights and finally as a political stalking horse on the domestic scene; and conservatives are fond of reproaching the bourgeois with a lack of nationalism, which from their point of view, is evaluated in a positive sense. Socialists, on the other hand, equally understandably exclude nationalism from their general ideology, because of the essential interests of the proletariat, and by virtue of their domestic opposition to the conservative stalking horse; they, in turn, not only reproach the bourgeoisie with an excess of nationalism (which they of course, evaluate in nationalism and even a negative sense) but actually identify nationalism and even the very idea of the nation with bourgeois ideology. The curious thing is that both of these groups are right in their criticism of the bourgeoisie. For, as we have seen, the mode of life that flows logically from the nature of capitalism necessarily implies an antinationalist orientation in politics and culture. This orientation actually prevails. We find a great many antinationalist members of the middle class, and even more who merely parrot the catchwords of nationalism.

In the capitalist world it is actually not big business and industry at all that are the carriers of nationalist trends, but the intellectual, and the content of *his* ideology is explained not so much from definite class interests as from chance emotion and individual interest. But the submission of the bourgeoisie to the powers of autocracy its alliance with them, its economic and psychological patterning by them—all these tend to push the bourgeois in a nationalist direction; and this, too, we find prevalent, especially among the chief exponents of export monopolism. The relationship between the bourgeoisie and militarism is quite similar. Militarism is not necessarily a foregone conclusion when a nation maintains a large army, but only when high military circles become a political power. The criterion is whether leading generals as such wield political influence and whether the responsible statesmen can act only with their consent. That is possible only when the officer corps is linked to a definite social class, as in Japan, and can assimilate to its position individuals who do not belong to it by birth. Militarism, too, is rooted in the autocratic state. And again the same reproaches are made against the bourgeois from both sides—quite properly, too. According to the "pure" capitalist mode of life, the bourgeois is unwarlike. The alignment of capitalist interests should make him utterly reject military methods, put him in opposition to the professional soldier. Significantly, we see this in the example of England where, first, the struggle against a standing army generally and, next, opposition to its elaboration, furnished bourgeois politicians with their most popular slogan: "retrenchment." Even naval appropriations have encountered resistance. We find similar trends in other countries, though they are less strongly developed. The continental bourgeois, however, was used to the sight of troops. He regarded an army almost as a necessary component of the social order, ever since it had been his terrible taskmaster in the Thirty Years' War. He had no power at all to abolish the army. He might have done so if he had had the power; but not having it, he considered the fact that the army might be useful to him. In his "artificial" economic situation and because of his submission to the sovereign, he thus grew disposed toward militarism, especially where export monopolism flourished. The intellectuals, many of whom still maintained special relationships with feudal elements, were so disposed to an even greater degree.

Just as we once found a dichotomy in the social pyramid, so now we find everywhere, in every aspect of the bourgeois portion of the modern world, a dichotomy of attitudes and interests. Our examples also show in what way the two components work together. Nationalism and militarism, while not creatures of capitalism, become "capitalized" and in the end draw their best energies from capitalism. Capitalism involves them in its workings and thereby keeps them alive politically as well as economically. And they, in turn, affect capitalism, cause it to deviate from the course it might have followed alone, support many of its interests.

Here we find that we have penetrated to the historical as well as the sociological sources of modern imperialism. It does not *coincide* with nationalism and militarism, though it *fuses* with them by supporting them as it is supported by them. It, too, is—not only historically, but also sociologically—a heritage of the autocratic state, of its structural elements, organizational forms, interest alignments, and human attitudes, the outcome of precapitalist forces which the autocratic state has reorganized, in part by the methods of early capitalism. It would never have been evolved by the "inner logic" of capitalism itself. This is true even of mere export monopolism. It, too, has its sources in absolutist policy and the action habits of an essentially precapitalist environment. That it was able to develop to its present dimensions is owing to the momentum of a situation once created, which continued to engender ever new "artificial" economic structures, that is, those which maintain themselves by political power alone. In most of the countries addicted to export monopolism it is also owing to the fact that the old autocratic state and the old attitude of the bourgeoisie toward it were so vigorously maintained. But export monopolism, to go a step further, is not yet imperialism. And even if it had been able to arise without protective tariffs, it would never have developed into imperialism in the hands of an unwarlike bourgeoisie. If this did happen, it was only because the heritage included the war machine, together with its sociopsychological aura and aggressive bent, and because a class oriented toward war maintained itself in a ruling position This class clung to its domestic interest in war, and the pro military interests among the bourgeoisie were able to ally themselves with it. This alliance kept alive war instincts and ideas of overlordship, male supremacy, and triumphant glory—ideas that would have otherwise long since died. It led to social conditions that, while they ultimately stem from the conditions of production, cannot be explained from capitalist production methods alone. And it often impresses its mark on present day politics, threatening Europe with the constant danger of war.

This diagnosis also bears the prognosis of imperialism. The precapitalist elements in our social life may still have great vitality; special circumstances in national life may revive them from time to time; but in the end the climate of the modern world must destroy them. This is all the more certain since their props in the modern capitalist world are not of the most durable material. Whatever opinion is held concerning the vitality of capitalism itself, whatever the life span predicted for it, it is bound to withstand the onslaughts of its enemies and its own irrationality much longer than essentially untenable export monopolism—untenable even from the capitalist point of view. Export monopolism may perish in revolution, or it may be peacefully relinquished; this may happen soon, or it may take some time and require desperate struggle; but one thing is certain—it *will* happen. This will immediately dispose of neither warlike instincts nor structural elements and organizational forms oriented toward war—and it is to their dispositions and domestic interests that, in my opinion, much more weight must be given in every concrete case of imperialism than to export monopolist interests, which furnish the financial "outpost skirmishes"—a most appropriate term—in many wars. But such factors will be politically overcome in time, no matter what they do to maintain among the people a sense of constant danger of war, with the war machine forever primed for action. And with them, imperialisms will wither and die.

It is not within the scope of this study to offer an ethical, esthetic, cultural, or political evaluation of this process. Whether it heals sores or extinguishes suns is a matter of utter indifference from the viewpoint of this study. It is not the concern of science to judge that. The only point at issue here was to demonstrate, by means of an important example, the ancient truth that the dead always rule the living.

PART TWO

IMPERIALISM IN CAPITALIST DEVELOPMENT AND UNDERDEVELOPMENT

THE
LEGACY
OF
MARX

8

PRIMITIVE ACCUMULATION
Toward a Theory of Capitalism and Its Development
Karl Marx

Marx elaborated an understanding of capitalism based on accumulation with the purpose of production being to achieve profit. He delineated a labor theory of value according to which the value of a commodity or product for sale is determined by the amount of necessary labor to produce it. In the production process the labor power of workers is assimilated into the newly produced commodity, but he showed how the value produced during a workday only partially goes to the worker in the form of wages, the remainder being surplus value available to the capitalist. Some of this surplus value must be reinvested in raw materials, machinery, and labor in order to expand production, while some of the surplus value will be consumed by the capitalist in the quest for personal luxuries and pleasure. The drive to accumulate may lead to problems such as tensions between the capitalist and workers; overproduction and crisis in the market that may result in layoffs, closing of factories, and so on.

WE HAVE SEEN HOW MONEY is changed into capital; how through capital surplus value is made and from surplus value more capital. But the accumulation of capital presupposes surplus value; surplus value presupposes capitalistic production; capitalistic production presupposes the preexistence of considerable masses of capital and of labor-power in the hands of producers of commodities. The whole movement therefore seems to be torn in a vicious circle out of which we can only get by supposing a

From Karl Marx, *Capital*, vol. 1, translated by Samuel Moore and Edward Aveling (New York: International Publishers, 1967), pp. 713–16.

primitive accumulation (previous accumulation of Adam Smith) preceding capitalistic accumulation; an accumulation not the result of the capitalist mode of production but its starting-point.

This primitive accumulation plays in Political Economy about the same part as original sin in theology. Adam bit the apple, and thereupon sin fell on the human race. Its origin is supposed to be explained when it is told as an anecdote of the past. In times long gone by there were two sorts of people; one, the diligent intelligent and, above all, frugal elite; the other, lazy rascals spending their substance, and more, in riotous living. The legend of theological original sin tells us certainly how man came to be condemned to eat his bread in the sweat of his brow; but the history of economic original sin reveals to us that there are people to whom this is by no means essential. Never mind! Thus it came to pass that the former sort accumulated wealth and the latter sort had at last nothing to sell except their own skins. And from this original sin dates the poverty of the great majority that, despite all its labor, has up to now nothing to sell but itself and the wealth of the few that increases constantly although they have long ceased to work. Such insipid childishness is everyday preached to us in the defense of property. M. Thiers, e.g., had the assurance to repeat it with all the solemnity of a statesman, to the French people, once *sospirituel*. But as soon as the question of property crops up, it becomes a sacred duty to proclaim the intellectual food of the infant as the one thing fit for all ages and for all stages of development. In actual history it is notorious that conquest, enslavement, robbery, murder, briefly force, play the great part. In the tender annals of Political Economy, the idyllic reigns from time immemorial. Right and "labor" were from all time the sole means of enrichment, the present year of course always excepted. As a matter of fact, the methods of primitive accumulation are anything but idyllic.

In themselves money and commodities are no more capital than are the means of production and of subsistence. They want transforming into capital. But this transformation itself can only take place under certain circumstances that center in this, viz., that two very different kinds of commodity-possessors must come face to face and into contact; on the one hand, the owners of money, means of production, means of subsistence, who are eager to increase the sum of values they possess, by buying other people's labor-power; on the other hand, free laborers, the sellers of their own labor-power, and therefore the sellers of labor. Free laborers, in the double sense that neither they themselves form part and parcel of the means of production, as in the case of slaves, bondsman, etc., nor do the means of production belong to them, as in the case of peasant-proprietors; they are, therefore, free from, unencumbered by, any means of production of their own. With this polarization of the market for commodities, the fundamental conditions of capitalist production are given. The capitalist system presupposes the complete separation of the laborers from all property in the means by which they can realize their labor. As soon as capitalist production is once on its own legs, it not only maintains this separation, but reproduces it on a continually extending scale. The process, therefore, that clears the way for the capitalist system, can be none other than the process which takes away from the laborer the possession of his means of production; a process that transforms, on the one hand, the social means of subsistence and of production into capital, on the other, the immediate producers into wage-laborers. The so-called primitive accumulation, therefore, is nothing else than the historical process of divorcing the producer from the means of production. It appears as primitive, because it forms the prehistoric stage of capital and of the mode of production corresponding with it.

The economic structure of capitalistic society has grown out of the economic structure of feudal society. The dissolution of the latter set free the elements of the former.

The immediate producer, the laborer, could only dispose of his own person after he had ceased to be attached to the soil and ceased to be the slave, serf, or bondman of another. To become a free seller of labor-power, who carries his commodity wherever he finds a market, he must further have escaped from the regime of the guilds, their rules for apprentices and journeymen, and the impediments of their labor regulations. Hence, the historical movement which changes the producers into wage-workers appears, on the one hand, as their emancipation from serfdom and from the fetters of the guilds, and this side alone exists for our bourgeois historians. But, on the other hand, these new freedmen became sellers of themselves only after they had been robbed of all their own means of production, and of all the guarantees of the existence afforded by the old feudal arrangements. And the history of this, their expropriation, is written in the annals of mankind in the letters of blood and fire.

The industrial capitalists, these new potentates, had on their part not only to displace the guild masters of handicrafts, but also the feudal lords, the possessors of the sources of wealth. In this respect their conquest of social power appears as the fruit of a victorious struggle both against feudal lordship and its revolting prerogatives, and against the guilds and the fetters they laid on the free development of production and the free exploitation of man by man. The chevaliers d'industrie, however, only succeeded in supplanting the chevaliers of the sword and by making use of events if which they themselves were wholly innocent. They have risen by means as vile as those by which the Roman freedman once on a time made himself master of his *patronus*.

The starting point of the development that gave rise to the wage-laborer as well as the capitalist, was the servitude of the laborer. The advance consisted in a change of form in servitude, in the transformation of feudal exploitation into capitalist exploitation. To understand its march, we need not go back very far. Although we come across its first beginnings of capitalist production as early as the fourteenth or fifteenth century, sporadically, in certain towns in the Mediterranean, the capitalistic era dates from the sixteenth century. Wherever it appears the abolition of serfdom has been long effected and the highest development of the middle ages, the existence of sovereign towns, has long been on the wane.

In the history of primitive accumulation, all revolutions are epoch-making that act as levers for the capitalist class in course of formation; but, above all, those moments when great masses of men are suddenly and forcibly torn from their means of subsistence, and hurled as free and "unattached" proletarians on the labor-market. The expropriation of the agricultural producer, of the peasant, from the soil, is the basis of the whole process. The history of this expropriation, in different countries, assumes different aspects, and runs through its various phases in different order; of succession, and at different periods. In England alone, which we take as our example, has it the classic form.

9

BACK TO MARX

Ellen Meiksins Wood

The following selection reminds us that Marx's theoretical contributions to under-standing of capitalist development and imperialism remain relevant today. Capi-talism and its logic of accumulation have become pervasive, suggesting either that the universalization of capitalism has resulted in its ultimate victory, as much of the Left has come to believe, or that it represents an opportunity to understand its successes as failures and that Marx was correct in his emphasis on a self-enclosed and contradictory system.

LET ME START WITH A provocative claim, which is contrary to all the con-ventional wisdom. The claim I want to make is that this historical moment, the one we're living in now, is the best not the worst, the most not the least appropriate moment to bring back Marx. I'll even claim that this is the moment when Marx should and can come fully into his own *for the first* time not excluding the historical moment when he actu-ally lived.

I'm making this claim for one simple reason: we're living in a moment when, for the first time, capitalism has become a truly uni-versal system. It's universal not only in the sense that it's global, not only in the sense that just about every economic actor in the world today is operating according to the logic of capitalism, and even those on the

From Ellen Meiksins Wood, "Back to Marx," *Monthly Review* 49 (June 1997): 1–6, 8–9. Copy-right © 1997 by Monthly Review Press. Reprinted with permission of Monthly Review Foundation.

outermost periphery of the capitalist economy are, in one way or another, subject to that logic. Capitalism is universal also in the sense that its logic—the logic of accumulation, commodification, profit-maximization, competition—has penetrated just about every aspect of human life and nature itself, in ways that weren't even true of so-called advanced capitalist countries as recently as two or three decades ago. So Marx is more relevant than ever, because he, more effectively than any other human being then or now, devoted his life to explaining the systemic logic of capitalism....

My main point is this: nearly every major development of Marxism in the twentieth century has been less about capitalism than about what is *not* capitalist. (I'll explain what I mean in a second.) This is especially true of the first half of the twentieth century, but I would argue that the tendency I'm talking about here has affected Marxism ever since. What I mean is that the major Marxist theories, like Marx, proceeded on the premise that capitalism with the most mature example and abstracted from it the systemic logic of capitalism, his major successors started, so to speak, from the other end. They were mainly interested—for very concrete historical and political reasons—with conditions that, on the whole, *weren't* capitalist. And there was an even more basic difference: whatever Marx may have thought about the global expansion of capitalism, or the possible limits on its expansion, that wasn't his primary concern. He was mainly interested in the internal logic of the system and its specific capacity to totalize itself, to permeate every aspect of life wherever it did implant itself. Later Marxists, besides being concerned with less mature capitalisms, generally started from the premise that capitalism would dissolve before it matured, or certainly before it became universal and total; and their main concern was how to navigate within a largely noncapitalist world.

Just think about the major milestones in twentieth century Marxist theory. For instance, the major theories of revolution were constructed in situations where capitalism scarcely existed or remained undeveloped and where there was no well-developed proletariat, where the revolution had to depend on alliances between a minority of workers and, in particular, a mass of precapitalist peasants. Even more striking are the classic Marxist theories of imperialism. In fact, it's striking that the theory of imperialism in the early twentieth century almost replaces or *becomes* the theory of capitalism. In other words, the object of Marxist economic theory becomes what you might call the *external* relations of capitalism, its interactions with noncapitalism and the interactions among capitalist states in relation to the noncapitalist world.

For all the profound disagreements among the classical Marxist theorists of imperialism, they shared one fundamental premise: that imperialism had to do with the location of capitalism in a world that wasn't— and never would be—fully, or even predominantly, capitalist. Take, for instance, the basic Leninist idea that imperialism represented "the highest stage of capitalism." Underlying that definition was the assumption that capitalism had reached a stage where the main axis of international conflict and military confrontation would run between imperialist states. But that competition was, by definition, competition over division and redivision of the world, that is, a largely noncapitalist world. The more capitalism spread (at uneven rates), the more acute would be the rivalry among the main imperialist powers. At the same time, they would face increasing resistance. The whole point—and the reason imperialism was the highest stage of capitalism—was that it was the *final* stage, which meant that capitalism would end before the noncapitalist victims of imperialism were finally and completely swallowed up by capitalism.

The point is made most explicitly by Rosa Luxemburg. The essence of her classic work in political economy, *The Accumulation of Capital,* is to offer an alternative to Marx's own approach. It is meant to be precisely an alternative to Marx's analysis of capitalism as a self-enclosed system. Her argument is that the capitalist system needs an outlet in noncapitalist formations—which is why capitalism inevitably means militarism and imperialism. Capitalist militarism, having gone through various stages beginning with the straightforward conquest of territory, has now reached its "final" stage, as "a weapon in the competitive struggle between capitalist countries for areas of noncapitalist civilization." But one of the fundamental contradictions of capitalism, she suggests, is that "although it strives to become universal, and, indeed, on account of this tendency, it must break down—because it is immanently incapable of becoming a universal form of production." It is the first mode of economy that tends to engulf the whole world, but it is also the first that *can't* exist by itself because it "needs other economic systems as a medium and soil" (Luxemburg, 1963, p. 467). So in these theories of imperialism, capitalism by definition assumes a noncapitalist environment. In fact, capitalism depends for its survival not only on the existence of these noncapitalist formations but on essentially precapitalist instruments of "extraeconomic" force, military and geopolitical coercion, and on traditional forms of colonial war and territorial expansion.

And so it goes on, in other aspects of Marxist theory, too. Trotsky's notion of combined and uneven development, with its corollary notion of permanent revolution, probably implies that the universalization of the capitalist system will be short-circuited by capitalism's own demise. Gramsci was writing very consciously in the context of a less developed capitalism, with a pervasive precapitalist peasant culture. And this surely had a lot to do with the importance he attached to ideology and culture, and to intellectuals, because something was needed to push class struggle beyond its material limits, something was needed to make socialist revolution possible even in the absence of mature material conditions of a well developed capitalism and an advanced proletariat. In a different way, the same is true of Mao. And so on.

What I'm saying, then, is that non- or precapitalism permeates all these theories of capitalism. Now all of these Marxist theories are profoundly illuminating in various ways. But in one way, they seem to have been proved wrong. Capitalism *has* become universal. It has totalized itself both intensively and extensively. It's global in reach, and it penetrates to the heart and soul of social life and nature. This doesn't, by the way, necessarily mean the disappearance of the nation-state. It may just mean new roles for nation-states, as the logic of competition imposes itself not only on capitalist firms but on entire national economies, which, with the help of the state, conduct their competition less in the old "extraeconomic" and military ways than in purely "economic" forms. Even imperialism now has a new form. People like to call it "globalization," but that's really just a code-word, and a misleading one at that, for a system in which the logic of capitalism has become more or less universal and where imperialism achieves its ends not so much by the old forms of military expansion but by unleashing and manipulating the destructive impulses of the capitalist market. Anyway, though this universalization of capitalism has certainly exposed some fundamental contradictions in the system, we have to admit that there's no sign of its demise in the near future.

So what theoretical response has there been to this new reality? Well, to begin with, you could say that there's been a real paradox here: the more universal capitalism has become, the more people have moved away from classical Marxism and its main theoretical concerns. This is certainly true of post-Marxist theories and their successors, but I suppose you could argue that it's true even of more recent forms of Marxism—say, the Frankfurt School, or the tradition of Western Marxism in general. For instance, the famous shift from the traditional Marxist concern with political economy to culture and philosophy in some of these cases seems to be related to the conviction that the totalizing effects of capitalism have penetrated every aspect of life and culture—and also that the working class has been thoroughly absorbed into that capitalist culture. (I happen to think, by the way, that there may be another explanation for this shift, which has to do not with the universalization of capitalism but, on the contrary, with the ways in which precapitalist forms still pervade the consciousness of thinkers like the Frankfurt School—but I don't have time to go into that here, and anyway, I'm far from being able to make a coherent argument about it.)

The point I want to make is this: there are, I think, two possible ways of responding to the universalization of capitalism. One is to say that if, contrary to all expectations, capitalism has after all become universal instead of dissolving before it had a chance to totalize itself, this is truly the end. This can only be the system's final triumph. I'll come back to the other possible response, but this one, the defeatist one, the one that represents the other side of the coin of capitalist triumphalism, is the one that has generally taken hold of the left today....

But if these theories seem to have bought into capitalist triumphalism, it may also be partly because of the intellectual background of twentieth-century Marxism....

But suppose we go back to Marx and to his internal analysts of capitalism as a self-enclosed system—which I think the very totality of capitalism actually entitles us to do. We really can begin to look at the world not as a relationship between what's inside and what's outside capitalism but as the working out of capitalism's own internal laws of motion. And that might make it easier to see the universalization of capitalism not just as a measure of success but as a source of weakness. Capitalism's impulse to universalize itself isn't just a show of strength.

It's a disease, a cancerous growth. It destroys the social fabric just as it destroys nature. It's a contradictory process, just as Marx always said it was. The old theories of imperialism may not have been strictly right to suggest that capitalism can't become universal, but it's certainly true that it can't be universally successful and prosperous. It can only universalize its contradictions, its polarizations between rich and poor, exploiters and exploited. Its successes are also its failures.

Now, capitalism has no more escape routes, no more safety valves or corrective mechanisms outside its own internal logic. Even when it's not at war, even when it's not involved in the old forms of interimperialist rivalry, it's subject to the constant tensions and contradictions of capitalist competition. Now, having more or less reached its geographic limits and ended the spatial expansion that supported its earlier successes, it can only feed on itself; and the more successful it is on its own terms—in other words, the more it maximizes profit and so-called growth—the more it devours its own human and natural substance. So maybe it's time for the left to see the universalization of capitalism not just as a defeat for us but also as an opportunity-and that, of course, above all means a new opportunity for that unfashionable thing called class struggle.

REFERENCES

Luxemburg, Rosa. 1963. *The Accumulation of Capital*. London: Routledge Kegan and Paul.

10

THE ROOTS OF IMPERIALIST THEORY IN MARX
Shlomo Avineri

While it is unclear that Marx was concerned with a theory of imperialism nor did he actually use the term imperialism, Marx and Engels in the the Manifesto came close to a conception of imperialism in reference to the need of the bourgeoisie to search for a constantly expanding international market. Avineri believes that an early understanding of imperialism can be discerned in Marx's attention to the non-European world, in particular his writing on the Asiatic mode of production which extends the analysis on primitive accumulation in the path of Western European capitalism out of feudalism. Marx seems to suggest that the combination of agriculture and home manufacture in China and India allowed each village to form self-sufficient, autonomous, inward-working economies incapable of creating conditions for their own overthrow and that the only way out would be an outside force, in the form of English colonialism and imperialism to destroy the old vestiges and establish the foundations for Western capitalism.

MARX'S VIEWS ON OVERSEAS EUROPEAN capitalist expansion is thus an extension of his dialectical understanding of the potentialities of capitalism in general, capitalist society is universalistic in its urges, and it will not change internally unless it encompasses the whole world; it is this that determines Marx and Engels's attitude to the concrete cases of nineteenth-century European expansion in India, China, North Africa, etc....

From *Karl Marx on Colonialism and Modernization* by Shlomo Avineri. Copyright © 1968 by Shlomo Avineri. Used by permission of Doubleday, a division of Bantam Doubleday Dell Publishing Group, Inc.

But the problem is not merely one of an internal inconsistency in Marx's philosophy of history. Since Oriental society does not develop internally, it cannot evolve toward capitalism through the dialectics of internal change; and since Marx postulates the ultimate victory of socialism on the prior universalization of capitalism, he necessarily arrives at the position of having to endorse European colonial expansion as a brutal but necessary step toward the victory of socialism. Just as the horrors of industrialization are dialectically necessary for the triumph of communism, so the horrors of colonialism are dialectically necessary for the world revolution of the proletariat since without them the countries of Asia (and presumably also Africa) will not be able to emancipate themselves from their stagnant backwardness.

Marx's view of European—and particularly British—colonial expansion is determined by these dialectical considerations. Consequently, Marx's views on imperialism can be painfully embarrassing to the orthodox communist; there certainly is a deep irony in the fact that while Marx's writings on European industrialization are always the first to be used and quoted by non-European Marxists, his writings on India and China are hardly known or even mentioned by them. The Maoists in particular seem to be totally unaware of them; they certainly make much of their particular brand of Marxism look very much out of touch with Marx himself.

Marx goes into considerable detail to discuss the various aspects of the impact of Western bourgeois civilization on Indian society. Marx argues that for the first time in its history political unity has been imposed on India by the British sword and strengthened by the introduction of modern means communication.

That this social transformation is being carried out by the European bourgeoisie, which is totally unaware of the ultimate consequences of its own acts, only brings out the basic dialectical nature of Marx's analysis. But the integration of India—and to a lesser degree of China as well— into the world market is a two-way road: not only is Asia becoming more dependent on Europe, Europe is also, dialectically, becoming more dependent on Asia....

The ultimate dependence of Europe on Asia is also implied by Marx when discussing the economic balance of payments regulating the flow of funds from the metropolis to the colonies, and especially to

India. It is here that Marx's sophisticated understanding of the dialectics of historical development proves itself so superior to the more linear analysis of Lenin's *Imperialism, the Highest Stage of Capitalism....*

The dialectical analysis of colonial expansion is thus merely an instance of realizing the internal structural tensions of capitalist society.

Marx's critique of colonial expansion thus avoids a mere moralistic stance and is deeply integrated into his general critique of European capitalist society; similarly, his insistence on the ultimate necessity of colonialism is divorced from his moral indignation of its horrors. This is surely a complex attitude to adopt, and it does not translate well into the necessarily more simple-minded language of political mass organizations, as the ideological writings on the subject by most European and non-European communist theoreticians amply show. The sophistication of Hegelian dialectics cannot be easily adapted to the more prosaic needs of Marxist parties of whatever coloration....

Anyone who has closely followed the main themes in Marx's writings about the non-European world cannot but be impressed by the mastery of detailed knowledge and by the breadth of the historical perspectives implied. It is true that one can criticize Marx on many counts: his understanding of Chinese society seems less profound than his grasp of Indian affairs, and certainly his central thesis about Oriental despotism being based on the absence of private property in land does not apply to China; yet the combination of agriculture with home manufacture, which he sees as determining the basic autarchy of village communities in Asia, is certainly as true of China as it is of India. Again, Japan hardly figures in his writings, mainly due, one would suppose, to the lack of sources and to the fact that Marx was, after all, covering current events for a newspaper, and Japan was not at that time making headline news; but one wonders how the successful case of defensive modernization in Japan would have affected Marx's judgment of the basic stagnant nature of society in Asia.

Yet with all these reservations in mind, one has to admit that few nineteenth-century thinkers and social theorists grasped as well the long-range implications of European colonial expansion for the socioeconomic structure of non-European society: even fewer had a comparable vision of the degree of world historical change brought about by the corrosive influence of Western commerce and the dialectical necessity for modernization and industrialization thus made imperative by European penetration into underdeveloped societies....

Yet Marx's basic failure to incorporate his insightful understanding of non-European society into the universal framework of his method of historical explanation is plainly visible. The nemesis of this failure is manifest in the contemporary quest for a Marxist interpretation of Asian history, and here the anti-Marxists sometimes join the Marxists in search of a conceptual framework that may not in fact be there. The ludicrous attempt to talk about Chinese "feudalism" or to explain the Indian caste system in terms of the European medieval guilds has lately been discarded by the Chinese Communists themselves. Yet the idea of overcoming this difficulty by postulating the revolution on the mobilization of the underdeveloped world against the industrialized nations, of discussing future history in terms of a war of the Villages of the World against the Cities of the World—all this is even more absurd when viewed in Marxian terms: it was, after all, Marx who talked about "the idiocy of village life" as the major epistemological obstacle for agrarian socialist revolutionary movements.

With all his understanding of the non-European world, Marx remained a Europe-oriented thinker, and his insights into Indian and Chinese society could never be reconciled with his general philosophy of history, which remained—like Hegel's— determined by the European experience and the Western historical consciousness. It may well be that a successful incorporation of the non-European world into a comprehensive system of history has ultimately to require the sort of rejection of the Western scale of values that is implied in Toynbee's philosophy of history. But such an approach poses other difficulties, since a reasonable argument could be made that the idea of history itself makes little sense outside the Western tradition.

Despite all this, it would be foolish to suggest that the attempt to make Marx relevant to the non-European world will fail because Marx's own writings give little comfort to such an approach. Such an attempt, forced as it may seem in terms of Marx's social philosophy, may yet turn out to be politically successful. If one looks for analogies, one has only to remember that it was among the Gentiles that the beliefs of the man who was crucified as King of the Jews became historically significant.

The irony of history may thus make Marx into a respectable, even fashionable, subject for academic discourse in a relatively affluent and bourgeois West, while in the non-European world an ideology relating itself to Marxism, yet overlooking most of what he said about the non-European world, may be politically triumphant. All this may have very little to do with the basic theoretical issues raised by Marx in his discussion of both the Western and the non-Western world. But these limitations of Marx may even, dialectically, vindicate his own dictum about man's consciousness being determined by his social existence. Or, as Hegel put it several decades before him, "every individual is a child of his time; so philosophy too is its own time apprehended in thoughts."

11

PROGRESSIVE AND NEGATIVE PERSPECTIVES OF CAPITALISM AND IMPERIALISM

Kenzo Mohri

Orthodox Marxist interpretations of development stress the progressive aspects of capitalism, along the line of the transformation of Europe from precapitalist and feudal formations to mercantile and eventually industrial capitalism. In a series of articles for the New York Daily Tribune *(1853), Marx examined this assumption in the cases of India and China where he analyzed communal village agriculture, handicrafts, and an absence of private property in land. These precapitalist forms could be overcome through British development of capitalism and imperialism. In contrast, Marx's writings on Ireland suggest that a national rather than socialist revolution in the form of tariffs and protection against British imports might lead to autonomy and self-sufficiency. These contrasting perspectives in Marx are analyzed by Kenzo Mohri in the following selection.*

RECENTLY A NEW CURRENT OF interpretation of Marx's view of British free trade in the nineteenth century seems to be on the rise among historians and theorists interested in the historical experiences of Third World peoples as "consumers of imperialism" (Hodgkin, 1972). One allegation usually shared by these interpreters is that Marx failed to grasp the historical function British free trade played in retarding or distorting the development of backward countries' economies through their integration into the world market system. In other words, Marx is criticized for having

From Kenzo Mohri, "Marx and Underdevelopment," *Monthly Review* 41 (October 1989): 32—41. Copyright © 1989 by Monthly Review Press. Reprinted with permission of Monthly Review Foundation.

optimistically believed that British free trade would promote industrialization throughout the world on the European model. It seems worthwhile to see if these critiques do indeed do justice to Marx or not. Before
reexamining Marx's theses on British free trade, however, I think I had
better briefly review how Marx's view is criticized by the aforesaid current of interpretations. Let us look at some of the most typical examples.

HOW MARX HAS RECENTLY BEEN CRITICIZED

Paul Baran characterizes Marx's argument as follows: "Whatever its
speed and whatever its zigzags, the general direction of the historical
movement seems to have been the same for the backward echelons as
for the forward contingents" (Baran, 1957, p. 140). With much the same
understanding of Marx's view, V. G. Kiernan points out: "So far as can
be seen, what he [Marx] had in mind was not a further spread of
Western imperialism but a proliferation of autonomous capitalism, such
as he expected in India and did witness in North America" (Kiernan,
1974, p. 198). B. Sutcliffe, too, maintains that "it is quite clear that for most
of the time Marx believed that capitalism would industrialize the
world" (Sutcliffe, 1972, pp. 180—81). Sutcliffe further points out that,
alongside this tendency of capitalism to industrialize the whole world,
Marx's writings emphasized another feature of capitalist penetration
which would de-industrialize the colonized lands. But Marx, according
to Sutcliffe, failed to spell out the full consequences of capitalist penetration in the case of India.

Commenting on the assertion Marx made in an article titled "The
Future Results of the British Rule in India"—i.e., that the "railway system
will...become, in India, truly the forerunner of modern industry"—M.
B. Brown argues that "this was almost precisely what did not happen, at
least for a hundred years" (Brown, 1972). What did take place in India,
emphasizes Brown, was the de-industrializing process forced by "the distorting effect of the international division of labor" (Brown, 1972, p. 69).

Samir Amin observes that "these distinctive problems of transition
to peripheral capitalism largely escaped Marx's notice, and this accounts
for his mistaken notion about the future development of the 'colonial
problem' " (Amin, 1974, p. 391). By Marx's "mistaken notion about the

future development of the colonial problem," Amin seems to mean Marx's assertion that "colonial rule would lead the East in the direction of full capitalist development" (Amin, 1974, p. 147)—in other words, his assertion that, regardless of the intentions and policies of colonial authorities, "no power would for long be able to hinder local development of capitalism *on the European model.*"

At this point, let us take note of the fact that the writings of Marx to which Amin directly refers here are "The Future Results of the British Rule in India" (1853) and Marx's letter to Engels dated October 8, 1858. Proper assessment of Amin's argument would of course require detailed examination of all his major writings. But here we have to content ourselves with simply taking note of Amin's understanding that "the pattern of transition to peripheral capitalism is, in fact, fundamentally different from that of transition to central capitalism" (Amin, 1974, p. 390).

The critiques of Marx noted above are enough for our present purpose, though the list could easily be expanded. In short, these critics blame him for having missed the historical function of British free trade in compelling "the development of underdevelopment" (Frank, 1962, chapter 1)—to use the term coined by A. G. Frank;—in underdeveloped countries and having tended to be overoptimistic about the future development of these countries.

REEXAMINATION OF MARX ON BRITISH FREE TRADE

To put my conclusion first, I prefer to side with H. B. Davis for the most part and consider Marx's view on this question to have undergone a significant change. Davis asserts that "down to the middle of the 1860s their [Marx's and Engels's] pronouncements on colonialism were ambivalent," and that "the shift from acceptance of colonialism to active opposition is nowhere more strikingly demonstrated than in the case of Ireland" (Davis, 1967, pp. 14, 16). To this I would like to add that the theoretical position Marx developed as he became more involved with the Irish question was further strengthened as a result of his more detailed studies of different societies, notably Russian society, in his last years. In what follows, however, I shall restrict myself to the Irish question, as the springboard which propelled him toward a deeper insight into British free trade.

MARX IN THE 1840s AND 1850s

First, I would like to examine briefly Marx's view of the historical significance of British free trade in the 1840s and 1850s. To begin with, the
following well-known passage from the "Speech on the Question of Free
Trade" (1848) ought to be recalled:

> But, generally speaking, the Protective system in these days is conser-
> vative, while the Free Trade system works destructively. It breaks up
> old nationalities and carries antagonism of proletariat and bourgeoisie
> to the uttermost point. In a word, the Free Trade system hastens the
> Social Revolution. In this revolutionary sense alone, gentlemen, I am
> in favor of Free Trade. (Marx-Engels, 1970, vol. 4, pp. 457–58)

There seems to be no doubt that Marx, up to the end of the 1850s,
firmly believed in the thoroughness and completeness with which the
British industrial capital would destroy noncapitalist societies in the
process of its worldwide expansion, and furthermore that he tool; this
"propagandistic (civilizing) tendency" (Marx, 1973, p. 542) of British capital positively and affirmatively. Marx maintained this same position in
(1) the well-known paragraph of the *Communist Manifesto* (1848) in which
he likens the cheap prices of British commodities to heavy artillery battering down all Chinese walls, and emphasizes that the British bourgeoisie creates a world after its own image; (2) in a series of splendid
writings on India produced in 1853; and (3) in numerous passages of the
Grundrisse, written in 1857–1858. (Due to space limitations, however, I
refrain from quoting all relevant passages here.)

What we can see in these writings is a clear-cut manifestation of
the positive view which Marx had of the historical role of British free
trade. One more point we should keep in mind in reexamining Marx's
views on British free trade is that Marx's understanding of the "revolutionary" role of British free trade was inseparably related to his prediction that British free trade was bound to fulfill "a double mission." "England," argued Marx, "has to fulfill a double mission in India: one
destructive, the other regenerating—annihilation of old Asiatic society,
and the laying of the material foundations of Western society in Asia"
(Marx, 1867, p. 84). This being so, when his belief in this thesis of a

"double mission" was shaken, his belief in the "revolutionary" role of free trade, too, would have to be shaken.

I have no intention of dismissing the fact that Marx, while viewing British capital as the "unconscious tool of history," pointed in the same article to the very important fact that "this loss of his old world, *with no gain of a new one*, imparts a particular kind of melancholy to the present misery of the Hindoo" (Marx, 1867, p. 34). But so long as this perception existed side by side with the prediction which Marx put forward a few weeks later, optimistically emphasizing the "regenerating " function of British capital—"the railway system will...become, in India, truly the forerunner of modern industry"—we cannot but conclude that what Marx referred to as "a particular kind of melancholy" was not yet grasped as a structurally inherent feature of the development of under-development but rather simply as a phenomenon of a temporary nature which would be wiped out sooner or later. Marx, during the 1850s, had not yet reached the deeper insight which both R. Palme Dutt and Paul Baran later formulated. Palme Dutt says that "the victory of for-eign capitalism in India differed from the victory of capitalism in Europe, in that the destructive process was not accompanied by any cor-responding growth of new forces" (Dutt, 1970, p. 87), and Baran observes that "accelerating with irresistible energy the maturing of *some* of the basic prerequisites for the development of a capitalistic system, the intrusion of Western capitalism in the now underdeveloped countries blocked with equal force the ripening of others" (Baran, 1957, p. 143). Both of them, while taking as their starting point the observation of Marx noted above, undoubtedly carried Marx's viewpoint much fur-ther. Marx, as we shall soon see, later explicitly disavowed his thesis on the "double mission" of British industrial capital.

MARX IN THE 1860s AND AFTER

In order to carry forward our discussion, let us pay attention to some aspects of Marx's treatises on the Irish question, which played the deci-sive role of a catalyst, causing him to deepen his understanding of world history. What did Marx think of the role that industrial capital played in Ireland, the "backyard" of Britain? One specific remark made in 1867 which is of special interest to us here is this: "Since 1846 the oppression, although it has become less barbaric in form, has been annihilating in substance, and there are no alternatives other than either voluntary emancipation of Ireland by England or the life-or-death struggle" (Marx, 1970, pp. 439—58). Further, "Every time Ireland was just about to develop herself industrially, she was 'smashed down' and forced back; into a mere 'agricultural country.' " The only industry that enjoyed a miserable prosperity in Ireland was the "coffin-making" industry.

"Ireland was compelled to contribute cheap labor power and capital for the establishment of 'the great factory of Britain.' " The inevitable outcome of such annihilating developments in Ireland was a socioeconomic structure in which the "system of usury rent" and a "general state of hunger" were dominant. Here, clearly, Marx was very close to perceiving the "development of underdevelopment" in Ireland. Needless to say, this perception is in line with the perception of the multilayered structure of the world market system described in section 7, chapter 15 ("Machinery and Modern Industry"), of the first volume of *Capital*: "A new and international division of labor, a division suited to the requirements of the chief center of modern industry, springs up and converts one part of the globe into a chiefly agricultural field of production, for supplying the other part which remains a chiefly industrial field."

With this understanding of the history as well as the existing situation of Ireland, Marx wrote as follows in a letter he sent to Engels at about the same time (November 1867):

What the Irish need is:

(1) Self-government and independence from England.
(2) An agrarian revolution. With the best intentions in the world the English cannot accomplish this for them, but they can give them the legal means of accomplishing it for themselves.
(3) *Protective tariffs against England.* Between 1783 and 1801 every branch of the Irish industry flourished. The Union which overthrew the protective tariffs established by the Irish Parliament, destroyed all industrial life in Ireland. The bit of linen industry is no compensation whatever....Once the Irish are independent, necessity will

turn them into protectionists, as it did in Canada, Australia, etc. (Marx, 1867, p. 324)

Marx quite explicitly brings up here a three-point program for ful-filling the needs of the Irish: (1) self-determination and independence, (2) an agrarian revolution *by the Irish themselves*, and (3) *protective tariffs against England*—as a prerequisite for the preceding two objectives—so as to lay the economic base for the survival of the nation. This viewpoint is *deci-sively different* from the one which Marx had in the 1850s, at least in three important respects. First, Marx's view about Ireland's independence changed drastically. In this regard, it seemed sufficient just to quote the well-known statement of Marx himself: "Previously, I thought Ireland's separation from Britain impossible. Now I think it inevitable" (Marx, 1867, p. 323).

The second important change is, in his opinion, about "protective tariffs." Marx at one time (in his 1853 letter to Engels) ridiculed the *New York Tribune* and H. C. Carey, and categorically denounced protectionism in general, on the grounds that "the destruction of the native industry [of India] by England is...revolutionary" (Marx, 1867, p. 311). There is a gulf between this view and the new one Marx had acquired. Admittedly, the historical implication of the demand of the protectionist bourgeoisie of the United States in the 1850s differed radically from that of the demand for "protective tariffs against England" which Marx thought appropriate for the Irish separationist movement as a necessary precondition for the fulfillment of the needs of the Irish people. I have not forgotten about this difference. The point I am trying to make clear here is rather that Marx, who once regarded the destruction of the native industry of India by the British capital as "revolutionary," does not regard the destruction of the native industry of Ireland by the same British capital as "revolu-tionary" anymore. On the contrary, the destruction of native Irish industry is now looked upon as the first step toward demolition of the base for the Irish revolution itself, or, we may dare to say, it is obviously taken as "counterrevolutionary" rather than as "revolutionary."

The third major change is in Marx's view about who should under-take social revolution. The logic which he employed in his article on India in 1853 is no longer present here. To repeat, his earlier view obvi-ously gave positive approval to the role British capital played as an "unconscious tool of history" and therefore assigned the role of a major vehicle for the social revolution of India to the very working of British industrial capital.

Of course, this is not meant to imply that Marx, even when he subscribed to such a view, forgot about the Indian people who should carry out revolution in their own society. In fact, in his 1853 article on India Marx explicitly asserted the importance of appropriation of the productive powers both by the British industrial proletariat and by the Indian people. However, what we are now concerned with is rather how Marx understood the relations between the destructive effects of British industrial capital on the one hand and the appropriate and further development of the productive powers by the Indian people on the other. In 1853 Marx thought that the former accelerated the latter, that is to say, the former would be an inevitable intermediary step on the way to the full realization of the latter. In 1867, on the contrary, Marx had come to realize that the destruction of the old world by British in industrial capital, far from bringing about the material base of the development of new productive powers as he once expected, is quite likely to result in the destruction and plundering of the very mechanism that assures the development of productive powers.

It is evident that Marx is no longer content with paying attention to destruction in general, but tries to make clear what results from that destruction and especially how it acts on the development of the very people who are expected to carry out future national development. Thus Marx, through his recognition of the importance of the indigenous people's initiative in carrying out their own social revolution, radically transformed his assessment of the historical role of British free trade. This will become all the more clear if we observe how his assessment of the Zamindari and Ryotwari systems changed between 1853 and 1881. In 1853 Marx wrote: "The Zamindari and Ryotwari themselves, abominable as they are, involve two distinct forms of private property in land—the great desideratum of Asiatic society" (Marx, 1867, p. 84). In sharp contrast, Marx wrote in 1881: "To take the case of India, for instance, no one with the exception of Sir H. Maine and others of the same stock, can be ignorant that there the extinction of the communal ownership of land was only an act of English vandalism which pushed the indigenous people not forward but backward" (Marx, 1970, p. 402). In 1853 Marx clearly had an affirmative view of what the British had been doing in India; in 1881, in contrast, his attitude toward the same conduct of the British was equally clearly negative. I would like to emphasize that this change derives from Marx's concern, which is stronger than ever, about the fate of the subjugated people, whether they were moving forward or backward. It is extremely significant that Marx now points to a destruction that "pushed the indigenous people *not forward but backward.*" He no longer takes the destruction and regeneration as two facets of the same process which are inseparably united, but instead perceives that they could be diametrically opposed to each other.

It is, then, only natural that Marx's awareness of the *subjective conditions* for social revolution, of the key role to be played be the colonized in achieving the radical reformation of their own society should lead him to pay attention to the *objective conditions* which would prepare these people for actually carrying out the task. The result is the emergence of a point of view which makes much of the formation of an independent national economy as an objective framework for economic development. This is the perspective Marx acquired on the basis of his analysis of the Irish question.

CONCLUSION

In the 1840s and 1850s Marx emphasized the "revolutionary" role of British free trade, basing himself upon a general expectation that it would destroy the framework of the old society which was an obstacle to the growth of productive forces, and would generate in its place the kind of development that would lay the basis for a new society. However, this view was discarded by Marx himself from the 1860s onward, as he became well aware that the destruction of the old society would not necessarily give rise to the material conditions for a new society. Rather, the theoretical position toward which Marx was rapidly moving in his later years may be characterized follows: the forcible integration of the old society into the world market system by the external pressure of British free trade and the resulting transformation of this society would determine a course of development of its economy and a structure of its productive powers completely dependent upon England "according to their greater or lesser suitableness for exportation" (Marx, 1970, p. 374). It might well be said that British free trade has played an essential role in depriving the precapitalist societies integrated into the world market system of the very preconditions for the balanced and systematic development of productive powers which would be indispensable for the construction an independent national economy. One is even tempted to assume that the "double mission" of British free trade should be interpreted not in the sense of a combination of "the destruction of the old society" and "the regeneration of a new society," as Marx thought up to the late 1850s, but rather in the sense of a *double mission of destruction*, meaning both "the destruction of the old society" and the destruction of some of the essential conditions for "regeneration of a new society."

What, then, can we conclude about the previously noted new current of critiques of Marx? First, they deserve criticism, primarily because they frown upon his "mistaken ideas" without making any effort to examine the development of his own understanding of British free trade through to the last years of his life. In contrast, what I have paid attention to and emphasized in this paper are the significant changes in Marx's thinking which are so clearly revealed in his later writings.

Second, however, if I were to limit myself to rejecting these critiques of Marx, I would be open to the justifiable charge of throwing the baby out with the bath water, of simply making an inflexible and sterile countercritique. My purpose in this paper has not been to contribute to such an unproductive attempt to "rescue" Marx dogmatically. On the contrary, my concern has been to call attention to various hints contained in these critiques of Marx which appear to be theoretically valuable and in this way to help reconstitute a critical perspective which can effectively tackle the question facing us today. What has become clear, as a result of what I may call the intercommunication of perspectives, is that (1) these critiques of Marx are basically right in their perception of the historical role of British free trade, and (2) the conclusions to which they lead are in fact virtually identical to those toward which Marx himself continued to strive throughout his untiring journey of theoretical inquiry in the latter half of his life.

REFERENCES

Amin, Samir. 1974. *Accumulation on a World Scale*. New York.

Baran, Paul. 1957. *The Political Economy of Growth*. Mexico: F.C.E., 1969.

Brown, Michael Barratt. 1972. "A Critique of Marxist Theories of Imperialism." In *Studies in the Theories of Imperialism*. Edited by R. Owen and B. Sutcliffe. London.

Davis, Horace, B. September 1967. "Capitalism and Imperialism: A Landmark in Marxist Theory." *Monthly Review*.

Dutt, R. Palme, ed. 1970. *India Today*. Calcutta.

Frank, André Gunder. 1962. *Latin America: Underdevelopment or Revolution*. New York.

Hodgkin, Thomas. 1972. "Some African and Third World Theories of Imperialism." In *Studies in the Theories of Imperialism*. Edited by R. Owen and B. Sutcliffe. London.

Kiernan, V.G. 1974. *Marxism and Imperialism*. London.

Marx, Karl, and Friedrich Engels. *On Colonialism*. Moscow: Foreign Languages Publishing House, 1960.

Marx, Karl. *Werke*. Berlin: Dietz, 1970.

———. 1859. *Grundrisse Foundations of the Critique of Political Economy*. Harmondsworth: Penguin, 1973.

Sutcliffe, B. 1972. "Imperialism and Industrialization in the Third World." In *Studies in the Theories of Imperialism*. Edited by R. Owen and B. Sutcliffe. London.

12

THE ROOTS OF DEPENDENCY THEORY IN MARX

Enrique Dussel

Enrique Dussel has systematically examined the original manuscripts and various editions of Marx's work and, in the following selection, he argues that revision of Marxist thought dates to 1932 with the publication of the previously unknown Economic and Philosophical Manuscripts of 1844 *and to 1939 with the publication for the first time of the* Grundrisse. *The ensuing debate has sought alternatives to the extreme economic determination that characterized interpretation and assessment of Marx's thinking to that time. Dussel believes that we can now transcend the first one hundred years of debate after Marx's death (1883) to rediscover the foundations of his scientific thinking that permit not only a critique of capitalism but of socialism as well. Thus, rather than dwelling upon the post-Marxism of the present moment, instead we need to return to Marx in order to comprehend his method and his categories, his theory and practice. The question of dependency serves as a point of departure for this endeavor.*

THIS ESSAY, WHICH AIMS TO re-pose the "dependency issue," asserts that a return to Marx is highly necessary. This work then should be seen as a "practice" or a "method" for trying to interpret the present using the categories slowly elaborated by Marx, especially from 1857 until the end of his life.

Marx began *Theories of Surplus Value* with a thesis that is reproduced

From Enrique Dussel, "Marx's Economic Manuscripts of 1861–63 and the 'Concept' of Dependency," *Latin American Perspectives* 17 (spring 1990): 62–101. Reprinted with permission of Sage Publications.

{145}

here by way of analogy. He wrote that "all economists share the error" (Marx, 1861—63, vol. 1, p. 40). I would say that many economists, historians, and sociologists share the error of examining dependency not as an international *social relation* and a *transfer of surplus value* between total national capitals of different organic composition, in the framework of competition in the world order, but through *its particular forms* or merely by means of aspects that are secondary phenomena. They thus confuse the essence with the appearance. Furthermore, they do not elaborate upon the concept nor do they first construct the necessary categories on an abstract, *logical*, and *essential* plane, but rather they got lost in a chaotic, unscientific, anecdotal history of dependency.

We can state at the outset that frequently in the debate on dependency Marx was notably absent. In some cases, as in the excellent work of Ruy Mauro Marini, the topic of "transfer of surplus value" was explicitly noted (Marini, 1973, p. 37), but that transfer became a compensation (that is, a secondary, derivative mechanism based on the essence of dependency): "the central thesis that is defended there…is that *the foundation* of dependency is the superexploitation of labor" (Marini, 1973, p. 101).

How can the consequence, or compensation, of the transfer of surplus value be the *foundation* (the essence) of dependency? A transfer of surplus value at a fundamental, essential level makes it necessary for dependent capital to superexploit its wage-labor. Superexploitation is a consequence. This mistake, Marx would call it "confusion," is due to there being no prior clear definition of the "concept"—in the sense that Marx gives this notion.

THE "ESSENCE" OF DEPENDENCY: TRANSFER OF SURPLUS VALUE AS A RESULT OF INTERNATIONAL SOCIAL RELATIONS

This section deals not with genetic or historical factors or determinants of the concept of dependency, be they partial or well founded, but only with the *essential* determinants, in Marx's sense. This question, which seems so simple because it is so obvious, has received practically no attention. Without clarifying the "essence" of dependency from its superficial, phenomenal, apparent or even causal determinants (the cause or determining factor is not the essence, itself), there could be no prior agreement on the concept of a dependency *as such*—even among those who called themselves Marxists.

So the matter of the *essential concept* of dependency was passed over, and the discussion centered on its secondary determinants. Since within these secondary determinants, on a concrete, genetic-historic plane or within the real historical formations, the problem is much more complex, a dead end was reached around 1975. It was simply impossible to go any further, and the question of dependency was abandoned as a theoretical problem without ever having been solved. The error was made back in the mid-1960s when the *dead-end* route was chosen by confusing the *essence* of dependency with its multiple, phenomenal, historical *appearances*. It was a question of method, therefore, and there were no philosophers in the dispute.

Insofar as we are of the opinion that the issue of current external debt is a mechanism for the *transfer of surplus value* via the payment of interest, it seems important to relaunch social science thinking toward correctly dealing with the "dependency question" and to clarify the *concept*. Let us start anew, then....

If one is to speak of the essential determinant of dependency as such, in the most abstract sense, one cannot forget that even the transfer of surplus value is a moment based upon a prior reality. Indeed, for Marx economic facts are above all human; they are human *relations*.... The capital-labor relation is, above all, a relation between persons (a face-to-face relation). It is a "social" relation insofar as the two persons in the relation are isolated and abstract without a community....That is, capital—as such and in the eyes of the capitalist—is *a thing* whose essence is value. When "two" capitals *compete*, *it* would merely be a matter of two *valuable* things—value would be inherent to it as capital. The transfer of value from one capital to another, via competition, appears in the eyes of both as a social relation between things. Capitals compete, the prices of their products are leveled, and the capitals transfer their surplus value from one to the other. It seems that nothing human takes place; or better, the fetishized capitals themselves have taken on the physiognomy of living, personal subjects in an active exchange.

In reality, however, the two capitals in competition are nothing but *things* that are held, appropriated, possessed by "two" capitalists in contradiction. To speak of two capitals, of two capitalists, or of two capitalist classes is here analogically the same (from a more abstract to a more concrete level).

That is, when we speak of "two" total national capitals in competition, in reality we are referring to the *social relation* (between persons who do not constitute a previous community) between the social classes that are the subject of appropriation by both capitals. It is a matter of the *national bourgeoisies confronting each other* (setting aside the states and other actors that must enter into a *more concrete* consideration of competition between *social formations*, which is not the same as between total national capitals).

From the outset and we have noted this earlier, the capital-labor social relation (which we shall call vertical) is one of exploitation. It is the relation in which labor *creates* new value, produces surplus value. The international social relation of a national bourgeoisie that possesses the more developed total national capital in competition with the bourgeoisie of the less developed total national capital is no longer one of exploitation; it is now horizontal. We shall call it a relation of international domination; it is the relation in which, via competition, surplus-value is *transferred* (but *not created*).

In the treatise on competition, the second one after that on capital in general, Marx would have dealt with this question: the domination of one capital over another in competition, which produces a transfer of surplus value from the weaker capital toward the stronger. This transfer, as we have said, is an effect of *domination*. The practical (ethical) relation by which one class dominates another (even if both are bourgeois) is realized in history by the apparatuses of the state (armies, naval forces, etc.). If the state was to be dealt with by Marx as a fourth part of his plan (after rent and wages, and in which the world market was to be the sixth part where international competition between total *national* capitals was to be carried out), it is evident that Marx was not about to study our question explicitly. Maybe it would have been a chapter in that sixth part or, simply, a seventh part, not even planned.

Now, competition between total national capitals of different [levels of] development does not happen naturally with equal willingness on both sides. And if living labor is violently coerced to sell itself (via the dissolution of previous ways of reproducing its life, and the destruction of the institutions that could have defended it by the direct and repressive action of the bourgeois state if need be), in an analogous way (although no longer as capital-labor exploitation, but as capital-capital domination) the less developed capital is coerced (violently in many cases, as, for example, in Paraguay in 1870, or under Latin American populisms since 1954, as in the case of Arbenz in Guatemala, or in Nicaragua in 1987) to *enter international competition*. The natural reaction of a less developed capital is to protect itself by refusing competition, fortifying its borders, and establishing a "nationalist" *national monopoly* (within which there may be international competition). This would be the only capitalist way to accumulate capital and develop autonomously. However, the more developed capital tends to destroy all of the less developed capital's protectionist barriers and imperiously shoves it into competition. Once *in competition* the more developed capital will extract surplus value from the less developed capital.

The international social relation of domination between national bourgeoisies determines, then, the transfer of value in world competition. What *is the fundamental law* of competition or of this transfer of capital with regard to dependency?

It must be recalled that this law is a particular application of the law of value and the law of competition in general. The law of value is fulfilled in dependency, contrary to what some think (even those Marxists pursuing Ricardo's mistaken road). Indeed, Ricardo thought that the transfer of "profit" took place only within a country and that between countries there was only equal exchange, or that one national capital could not benefit from its advantage over another:

> Capital, if there were any difference in profit, would *transfer* (Übertragen) rapidly from London to Yorkshire; but if as a consequence of the growth of capital and population wages increase, and profits fall, capital and population would *not because of this* necessarily move from England to Holland or to Spain or to Russia, where profits would be greater.... The *emigration of* capital (from one country to another) *finds obstacles* in the imaginary or real insecurity of capital when it is not under the direct control of the possessor together with his natural reticence which any person feels upon abandoning the place of his birth and relations, and trust himself with all his established habits to a

strange government and to new laws. (Ricardo, quoted in Marx, 1974, pp. 811, 812)

When "it is a matter of different countries" (Marx, 1974, p. 811), then, it would appear, according to Ricardo, that we are in a situation of pure and simple barter, because in exchange "we cannot create any value" (Marx, 1974, p. 809). This leads him to conclude that "through foreign trade values can never be increased" (1974, p. 810). Marx, who disagrees, sees advantage in exchange. The profit achieved by the stronger country is not spent only unproductively as consumed income, but the capital achieved can be invested to put "in movement new labor with the new value, and thus bring to light *new values*" (1974, p. 810). For Marx, then, the law of value continues to rule international relations, and there can be profit in exchange between nations. What is the law that rules this exchange? It is the same as that of *competition* in general.

To study Marx's answer we must look at two chapters which are methodically *more concrete*, no longer at the extremely abstract level of capital *in general* (or of the concept in itself), but at the level of the confrontation of *many* capitals (which was to have been laid out in the second, unwritten, treatise on competition, or in the much later section on exchange in the world market). Indeed, to understand the *fundamental law* of dependency, or of competition in general at the international level (a determination derived from the international social relation of the respective bourgeoisies), it is necessary for certain conditions to be met: first, that there be *different values* in a product (e.g., in Houston and in Mexico); second, this difference must be the fruit of a *different degree of organic composition* of the capitals involved (of the more developed total national capital of the United States, and Mexico's less developed total national capital), at a material, objective level, or due to the technological determination of the mode of production in terms of its value; third, as codetermination of the preceding (dialectically intertwined, as Palloix indicated), that there be *different wages*—a higher absolute or subjective wage (that which is received by each worker) in the more developed capital, and a higher relative or objective wage (the proportion of wage-value contained in *each* product) in the less developed capital; fourth, both the organic composition and the wage are established within the *national* context (an oft-forgotten issue; at the concrete level this determination is fundamental—the total capital is *national*).

That certain products may have different values (commodity value) and nevertheless the same price ("cost-price" at the beginning of the *Manuscripts of 1861–63* and "price of production" in Marx's definitive denomination) is the theoretical solution to this apparent antinomy.

Let us look more closely at the first aspect: the existence of products or commodities with different values Marx deals with this when he says that the *"greater" the organic composition, the "lower" the value of the product.* This is Bettelheim's position versus Emmanuel, and it is correct. It would determine the first type of unequal exchange (by the mere difference in organic composition). In this case we are not interested in the rates of surplus value or of profit, since in an abstract manner we are only considering the total value of the product.

On the other hand, products also have a different value because of the difference in wages. This is the aspect highlighted in a unilateral way by Emmanuel (and therefore Palloix is right in showing that it is complementary to the previous aspect), which would determine a second type of unequal exchange (for Emmanuel, strict unequal exchange):

> What appears within the movement of wages as a series of varying combinations may appear for different countries as a set of simultaneous differences in *national wage levels....* It will frequently be found that the daily or weekly wage in the first *nation* [with a more developed capitalist mode of production] is higher than in the second [with a less developed capitalism], while the relative price of labor, ie., the price of labor as compared both with surplus value and with the value of the product, stands higher in the second than in the first. (Marx, 1866–67, pp. 701, 702, emphasis added)

It is here that the conditions resulting from "natural and historical development" (Marx, 1866–67, p. 701), the historical reality of the nation, of the state, establish *national* borders that capital cannot easily transcend. The fluidity of capital (as was indicated by Palloix in 1970, although he would incorrectly deny this later) is not total: It cannot go from "England to Holland" with the same speed that it goes from "London to Yorkshire." There is *a fundamental barrier* which must be studied very closely in Latin America today: the *national* border. It is not merely a juridical or geographic border. It is a border that is historical, social, cultural, technological, of "modes of consumption" (the *national* bourgeois state), military, and fundamentally economic. The *national* market, as a moment of total *national* capital, has been passed over by a certain abstract internationalist Marxism. Marx speaks to us of an "average wage," and also of an "average national wage." Emmanuel studies this point and allows us to discover the *national* aspect, not only of wages but of the entire "total *national* capital," within which the national average of a country's (absolutely or subjectively) lower wages have to do with the low organic composition of capital and with the international *social relation* of domination (since the metropolitan states with regard to the colonies, or the imperialist states with regard to dependent nations, exercise a coercion that is *internal* to the world market and *external* to the dependent domestic market: a political, practical, ethical relation).

Having accepted the position that commodities can have a different value but the same price, whether as a result of different organic compositions or of the different wage levels in the international order, we can take up the law of dependency. Given the diversity noted in the value of products or commodities, a particular phenomenon occurs upon entering competition:

> Capital invested in foreign trade can yield a higher rate of profit, firstly, because *it competes* with commodities produced by other countries with *less developed production facilities, so* that the more advanced country sells its goods above their value, even though still more cheaply than its *competitors....* The privileged country receives more labor in exchange for less, even though this difference is pocketed by a particular class. (Marx, 1865–70, pp. 344, 345)

This "particular class" is the national bourgeoisie of the more developed country.

Competition, or the movement that confronts two total national capitals, *does not create value*; rather, it *distributes value* via the *equalization of prices.* To create *value*, to distribute (or transfer) *value*, therefore, is not the same as to equalize *prices.* It is, once again, the whole question of the passage *from value to price.*

Let us repeat. The *"development* of the *concept* of dependency" demands order in the constitution and exposition of categories. The first aspect is the possibility of the existence of products or commodities of different value. The second aspect is to place these products in competition. Thus placed face to face (in reality, so as not to fetishize the unequal exchange of international values, it is not the products but the corresponding national bourgeois classes which are face to face) an *equalization* takes place, although not of values (which can never be equalized), but of *prices*. The law of value regulates or controls this equalization. In the *Manuscripts of 1861–63*, contrary to Rodbertus (chapter 9 on rent), Marx discovers the category of "average profit." If we apply this at the international level we will have enunciated the fundamental law of competition, of equalization, of the distribution of value, and, therefore, of dependency insofar as it is a transfer of surplus value:

> When there is an international exchange of commodities which are products of total national capitals of different levels of development (i.e., of different organic composition and with different average national wages) the commodity of the more developed capital will have a lower *value*. Competition, however, equalizes *the price* of both commodities at a single average price. In this manner, the commodity with a lower value (that of the more developed national capital) obtains a price greater than its value, which it realizes by extracting surplus value from the commodity with a higher value. Therefore the commodity of the less developed capital although it may realize a profit (if its price is less than the international average price), *transfers surplus value* because the average international price is less than the national value of the same commodity.

This fundamental law is *explicit* in various forms in Marx, and it is usual in classical Marxism such as Grossman (1979), for example. We can thus conclude that dependency, in the logic of Marx's own thought, is an irrefutable concept. Therefore, the whole Latin American polemic around this issue simply manifested a lack of methodological rigor. That is, *dependency exists* at an abstract, essential, or fundamental level, and it is the international social relation between bourgeoisies possessing total national capitals of different degrees of development. In the framework of competition, the less developed total national capital finds itself *socially dominated* (a *relation* between persons), and, in the final analysis, *transfers surplus value* (an essential *formal* moment) to the more developed capital, which realizes it as extraordinary profit.

Some might say that this is obvious, that nobody has denied it. But this is not so. Because these *obvious, essential,* and abstract questions were not defined beforehand, and the discussion proceeded directly to *history* (instead of to the essential *logic*), mistakes and confusions were committed that were naive from the standpoint of good Marxism....

NEW POLITICAL CONCLUSIONS: "NATIONAL" AND "POPULAR" LIBERATION

Earlier I said that the debate on the "theory of dependency" came to a dead end.... For the present crises—the international external debt and the need for a revolutionary theory articulated to the praxis of liberation in Central America, the Caribbean, and increasingly in other parts of Latin America—there is no theory to explain them (Marxism just as Marx left it is not sufficient). The contradiction between theory and praxis lies in the following: An international class struggle (capitalist-proletarian) was enunciated as the only possibility, while every attempt at "national" or "popular" liberation was branded as populist. The "question of dependency" would be a bourgeois problem of interest only to peripheral national capitalism; it would not be a Marxist question. Nevertheless, the revolution that will overcome capitalism is not *immediately* a world revolution, nor is it carded out at the level of the factory.

Proletarians liberate themselves from the capitalist class only through *national* revolutions by taking *state power.* Frequently revolutionary vanguard movements have not been only proletarian but also peasant and petty-bourgeois (since Marx or Lenin, through Mao, Agostinho Neto, or *comandante* Borge; one must recall that Fidel Castro and Engels were, strictly speaking, bourgeois, one during his youth and the other throughout his life). The concept of *peripheral dominated "nation"* and of *exploited "people" (complex* political categories at the concrete level of *reproduction)* as a "social bloc of the oppressed" subsumes the (more abstract) category of "class." All of this could have been theoretically grounded had the *concept* of dependency been developed correctly. The process of national and popular liberation is the only way to destroy the mechanisms of constant and increasing *transference of surplus value* from the less developed total national capital. This assumes overcoming capitalism as such, since the extraction of surplus value (a living capital-labor relation) is articulated to the transfer of surplus value in the competition between total national capitals of different levels of development. The *weakness* of peripheral capital (due to its structural transfer of surplus value) does not mean we can subsume the entire population as a wage-earning class: The *marginal popular* masses play a leading role in the process of change. The popular movement and popular organization become political priorities.

When one speaks of liberation one thinks in terms of a situation of domination. Dependency represents this situation of domination in the world capitalist system. We think that, in the strict sense, the dependency relationship needs two industrial capitals (one in the center and the other in the periphery)....

The concept of dependency is the only one that can provide a theoretical framework for a political understanding of the situation of domination in which our Latin American nations find themselves today. (Let it be said in passing that the same is true for the African and Asian nations.) The concept of "class struggle" is not sufficient to give a fundamental diagnosis. It must not be forgotten that the "competitive *struggle*" (Marx, 1865–70, p. 353, emphasis added) situates the peripheral countries in a very precise manner, and their weak and weakened capitalism lends itself to processes of liberation. It is liberation *from dependency* (as *national* domination, via the national bourgeoisies and the total capital of the country), and liberation *of the oppressed people* in the nation (the social bloc of those who with their labor, be it wage-labor or available labor, create all the transferable value and surplus value).

This is why the Frente Sandinista de liberacion Nacional (FSLN) defines itself as a *national end popular* liberation movement. *National* in that, by overcoming capitalist dependency, the country can accumulate the fruit of the labor of its workers as its own wealth. *Popular* in that not only the classes oppressed by past capitalism, but even all those who were *nothing* for total national capital (the unemployed, the ethnic minorities, the marginal population, etc.), in Nicaragua can organize a new, liberated way of life on the basis of their *culture*—and of their religion as a part of their popular *culture*—as an affirmation of the exteriority of concrete, historical *living labor*.

To continue Marx's theoretical discourse beyond Latin America and not merely to apply it (which is an error because it was "open" and "unfinished"), and to discover in it new possibilities *based on the people's praxis of national liberation,* based on the "logic of the majorities" (but of the majorities as subjects of the history of liberation), is the task of a philosophy of liberation.

The concept of dependency, therefore, from *a political* perspective (in the correct praxis of national and popular liberation) and from a *theoretical* perspective (in a philosophy of liberation that methodically thinks about Latin American reality as a process of liberation) is fundamental. At the level of political economy, it is the very starting point for the concept of liberation. It is the theoretical moment from which and *from where* the process of liberation on our continent originates and starts.

REFERENCES

Marini, Ruy Mauro. 1973. *Dialéctica de la dependencia.* Mexico City: Ediciones Era.

Marx, Karl. 1861–63. *Theories of Surplus Value.* 3 vols. Translated by Emile Burns. Moscow: Progess Publishers, 1963.

———. 1865–70. *Capital: A Critique of Political Economy.* Vol. 2. Introduction by Ernest Mandel. Translated by David Fernbach. New York: Vintage Books, 1981.

———. 1866–67, *Capital: A Critique of Political Economy.* Vol. 1. Introduction by Ernest Mandel. Translated by Ben Fowkes. New York: Vintage Books, 1977.

———. 1974. *Grundrisse.* Berlin: Dietz.

THE
LEGACY
OF
LENIN

13

UNEVEN CAPITALIST DEVELOPMENT
The Case of Capitalist Russia

V. I. Lenin

The following selection from Lenin's analysis of Russian development reflects the impacts of capitalism upon an underdeveloped country. In particular, he identifies processes at work in the uneven transition to capitalism. Further understanding of Lenin's contribution is included in "Marxist Theory and Imperialism" by Anthony Brewer (see chapter 17).

THIS WORK WAS WRITTEN IN the period preceding the Russian Revolution, during the slight lull that set in after the outbreak of the big strikes of 1895–1896. At that time the working-class movement withdrew, as it were, into itself, spreading in breadth and depth and paving the way for the beginning in 1901 of the demonstration movement.

The analysis of the social-economic system and, consequently, of the class structure of Russia given in this work on the basis of an economic investigation and critical analysis of statistics, is now confirmed by the open political action of all classes in the course of the revolution. The leading role of the proletariat has been fully revealed. It has also been revealed that the strength of the proletariat in the historical movement is immeasurably greater than the share it constitutes of the total mass of the population. The economic basis of the one phenomenon and the other is demonstrated in the present work.

From V. I. Lenin, *History of Capitalism in Russia* (1899; reprint Moscow: Foreign Languages Publishing House, 1956), pp. 6–9, 594–95, 596–603, 604–605.

Further, the revolution is now increasingly revealing the dual position and dual role of the peasantry. On the one hand, the tremendous relics of corvee economy and all kinds of survivals of serfdom, with the unprecedented impoverishment and ruin of the peasant poor, fully explain the deep sources of the revolutionary peasant movement, the deep roots of the revolutionary character of the peasantry as a mass. On the other hand, in both the course of the revolution, the character of the various political parties, and the numerous ideological-political trends is revealed the inherently contradictory class structure of this mass, its petty-bourgeois character, the antagonism between the employer and the proletarian trends within it. The vacillation of the impoverished small master between the counterrevolutionary bourgeoisie and the revolutionary proletariat is as inevitable as the phenomenon existent in every capitalist society that an insignificant minority of small producers wax rich, "get on in the world," turn into bourgeois, while the overwhelming majority are either utterly ruined and become wage-workers or paupers, or eternally eke out an almost proletarian existence. The economic basis of both these trends among the peasantry is demonstrated in the present work.

With this economic basis the revolution in Russia is, of course, inevitably a bourgeois revolution. This Marxist proposition is absolutely irrefutable. It must never be forgotten. It must always be applied to all the economic and political problems of the Russian Revolution.

But one must know how to apply it. A concrete analysis of the position and the interests of the different classes must serve as a means of defining the precise significance of this truth when applied to this or that problem. The opposite mode of reasoning frequently met with among the Right-wing Social-Democrats headed by Plekhanov, i.e., the endeavor to seek for answers to concrete questions in the simple logical development of the general truth about the basic character of our revolution, is a vulgarization of Marxism and downright mockery of dialectical materialism. Of such people, who from the general truth of the character of this revolution deduce, for example, the leading role of the "bourgeoisie" in the revolution, or the need for Socialists to support the liberals, Marx would very likely have repeated the words once quoted by him from Heine: "I sowed dragons and reaped fleas."

With the present economic basis of the Russian Revolution, two main lines of its development and outcome are objectively possible:

Either the old landlord economy, bound as it is by thousands of threads to serfdom, is retained and turns slowly into purely capitalist, "Junker" economy. The basis of the final transition from otrabotki to capitalism is the internal metamorphosis of feudalist landlord economy. The entire agrarian system of the state becomes capitalist and for long retains feudalist features. Or the old landlord economy is broken up by revolution, which destroys all the relics of serfdom, primarily large landownership. The basis of the final transition from otrabotki to capitalism is the free development of small peasant farming, which has received a tremendous impetus as a result of the expropriation of the landlords' estates in the interests of the peasantry. The entire agrarian system becomes capitalist, for the more completely the vestiges of serfdom are destroyed the more rapidly does the disintegration of the peasantry proceed. In other words: either—the retention in the main of landlordism and of the main supports of the old "superstructure"; hence, the predominant role of the liberal-monarchist bourgeois and landlord, the rapid transition of the well-to-do peasantry to their side, the degradation of the peasant masses, not only expropriated on a vast scale but enslaved, in addition, by one or other kind of Cadet-proposed land-redemption payments, and downtrodden and dulled by the dominance of reaction; the executors of such a bourgeois revolution will be politicians of a type approximating to the Octobrists. Or—the destruction of landlordism and of all the main supports of the corresponding old "superstructure"; the predominant role of the proletariat and the peasant masses, with the neutralizing of the unstable or counterrevolutionary bourgeoisie; the speediest and freest development of the productive forces on a capitalist basis, under the best circumstances at all conceivable under commodity production for the worker and peasant masses;—hence, the establishment of the most favorable conditions for the further accomplishment by the working class of its real and fundamental task of socialist reorganization. Of course, infinitely diverse combinations are possible of elements of this or that type of capitalist evolution, and only hopeless pedants could set about solving the peculiar and complex problems arising merely by quoting this or that opinion of Marx about a different historical epoch.

The work here presented to the reader is devoted to an analysis of the prerevolutionary economy of Russia. In a revolutionary epoch, life in a country proceeds with such speed and impetuosity that it is impossible to define the major results of economic evolution in the heat of political struggle.

THREE STAGES IN THE DEVELOPMENT OF CAPITALISM IN RUSSIAN INDUSTRY

There are three main stages in this development: small commodity-production (small, mainly peasant industries); capitalist manufacture; and the factory (large-scale machine industry). The facts utterly refute the view widespread here in Russia that "factory-and-works" and "kustar" industry are isolated from each other. On the contrary, to divide them is purely artificial. The connection and continuity between the forms of industry mentioned is of the most direct and intimate kind. The facts quite clearly show that the main trend of small commodity-production is toward the development of capitalism, and in particular, toward the rise of manufacture; and manufacture is growing with enormous rapidity before our eyes into large-scale machine industry. Perhaps one of the most striking manifestations of the intimate and direct connection between the consecutive forms of industry is the fact that a whole number of big and of the biggest factory-owners were at one time the smallest of small industrialists and passed through all the stages from "popular production" to "capitalism...."

The three main forms of industry enumerated above differ first of all in their different systems of technique. Small commodity-production is characterized by its totally primitive, hand technique that remained unchanged almost from time immemorial. The industrialist remains a peasant who follows tradition in his methods of processing raw material. Manufacture introduces division of labor, which effects a substantial change in technique and transforms the peasant into an artisan, a "detail laborer." But production by hand remains, and, on its basis, progress in methods of production is inevitably very slow. Division of labor springs up spontaneously and is passed on by tradition just as peasant labor is. Large-scale machine industry alone introduces a radical change, throws manual skill overboard, transforms production on new, rational principles, and systematically applies science to production. So long as capitalism failed in Russia to organize large-scale machine industry, and in those industries in which it has not done so yet, we observe almost complete stagnation in technique, we see the employment of the same handloom and the same watermill or windmill that were used in production centuries ago. On the other hand, in those industries where the factory holds sway we observe a complete technical revolution and extremely rapid progress in the methods of machine production.

Connected with the different systems of technique we see different stages of development of capitalism. Small commodity-production and manufacture are characterized by the prevalence of small establishments, from among which only a few large ones are generated. Large-scale machine industry completely eliminates the small establishments. Capitalist relationships arise in the small industries, too (in the shape of workshops employing wage-workers and of merchant capital), but these are still slightly developed and are not crystallized in sharp contradictions between the groups of persons participating in production. Neither big capitals nor extensive proletarian strata yet exist. In manufacture we see the rise of both. The gulf between the one who owns the means of production and the one who works already attains considerable dimensions. "Wealthy" industrial settlements spring up, the bulk of whose inhabitants are entirely propertyless working people. A small number of merchants, who do an enormous business buying raw materials and selling finished goods, and a mass of detail workers living from hand to mouth—such is the general picture of manufacture. But the multitude of small establishments, the retention of the tie with the land, the adherence to tradition in production and in the whole manner of living—all this creates a mass of intermediary elements between the extremes of manufacture and retards the development of these extremes. In large-scale machine industry all these retarding factors disappear; the acuteness of social contradictions reaches the highest point. All the dark sides of capitalism become concentrated, as it were: the machine, as is known, gives a tremendous impulse to the uttermost extension of the working day; women and children are drawn into industry; a reserve army of unemployed is formed (and by virtue of the conditions of factory production must be formed), etc. However, the socialization of labor brought about on a vast scale by the factory, and the transformation of the sentiments and conceptions of the people it employs (in particular, the destruction of patriarchal and petty-bourgeois traditions) cause a reaction: large-scale machine industry, unlike the preceding stages, imperatively calls for the planned regulation of production and public control over it (a manifestation of the latter tendency is factory legislation).

The very character of the development of production changes at the various stages of capitalism. In the small industries this development follows in the wake of the development of peasant economy; the market is extremely narrow, the distance between the producer and the consumer is short, and the insignificant scale of production easily adapts itself to the slightly fluctuating local demand. That is why the greatest stability characterizes industry at this stage, but this stability is tantamount to stagnation in technique and the preservation of patriarchal social relationships enmeshed in all sorts of survivals of medieval traditions. The manufactories work for a big market—sometimes for the whole country—and, accordingly, production acquires the instability characteristic of capitalism, an instability which attains the greatest intensity under factory production. The development of large-scale machine industry cannot proceed except in spurts, in alternations of periods of prosperity and of crisis. The ruin of small producers is tremendously accelerated by this spasmodic growth of the factory; the workers are now drawn into the factory in masses during a boom period, and now thrown out. The formation of a vast reserve army of unemployed, ready to undertake any kind of work, becomes a condition for the existence and development of large-scale machine industry....
The "instability" of large-scale machine industry has always evoked, and continues to evoke, reactionary complaints from individuals who continue to look at things through the eyes of the small producer and who forget that it is this "instability" alone that replaced the former stagnation by the rapid transformation of methods of production and of all social relationships.

One of the manifestations of this transformation is the separation of industry from agriculture, the release of the social relationships in industry from the traditions of the feudal and patriarchal system that weigh down on agriculture. In small commodity-production the industrialist has not yet emerged at all from his peasant shell; in the majority of cases he remains a cultivator, and this connection between small industry and small agriculture is so profound that we observe the interesting law of the parallel disintegration of the small producers in industry and in agriculture. The generation of a petty bourgeoisie and of wage-workers proceeds simultaneously in both spheres of the national economy, thereby preparing the way, at both poles of disintegration, for the break of the industrialist with agriculture. Under manufacture this break is already very considerable. A whole number of industrial centers arise that do not engage in agriculture. The chief representative of industry is no longer the peasant, but the merchant and the manufactory-owner on the one hand, and the "artisan" on the other. Industry and the relatively developed commercial intercourse with the rest of the world raise the standard of living of the population and their culture; the peasant cultivator is now regarded with disdain by the manufactory workman. Large-scale machine industry completes this transformation, separates industry from agriculture once and for all, and, as we have seen, creates a special class of the population totally alien to the old peasantry and differing from the latter in its manner of living, its family relationships and its higher standard of requirements, both material and spiritual. In the small industries and in manufacture we always find survivals of patriarchal relations and of diverse forms of personal dependence, which, in the general conditions of capitalist economy, exceedingly worsen the condition of the working people, and degrade and corrupt them. Large-scale machine industry, which concentrates masses of workers who often come from various parts of the country, absolutely refuses to tolerate survivals of patriarchalism and personal dependence, and is marked by a truly "contemptuous attitude to the past." And it is this break with obsolete tradition that is one of the substantial conditions which has created the possibility and evoked the necessity of regulating production and of public control over it. In particular, speaking of the transformation brought about by the factory in the conditions of life of the population, it must be stated that the drawing of women and juveniles into production is, at bottom, progressive. It is indisputable that the capitalist factory places these categories of the working population in particularly hard conditions, and that for them it is particularly necessary to regulate and shorten the working day, to guarantee hygienic conditions of labor, etc.; but endeavors to completely ban the work of women and juveniles in industry, or to maintain the patriarchal manner of life that ruled out such work, would be reactionary and utopian. By destroying the patriarchal isolation of these categories of the population who formerly never emerged from the narrow circle of domestic, family relationships, by drawing them into direct participation in social production, large-scale machine industry stimulates their development and increases their independence, in other words, creates conditions of life that are incomparably superior to the patriarchal immobility of precapitalist relationships.

The first two stages of industrial development are characterized by the population being settled. The small industrialist, remaining a peasant, is bound to his village by his farm. The artisan under manufacture is usually tied to the small, isolated industrial area which is created by manufacture. In the very system of industry at the first and second stages of its development there is nothing to disturb this settled and isolated condition of the producer. Intercourse between the various industrial areas is rare. The transfer of industry to other areas only takes place by the migration of individual small producers, who establish new small industries in the outlying parts of the country. Large-scale machine industry, on the other hand, necessarily creates mobility of the population; commercial intercourse between the various districts grows enormously; railways facilitate travel. The demand for labor increases on the whole—rising in periods of boom and falling in periods of crisis, so that it becomes a necessity for workers to go from one factory to another, from one part of the country to another. Large-scale machine industry creates a number of new industrial centers, which arise with unprecedented rapidity, sometimes in unpopulated places, a thing that would be impossible without the mass migration of workers.

The above-described characteristic features which distinguish large-scale machine industry from the preceding forms of industry may be summed up in the words—socialization of labor. Indeed, production for an enormous national and international market, development of close commercial ties with various parts of the country and with different countries for the purchase of raw and auxiliary materials, enormous technical progress, concentration of production and of the population in colossal enterprises, demolition of the worn-out traditions of patriarchal life, creation of mobility of the population, and enhancement of the worker's standard of requirements and development—all these are elements of the capitalist process which is increasingly socializing production in the country, and with it those who participate in production.

On the problem of the relation of large-scale machine industry in Russia to the home market for capitalism, the data given above lead to the following conclusion. The rapid development of factory industry in Russia is creating an enormous and ever-growing market for means of production (building-materials, fuel, metals, etc.), is increasing with particular rapidity in the part of the population engaged in making articles of productive and not personal consumption. But the market for articles of personal consumption is also growing rapidly, owing to the growth of large-scale machine-industry, which is diverting an increasingly large part of the population from agriculture into commercial and industrial occupations.

14

ASSESSING LENIN'S THEORY

John Willoughby

This essay argues that the Leninist emphasis on political domination cannot be reduced to economic tendencies. While emphasis on evolving forms of capital accumulation remains fundamental, a materialist theory of imperial domination in the capitalist era necessitates analysis of evolving state structures. Lenin did not intend to suggest a definitive theory of imperialism, but instead presented a popular synthesis of many ideas and issues. Willoughby identifies confusions in Lenin's definition and the relevance of his thinking to twentieth-century Marxism. He argues that imperialism is a political phenomenon and should be examined in light of how economic trends affect political options in changing times and conditions. Rather than imperialism contributing to the fall of capitalism, he argues, the state and its policies suggest a tendency toward integration rather than imperial pretensions leading to conflict among dominant nations.

MANY OF US WHO HAVE written about *Imperialism, the Highest Stage of Capitalism* have noted that the work was never meant to represent the final scientific statement on the problem of capital expansion and advanced capitalist state coercion. Indeed, Lenin was too careful a student of Marx to claim that any body of thought could represent the ultimate solution to any problem. Moreover, this World War I-era pamphlet was primarily written to synthesize certain important theoretical writings on

From John Willoughby, "Evaluating the Leninist Theory of Imperialism," *Science and Society* 59 (fall 1995): pp. 321–25, 326–27, 328–30, 330–31, 332, 333, 335, 336. Reprinted with permission of Guilford Publications.

the subject of imperialism and to draw out their political implications as sharply as possible. The subtitle states that *Imperialism, the Highest Stage of Capitalism* was intended as a popular outline.

Why did Lenin write a succinct, synthetic popularization of the newly developed Marxian theory of imperialism? He believed that the Great War was laying the basis for a new revolutionary era. Workers and Marxist activists had to understand that the defeat of the imperialist impulses that led to World War I *required* the overthrow of capitalism and the establishment of workers' republics which could inaugurate a socialist political economic order. All of Lenin's writings were imbued with a furious political purpose, but *Imperialism* shakes with even more passion than usual. This energy is one reason why this pamphlet is perhaps Lenin's best known writing.

There are historical reasons as well for the continued salience of Lenin's analysis of imperialism. In the first place, Lenin's arguments about the inevitability of capitalist war, the statist character of contemporary capital accumulation, and its increasingly moribund and parasitic nature seemed right on target to many Communists and non-Communists caught up in the maelstroms of depression and Fascism during the interwar years.

Second, Lenin continued to develop his views on imperialism until his stroke in 1922 in ways which became very attractive to anticolonialist activists. At the meeting of the Second Congress of the Communist International in 1920, for example, Lenin argued that the world was becoming divided between the oppressor nations of the West and the colonial peoples of the East. This dichotomy was very suggestive and grew increasingly popular in the post-World War II era of colonial liberation struggles. Lenin is rightly viewed as the inspiration behind many theories of neocolonialism. *Imperialism* seemed particularly relevant during the interwar period of capitalist barbarism and the immediate postwar era that saw the dismantling of colonial structures of domination.

The final reason for the strong following accorded Lenin's theory was his status as the only Communist "saint" embraced by nearly all Marxian movements. Trotskyists, Stalinists, and Maoists could all agree that Lenin's *Imperialism* represented a profound scientific achievement. His work on this subject achieved a canonical status which is only now eroding. To the world of bureaucratic Communist societies, *Imperialism* often represented the most scientific statement on trends within advanced capitalist society. Stalin argued that Lenin's work on imperialism and party organization created a higher body of thought which he labeled Marxism-Leninism. Lenin's contributions, according to this view, contributed categories of analysis that were singularly appropriate for the understanding of monopoly capitalism.

More nuanced and circumspect academic Marxists have also maintained that Lenin's contributions to the theory of imperialism established him as a theorist of the first. Certainly, Lenin's analysis of imperialism has had a profound political and academic impact. It is not difficult to trace the effect of Lenin's writings on conceptualizations of neocolonialism, monopoly and state monopoly capitalism, dependency theory, regulation theory, and world system theory. The writings of many of those working within the United Nations Council on Trade and Development have also borrowed heavily, if indirectly, from Lenin's writings. There is no doubt that his work on imperialism will provide a framework of analysis for many well into the next century. This is quite a legacy for a popular pamphlet and a few short articles or speeches.

LENIN IN ANALYTICAL CONTEXT: THE REDUCTIONIST LOGIC OF THE EARLY TWENTIETH-CENTURY MARXIST TRADITION

> If it were necessary to give the briefest possible definition of imperialism, we should have to say that imperialism is the monopoly stage of capitalism.
>
> —Lenin, 1971, p. 85

This famous statement by Lenin has often been cited as his unique contribution to the Marxist theory of imperialism. In fact, this formulation, while rhetorically compelling, is monumentally confusing. To suggest that imperialism is a stage of capitalism obviously implies that eliminating imperialism requires the elimination of capitalism, since imperialism is capitalism. But this verbal sleight of hand actually can inhibit a study of the connection between two distinct social institutions: a mode of production based on the exploitation of free labor and a system of political domination by the rulers of a capitalist polity or polities over the peoples of other states in order to maintain favorable conditions of exploitation. Perhaps imperialism grows out of "monopoly capitalism," but this, as Arrighi points out, should be treated as a "hypothesized statement of fact," not an axiomatic statement which *must* be true (Arrighi, 1987).

Despite the confusions of Lenin's definition, his linkage of imperialism to a stage of capitalism is squarely within the early twentieth-century tradition of Marxian thinking. He is not the initiator of this view. Rather, the link between imperialism and changes in the mode of capital accumulation was first made by Rudolf Hilferding. Although this argumentation was vigorously contested by Rosa Luxemburg, Hilferding's *Finanzkapital* became the consensus statement for most of the high priests of Marxism's "golden age."

Hilferding defined finance capital as "bank capital (thus capital in money form), that in reality has been transformed into industrial capital" (Hilferding, 1981, p. 225). Concretely, this meant that the age of finance capital required the development of institutions that facilitated the mobility of capital ownership. As ownership became centralized, it was necessary to develop ways for capitalists to switch relatively smoothly from one branch of production to another. Entrepreneurial activity was, according to Hilferding, now defined as the ability to control a whole range of socialized production activities through the manipulation of money capital flows.

Hilferding argued that the emergence of finance capital in the early twentieth century intensified nation-state competition and imperial practices. The emergence of huge pools of liquid capital was linked to the concentration and centralization of production in the United States and Germany, which took place behind high tariff barriers. This attenuated price competition, but also limited the quantity of sales within national boundaries. Thus, national monopolies attempted to use their domestic profits to subsidize the selling of goods abroad. This competitive dumping process intensified international rivalries and accelerated capital export: "Thus the export of capital which receives a powerful stimulus from the productive tariff…contributes to the penetration of capital into all parts of the world and the internationalization of capital" (Hilferding, 1981, p. 314).

This historically contingent analysis helps explain Lenin's cryptic linkage between the merger of bank and industrial capital, capital export, and the cartellization of the world economy. Lenin's five point description of imperialism closely follows Hilferding's logic. It is likely that Lenin stressed this dialectic between cartellization and violent rupture because of the interpretive work of Nikolai Bukharin in his book *Imperialism and World Economy*. In this quite interesting "take-off" from Hilferding, Bukharin posits a dialectic between nationalization and internationalization. The globalization of networks of accumulation becomes linked with the ever-increasing power of national monopoly interests and the regulatory power of the state. Bukharin followed Hilferding in suggesting that the anarchy of accumulation would *normally* give rise to imperial conflict. Lenin was far less circumspect. For him, uneven development must *always* predominate:

> Finance capital and trusts have not diminished but increased the differences in the rate of growth in various parts of the world economy. Once the relations of forces are changed, what other solution to the contradiction can be found *under capitalism* than that of force? (Lenin, 1970, p. 93)

Lenin was not innovating here, but following the reductionist logic of the early twentieth-century theorists. There are three key political arguments in Lenin's work: that capital export leads to the imperial domination of subordinated territories, that uneven development leads to imperialist war, and that monopolistic stagnation leads to political economic parasitism.... The point here is that every argument about imperial politics rests on an economic law. The link between economic tendencies and political outcome is unproblematic....

It sill remains to define the economic contradictions correctly and identify those that require capital export and imperialism. Many favorable and unfavorable commentaries on the early Marxian tradition have focused their attention on the variety of economic contradictions that different theorists have selected as dominant. Thus, Luxemburg is rightly criticized for failing to prove that there must always and necessarily be insufficient demand to purchase the additional product that any expanding capitalist economy places on the market, and Hobson is faulted for failing to demonstrate clearly why a skewed income distribution must necessarily generate inadequate domestic demand. Theorists such as Bukharin who emphasize raw material shortage are often criticized for focusing on short-term trends rather than on any inherent tendency. Finally, the problems with the falling rate of profit thesis, emphasized by Hilferding, are well known, although there does seem to be a consensus that the rate of profit *was* falling during the prewar period. Lenin stressed all of these contradictions (except Luxemburg's) in his pamphlet, although he placed priority on the "law of the tendency of the rate of profit to fall."

These critiques are useful in sharpening our understanding of the status of particular contradictions in our theorizing. The result, however, has been largely destructive. No particular contradiction can take logical priority, but all of them can be thought of as helping to create a tendency toward capital expansion. This is not even a Marxian conclusion, however. Emphasis on capital's expansive tendency is an integral part of the pre-Marxian classical tradition.

On the other hand, all of the contributors to this body of thought were too well trained in Marx's method to ignore historical context. The contextualized arguments made by all of them stress the importance of the changing form or mode of economic expansion. I take the following to be Hilferding's, Bukharin's, Lenin's, and Luxemburg's major contribution to our understanding of the logic of the world economy's evolution....

We cannot deduce imperial domination from capital export or capitalist rivalry from the logic of uneven development without additional arguments connecting the evolution of national social formations to the world accumulation process. And this, in turn, means that the roots of metropolitan territorial domination are still obscure. We have neither a general explanation of capitalist imperialism, nor an accounting of its heterogeneous character. *This is a fundamental failure.* No theory of imperialism can be complete without a compelling explanation of the varying forms of metropolitan capitalist state domination. And this requires that attention be paid to the formation of varying political structures throughout the world economy—an attention that is diverted by the reductionist theories of capitalist imperialism and, in Lenin's case, by the actual definition of imperialism itself.

What of the "Third Worldist" aspect of Lenin's theory? Here, Lenin stressed economic parasitism and the exploitation of poor nations by the rich. This part of his work is much more closely linked to John Hobson's argumentation than to Hilferding's. Lenin never attempted to document the extent of parasitism or even to define this phenomenon clearly. He also never linked his Comintern writings to his earlier stress on intercapitalist competition....

We should not be too critical of these theoretical failings. Historical context changes, and Lenin was certainly more sensitive to these changes than most. It may also be hard to expect an overworked Prime Minister of the first "workers' state" to worry too much about the relation of a speech to earlier theoretical syntheses.

Still, this emphasis on parasitism did suffer from some of the same failings that also weakened Lenin's previous stress on capitalist rivalry. Lenin's assumption that capital accumulation was no longer progressive could not explain why most capital flows remained within the advanced capitalist world. Moreover, the traditional emphasis on capital flows and stagnation tended to obscure the political and cultural dimensions of the creation of the capitalist world economy. The transformation of new networks of commodity production and distribution was (and is) associated with the simultaneous creation of new state structures and cultural identities (Anderson, 1983). Given the importance of the Leninist emphasis on state power, this lacuna is surprising. The early twentieth-century Marxian tradition has left all contemporary Marxian theorists with a flawed legacy.

To summarize: the strength of the classical Marxian theory rests on its evolutionary perspective. It focuses on the changing dynamics of capital accumulation and then explores the changing forms of spatial expansion that flow from these evolving contradictions. This emphasis on the economic "base" helps the analyst and activist identify what processes are most dynamically affecting global political economic relations. The attempt to develop a new law of motion in monopoly capitalism was not successful. Still, the focus on the growing importance of capital export and the technological developments that accompanied it provides an important framework for the understanding of the global political contradictions associated with the expansion of capitalist networks of accumulation.

If the evolutionary aspect of the classical Marxian theory points the analyst in the correct direction, the attempt of this theory to *explain*

imperial conflict or oppression by reference to these economic tendencies alone is not successful. No economic tendency implies a given political result. *Lenin's Hilferding's, Bukharin's, Hobson's, and Luxemburg's attempts to*
explain the imperialist phenomenon are written at the wrong level of abstraction. Imperialism is a political phenomenon. To understand it, one must explore
the ways in which economic trends affect political *options.* Historically
contingent issues such as the recent history of international tension, the
nature of military technology, the balance of class forces within different
social formations, and the motivations of rival state officials will all
determine the form which imperialism takes in a particular epoch.

UNDERSTANDING ECONOMICS AND POLITICS OF CAPITALIST IMPERIALISM TODAY: HOW MUCH GUIDANCE DOES THE LENINIST TRADITION GIVE US?

...There are still serious theoretical issues to be resolved. Recent studies of
profitability have not shown convincingly that transnational corporations
possess a clear competitive advantage over more regionally bounded
firms. Still, the Marxian emphasis on different moments of accumulation
permit a more thorough accounting of the social and political impact of
the integration of commodity capital circuits through trade, of money
capital circuits through portfolio and banking investments, and of productive capital circuits through direct foreign investment.

There can be little doubt that these trends have only been significantly interrupted once in the history of global capitalism—during the
period of twentieth-century global war, which lasted, with one inter-
ruption during the 1920s and early 1930s, from 1914 through 1945. Moreover, no serious student can deny the importance of powerful private
accumulation units in intensifying these trends of capital interpenetration. This organizational/institutional perspective on the accumulation
process has proven to be immensely important to our understanding of
global economic trends. Mainstream economic theory is only beginning
to realize this with its launching of the New Institutional Economics.

Economic globalization and global exploitation? At first glance, the Leninist tradition's emphasis on regional exploitation has also stood the test of time
well. Even though Arghiri Emmanuel's *Unequal Exchange* has been subjected
to many mainstream and radical criticisms, Emmanuel's argument can be

accepted if one defines exploitation as existing when one group works more for a given bundle of goods than another. John Roemer, while extremely critical of resting any theory of exploitation on value theory, has demonstrated that a country experiences exploitation if it imports capital and/or exports labor. Many Third World countries do both.

Still, a closer look at this issue raises serious questions. Lenin's original argument appeared to link exploitation to *stagnation*—the implication being that a country could only develop by breaking out completely of capital accumulation circuits. Samir Amin has drawn precisely this conclusion, but an examination of the data suggest that those "Third World" countries most enmeshed in capital circuits are also the most dynamic. It is a common joke in development circles that most poor nations would love to be exploited by an infusion of capital from the North. More seriously, most of those countries that have either purposefully isolated themselves from the world economy or been isolated by imperial action have suffered disastrously.

Space does not permit an elaboration of this point. Nevertheless, radical economists are increasingly realizing that *it is not true* that global capital accumulation must coerce the Third World into a position of permanent economic backwardness. On the level of the abstract theory of capital expansion and exploitation, it is not possible to argue for the inevitable necessity of the North-South divide.

The Frustrated Search for a Repeat of the Old Scenario of Liberal Capitalist Collapse

...I was determined to prove that the serious disruptions in the institutional structure of accumulation during this period [early 1970s] were a product of uneven development, i.e., the decline of American economic power; and that global capitalism would soon devolve into three competing zones of economic conflict, dominated by the so-called European Community, the United States, and Japan.

My research into economic trends of division during the 1970s in fact demonstrated the opposite of what I expected. The world economy was becoming more integrated, except in those economic ions that were backwaters. Nothing in the data since then has persuaded me that these integrative trends have reversed themselves. There is little evidence that nation-state authorities have any interest in creating zones of exclusion. And the collapse of the "Iron Curtain" has hardly signaled a decline in U. S. hegemony.

This has not stopped many Marxian and non-Marxian theorists from predicting the ultimate breakdown of liberal capitalism....

Is Capitalism still not Progressive?

Much of Lenin's work was meant to suggest that capitalism had reached a moribund stage. This intuition made perfect sense to many during the interwar period. The continued immiseration of much of the populations of South America, Africa, and South Asia also provide intuitive support for this perspective. Nevertheless, other developments cast serious doubt on the stagnationist perspective of the Leninist tradition.

The most obvious challenge to this perspective is the continued technological dynamism of the accumulation process. Moreover, certain regions of the world continue to experience sustained increases in living standards, and in nearly every case, these areas are dominated by a capital accumulation process. Recent political developments—such as the destruction of the political part of the apartheid regime in South Africa—also call into question the simple link many of us have made between the establishment of capitalism and the strengthening of authoritarian political institutions. Significant democratic reform need not impede the tyrannical economic authority of capital; indeed such reform may strengthen and rationalize accumulation.

The Leninist tradition suggests that we are necessarily living in the twilight of capitalism; this gives little assistance to anyone attempting to understand the more complex dynamics of capital accumulation and political evolution.

GUIDELINES FOR AN ALTERNATIVE THEORY OF IMPERIALISM

The two most positive legacies of the Leninist theory of imperialism are its insistence that the nature of *capitalist* imperialism is ineluctably linked to changing forms of accumulation and that eliminating the coercive political processes associated with imperialism requires profound structural transformation. These two "findings" provide us with guidelines for constructing a theory that does not insist on "knowing" the coming crisis of capitalism, and that is more acute in identifying the actual source of political coercion—the state....

First, capital expansion may encourage or even stimulate imperial intervention by rapacious state officials, but there is nothing inevitable about this connection. Political intervention can matter by raising the costs of such policies to unacceptable levels.

Second, imperialism rests on a discrete number of state officials to keep control of the levers of power. A real democratizaion of foreign policy could deal a serious blow to imperial pretensions, although to implement such a political transformation would transform more than foreign policy.

Third, even if imperialism persists, the coercive form a particular policy may take can vary according to the level of knowledge and activism of a constituency opposed to or in support of such a policy.

None of these commonsense findings—which can explain the actual political practice of anti- and pro-imperialist movements—very readily flow from the Leninist traditions' explanations of imperialism. If this old Marxian tradition once helped to explain imperfectly the logic of imperial conflict during the first half of the twentieth century, it does not do a particularly good job now. It is time learn what we can from this school of thought and move on.

REFERENCES

Anderson, Benedict R. 1983. *Imagined Communities: Reflections on the Origins and Spread of Nationalism*. London: Verson.

Arrighi, Giovanni. 1987. "A Crisis of Hegemony." In *Dynamics of Global Crisis*. New York: Monthly Review Press.

Hilferding, Rudolph. 1981. *Finance Capital*. London: Routledge Kegan and Paul.

Lenin, V. I. 1970. *Imperialism, the Highest Stage of Capitalism*. Moscow: Progress Publishers.

15

LENIN, IMPERIALISM, AND THE
STAGES OF CAPITALIST DEVELOPMENT

Terrence McDonough

This essay emphasizes Lenin's identification of a new stage of capitalism as the solution to the theoretical crisis within Marxism that emerged at the turn of the twentieth century. The influence of this contribution is examined in the light of several contemporary schools of development and their attention to stages of development. McDonough shows how Lenin's understanding of a stage of capitalism influenced theory throughout the twentieth century. In particular, he examines the social structure of accumulation framework, late capitalism, and the abstraction of imperialism in contemporary thought.

LENIN'S IMPERIALISM, THE HIGHEST STAGE *of Capitalism* has usually been discussed in the context of the metropolitan-satellite relations of international. That such a statement seems painfully obvious demonstrates how easy it is to forget that Lenin took as his subject the totality of the development of monopoly capitalism in his time. Rather than addressing an academic specialism the early Marxist writers were attempting to provide the theoretical basis for a socialist political strategy of the working class. In pursuit of this goal, the classical Marxist writers were compelled to deal with a range of Marxist concerns in the context of a single argument. It should thus not be surprising that a work like *Imperialism* might

From Terrence McDonough, "Lenin, Imperialism, and the Stages of Capitalist Development," *Science and Society* 59 (fall 1995): 339–40, 346–51, 352–53, 354–55, 358–60, 361–62, 363–64. Reprinted with permission of Guilford Publications.

be found in a pivotal position in more than one of today's more specialized traditions in Marxian economic thought.

This article will argue that an analysis of the contribution of Lenin's *Imperialism* cannot be limited to a consideration of theories of imperialism. *Imperialism*'s contribution to stage theories of capitalist development must also be examined. Lenin's concept of a stage of capitalism was a significant contribution to the resolution of the first major crisis in Marxian theory. This crisis was initiated by the capitalist recovery from the Great Depression of the late nineteenth century and Bernstein's revisionist response. Lenin's solution to this controversy has been a seminal influence on subsequent Marxian discussion of stages within capitalist history. Lenin's concept of the imperialist stage of capitalist history is the ancestor, through the Baran-Sweezy monopoly capital school, of the American social structures of accumulation framework for Marxian stage theory. Ernest Mandel's theory of the stage of late capitalism was directly inspired by Lenin's theory of the era of classical imperialism. Finally, Lenin's influence on stage theory has not been confined to the West. The Uno school's theory of mercantilism, liberalism, and imperialism as stages of capitalism is also traceable directly to Lenin's work in *Imperialism*.

Understanding the response of the socialist movement to the capitalist recovery is essential to understanding the important place Lenin's *Imperialism* holds in the history of Marxian thought. The failure of capitalism to enter a final crisis at the end of the nineteenth century stood as a challenge to the scientific character of Marx's understanding of capitalism as received by the Second International. The seriousness of this challenge was compounded when two of Marxism's foremost theoreticians responded as they did. Kautsky refused to face up to the task of explaining the new conjuncture, thus denying the crisis. Bernstein took the new situation more seriously but sought the solution essentially outside the frame of Marxist theory. When the debate between the two merely reproduced itself within the Marxist movement in an insular kind of dogmatist-revisionist tension, Marxism had reached a serious impasse. A way out of this cul de sac was desperately needed. Building on the work of Hilferding and Bukharin, it was Lenin's analysis of the new conjuncture as the movement of capitalism to a new stage of accumulation that restored the ability of the Marxist paradigm to advance as a scientific understanding of the economy and society.

More specifically, the breakdown controversy had left several important theoretical tasks unaccomplished. The most pressing of these was the explanation of the end of the Great Depression and the renewal of capitalist growth. This explanation would, on the one hand, have to go beyond the assertion that nothing had really changed. On the other hand, it would have to avoid the revisionist trap of seeing the recovery as evidence of the basically harmonious character of future capitalist economic and social development. Such a theoretical advance would have to analyze the contradictory nature of capitalist class society while simultaneously explaining a period of relatively unproblematic capitalist accumulation. A second theoretical task highlighted by the course of the revisionism debate is the inadequacy of the existing Marxist theory of the state. Both parties to the revisionism debate had a mechanistic and instrumentalist view of the state and merely debated how best to replace the engine driver. Lenin was to address both these tasks. The Marxist theory of the state was reformulated in *The State and Revolution* (1968). *Imperialism, the Highest Stage of Capitalism* undertook to explain why capitalism had recovered around 1900. Far from denying the continuing relevance of class contradiction, Lenin sought to explain how the new stage of imperialism arose from changes generated by class conflict at the end of the nineteenth century. In this way, Lenin is very much a central figure in overcoming the first crisis of Marxism.

FINANCE CAPITAL AND THE WORLD ECONOMY

In examining the precise nature of *Imperialism*'s contribution to Marxist theory, it is important to recognize that Lenin was building on the work of two other authors who had started to address some of the same problems. It is essential to consider Rudolf Hilferding's *Finance Capital* (1980) and Nikolai Bukharin's *Imperialism and World Economy* (1973). A casual perusal of these works makes it clear that *Finance Capital* was a foundation for both of the later volumes. While Lenin makes only brief reference in *Imperialism* to Bukharin's work, the laudatory preface he wrote for the book in 1915 makes clear that he had read the manuscript closely and admired it.

Hilferding and Finance Capital

...Hilferding clearly saw his task as closely related to the one undertaken by Marx. Just as Marx had analyzed the emergence and dynamic growth of industrial capital in contrast to the previously dominant merchant capital in Das Kapital, Hilferding set out in Das Finanzkapital to analyze the emergence from industrial capital of the new form of finance capital. Such a study, Hilferding writes, is essential to achieving a "scientific understanding of the economic characteristics of the latest phase of capitalist development" (Hilferding, 1910, p. 21).

Hilferding begins his study with a lengthy consideration of the role of money and bank credit in capitalist economies. In addition, with the advent of the joint-stock company, banks become involved in raising industrial capital through the promotion of stock issues. The pooling of capitals which the sale of stock makes possible opens the way for an enormous expansion of the scale of capitalist enterprise. The increasing unification of bank capital and industrial capital generates finance capital. Increasing bank involvement with industrial production creates a change in business principles: "The professional banking principle of maximum security makes the banks inherently averse to competition and predisposed in favor of the elimination of competition in industry through cartels, and as replacement by a 'steady profit.'" In Hilferding's analysis there is an intimate relationship between the growth of the corporate form of ownership, the increasing concentration and centralization of industry, and the merging of previously separate spheres of capital activity into finance capital under the control of the banks.

While the basic capitalist tendencies toward crises still exist, the concentration of industries tends to mitigate the negative effects for capital. Hilferding observes that the ability of an enterprise to survive increases with its size. Joint-stock companies can attract additional capital and accumulate reserves in good years. The diversification of business activity on the part of banks and industries allows for the spreading of risk. Concentrated banking is also in a position to confine speculative movements within certain limits. The ability of cartels to maintain prices means that they can divert the main burden of a crisis to the non-cartelized industries. The existence of capitalist crisis then accelerates the process of concentration.

Having undertaken the comprehensive description of transformations at the economic level of society, Hilferding turns to political analysis. Under the sway of finance capital, tariffs support cartelization directly by reducing the number of foreign competitors, and indirectly by providing increased revenue which can then be invested in concentration. The generalization of the protective tariff increases the importance of the size of the protected area and hence the size of the national territory and the control of colonial areas.

Monopoly profits increase the volume of capital potentially available for investment at the same time as the monopolization of markets restricts investment opportunities. Simultaneously, opportunities for higher profit exist in undeveloped areas. The overseas expansion of economic activity can only be accomplished through the threat or actual use of military force. As the world is increasingly divided up among the major economic powers, political and military conflicts become increasingly bitter. The redistribution of territory can only be accomplished by force, and war becomes likely.

Hilferding also seeks to understand the ideological changes that accompany the economic and political transformations associated with finance capital. The new ideology abandons liberalism, demanding organization rather than the freedom of the individual capitalist. Finance capital requires a politically powerful state that can protect its interests both at home and abroad. Nationalism in the hands of finance capital ceases to be a defense of the right of nations to self-determination and becomes the right of one's own nation to dominate all others. This new nationalism inevitably takes on racialist overtones.

Hilferding also examines the changes in the relation of the various classes to one another in the era of finance capital. Support for the tariff, a strong state, and opposition to the working class increasingly unites capital and large landowners. Small business is increasingly subordinated to big capital and also shares its opposition to labor. A new middle stratum arises, consisting of the salaried managerial and technical employees in commerce and industry. This rapidly growing stratum is still politically aligned with big capital and the policy of imperialism. Thus, along with economic changes, the dominance of finance capital brings with it political and ideological transformations.

Bukharin and the World Economy

According to Bukharin's biographer, Hilferding's *Finance Capital* was "the starting point and essential inspiration" (Cohen, 1980, p. 25) for Bukharin's (1973) contribution, *The World Economy and Imperialism*. The major difference between Bukharin's treatment and that of Hilferding was that Bukharin reversed the order of Hilferding's presentation. Hilferding had argued from finance capital to concentration to the world economy and imperialism. Bukharin started with the world economy: "Thus the problem of studying imperialism, its economic characteristics, and its future, reduces itself to the problem of analyzing the tendencies in the development of the world economy, and of the probable changes in its inner structure" (Bukharin, 1973, p. 18—19). He then set about drawing the connections between the world economy, state policy, class relations, concentration, and finance capital. Despite the different starting point, the connections drawn are similar to those made by Hilferding. Bukharin's argument does, however, lay more causal stress on the development of the world economy than does Hilferding's analysis. From the point of view of stages theory, Bukharin's volume serves to reaffirm, further document, and update Hilferding's position.

LENIN AND IMPERIALISM

Only after identifying the respective contributions of Hilferding and Bukharin is it possible to assess the specific contribution of Lenin in *Imperialism, the Highest Stage of Capitalism* (1917). Lenin's volume draws extensively on the previous two works....

Nevertheless, from the point of view of advancing a Marxist theory of stages of capitalism, *Imperialism* makes two very significant contributions. The first is to identify imperialism specifically as a "stage" of capitalism. The second is to identify the imperialist stage with monopoly capitalism.

Imperialism as a Stage

The concept of a stage of capitalism is used in Lenin's subtitle and appears frequently throughout the work. This is not merely a matter of terminology. Lenin gives substance to his use of the new term by seeking to identify more sharply the boundary between the imperialist stage of capitalism and its predecessor. Lenin is abstractly cautious in approaching this task, contending at one point that "it would be absurd to argue, for example, about the particular year or decade in which imperialism 'definitely' became established" (Lenin, 1968, p. 233). Yet throughout *Imperialism*, Lenin is concerned to identify the time of the transition between stages as closely as possible. For instance, he argues that "for Europe, the time when the new capitalism *definitely* superseded the old can be established with fair precision; it was the beginning of the twentieth century" (Lenin, 1968, p. 180, Lenin's italics).

Lenin offers the following extended definition of imperialism, which he says embodies its five basic features:

> Imperialism is capitalism at that stage of development at which the dominance of monopolies and finance capital is established; in which the export of capital has acquired pronounced importance; in which the division of the world among the international trusts has begun; in which the division of all territories of the globe among the biggest capitalist powers has been completed. (Lenin, 1968, p. 232)

These five characteristics form the basis of the organization of much of the pamphlet. Lenin is concerned to locate the turning point at which each of these characteristics of imperialism can be said to have been established.

In discussing the dominance of monopolies, Lenin argues that cartels are a transitory phenomenon until

> the boom at the end of the nineteenth century and the crisis of 1900–03. Cartels become one of the foundations of the whole of economic life. Capitalism has been transformed into imperialism. (Lenin, 1968, p. 181)

Later he says, more narrowly, the crisis of 1900 "marked the turning-point in the history of modern monopoly" (Lenin, 1968, p. 187).

Regarding the importance of finance capital, Lenin quotes Jeidels to the effect that the crisis of 1900 "enormously accelerated and intensified the process of concentration of industry and of banking, consolidated that process, for the first time transformed the connection with industry into the actual monopoly of the big banks, and made this connection much closer and more active" (Lenin, 1968, p. 200). From this Lenin concludes that "the twentieth century marks the turning-point from the old capitalism to the new, from the domination of capital in general to the domination of finance capital."

...This concern with the identification of the turning point marking the transition from one stage of capitalism to another cannot be found in either Hilferding's or Bukharin's treatments. The location of the point of transition from the previous stage of capitalism to the new stage of imperialism emphasizes the qualitative rather than the quantitative nature of the transition. This contribution is specifically Lenin's. It is this difference which lends a different content to Lenin's change in terminology in designating imperialism as a stage of capitalism rather than a phase or an epoch.

Imperialism as Monopoly Capital

The other major difference in Lenin's work is in the role given specifically to the development of monopoly market structures. I have already discussed how Hilferding began his analysis with finance capital while Bukharin analyzed virtually the same set of institutions using the world economy as his starting point. Lenin adopts still another starting point by emphasizing the role of monopoly capital in imperialism. Indeed, in one of the most often-quoted passages from *Imperialism* Lenin equates the two: "If it were necessary to give the briefest possible definition of imperialism we should have to say that imperialism is the monopoly stage of capitalism" (Lenin, 1968, p. 232).

Lenin begins his discussion of the highest stage of capitalism with a discussion of "concentration of production and monopolies" (Lenin, 1968, p. 176). This transposition of the order of the discussion of monopolies would not have great significance except that Lenin also gives the emergence of monopoly a causative significance in the development of the rest of the basic features of imperialism. Finance capital, the export of capital, and the imperialist division of the world all stem from the emergence of the monopoly market structure. Toward the end of the pamphlet Lenin sums up this argument in the following way:

We must take special note of the four principal types of monopoly, or principal manifestations of monopoly capitalism, which are characteristic of the epoch we are examining. Firstly, monopoly arose out of the concentration of production at a very high stage....Secondly, monopolies have stimulated the seizure of the most important sources of raw materials....

Thirdly, monopoly has sprung from the banks....A financial oligarchy, which throws a close network of dependence relationships over all the economic and political institutions of present-day bourgeois society without exception—such is the most striking manifestation of this monopoly. Fourthly, monopoly has grown out of colonial policy.

To the numerous "old" motives of colonial policy, finance capital has added the struggle for the sources of raw materials, for the export of capital, for spheres of influence, i.e., for spheres of profitable deals, concessions monopoly profits, and so on, economic territory in general. (Lenin, 1968, p. 258)

This identification of monopoly capital as the key factor in determining the character of the new stage would have a profound influence on subsequent generations of Marxist stage theorists.

Finally, Lenin takes explicit note of the effect of the monopoly regime on the rate of growth in the capitalist countries. Bukharin and especially Hilferding had done this implicitly in emphasizing the positive impact of the various aspects of finance capital on the profit rate. In emphasizing the uneven character of capitalist growth, Lenin points out that "on the whole, capitalism is growing far more rapidly than before" (Lenin, 1968, p. 259).

THE STAGES THEORY OF CAPITALISM

We have seen Lenin's role to be crucial in completing the initial formulation of a Marxist theory of stages of capitalism. Hilferding and Bukharin develop a theory of finance capital/imperialism which sees its development as a comprehensive set of interlocked changes in capitalism in the realm of economics, politics, ideology, and international relations. It is Lenin who designates the theory as a stage theory and sharpens the temporal division between imperialism and the previous stage of capitalism. Lenin also argues that it is the transition to monopoly capital that drives the other changes in capitalist society. Finally, Lenin explicitly links the new stage of capitalism to renewed economic growth without downplaying the conflictual nature of capitalist class relations and capitalism's consequent tendency toward crisis.

New Approaches to Stages Theory

The deep recession of 1974 marked the definitive end of the long period of postwar prosperity. The end of the impressive capitalist expansion that followed the Second World War revived interest in long cycle. Building on the historical experience of the recoveries that followed the two great depressions (the late nineteenth century and the 1930s), it seemed unwise to identify the stagnation of the 1970s with the final crisis of capitalism. Any explanation of the ongoing economic crisis had to recognize its distinctive character as more than an ordinary downturn in the business cycle. At the same time, such an explanation would also have to allow for the possibility of renewed expansion in the future. Analyzing the possible existence of a long cycle in capitalist history fit this bill perfectly.

The social structure of accumulation framework. At the end of the 1970s David Gordon (1978; 1980) published two articles linking long cycle theory with the concept of stages of capitalism. In this context, the advent of monopoly capital at the turn of the century coincides with the completion of the long wave trough at the end of the nineteenth century and the inauguration of the long wave expansion which ended with the Great Depression of the 1930s. As argued above, it is completely consistent with the monopoly capital tradition established by Lenin to explain the beginning of the expansion around 1900 through the establishment of monopoly and the institutional changes accompanying it.

The new question posed by the adoption of a long-wave perspective to the monopoly stage of capitalism tradition was whether the postwar expansion was associated with a similar set of multidimensional institutional changes. Gordon (1978) answers this question by proposing a set of postwar institutions whose establishment accounted for the long period of postwar prosperity. These institutions included, among others, multinational corporate structures dual labor markets associated with a bread-and-butter industrial unionism, American international economic and military hegemony easy credit, conservative Keynesian state policy, and bureaucratic control of workers.

In this way, Gordon established the possibility of articulating a postwar set of institutions that conditioned the subsequent expansion of the economy in a way similar to the manner in which the set of institutions analyzed by Hilferding, Bukharin, and Lenin accounted for the turn of the century expansion. Thus the multi-institutional analysis of monopoly capital is implicitly used by Gordon as a model for explaining the postwar expansion.

The repetitive use of this kind of explanation raised the question of whether the assembling of such sets of institutions could be generalized as the basis of a comprehensive theory of stages of capitalism. Gordon (1978; 1980) answers this question by proposing that both the institutions comprising monopoly capital and those making up the postwar social order constituted examples of social structures of accumulation (SSAs). The construction of a new SSA provided the basis for a new stage of capitalism. The disintegration of this set of institutions marks the end of each stage. The argument in the foregoing paragraph establishes Lenin's analysis in *Imperialism* as the direct ancestor of the SSA approach to analyzing stages of capitalism.

The SSA approach achieved its definitive form shortly thereafter with the publication of Gordon, Edwards, and Reich's *Segmented Work, Divided Workers* (1982). This volume used Gordon's SSA approach to capitalist stages to reformulate these authors' earlier analysis of the history of capital-labor relations in the United States. The authors' exposition of the SSA that dominated the capitalist world at the beginning of the twentieth century clearly owes a great deal to Lenin's original description of the era of imperialism.

Recent developments within the SSA school have brought the SSA framework even closer in character to Lenin's framework. The notion of long cycles or long waves has been deemphasized in favor of a conception of periods of alternating growth and stagnation in capitalist history. The length of these periods is not determined in advance. They do not follow on from one another with the strict logic that a cycle theory would demand. The eclipse of the long cycle argument refocuses attention on Lenin's concept of stages of capitalism.

In my own work examining the construction of the monopoly capitalist SSA in the United States, I have found some of Lenin's formulations
concerning the transition from the competitive stage to the monopoly
stage to be closer to events than Gordon et al.'s reading of this transition.
While Gordon et al. emphasize the diversity of institutional change
involved in this transition period, I have argued (McDonough, 1994) that
the organizing principle of the SSA put into place at the turn of the century in the United States can be found in the monopoly market structure established in the merger wave of 1898 to 1902. Each of the other
core institutions in the SSA was constructed around the emergence of the
new monopoly structure of capital (see McDonough, 1994). Thus as Lenin
argued in *Imperialism*, monopoly capital can be regarded as the linchpin of
the new stage of capitalism. Gordon et al. tend to see the important institutions of the monopoly SSA in the United States as achieving consolidation during the First World War years. I have argued (McDonough,
1994b), in agreement with Lenin's dating of the monopoly stage of capital to the turn of the century, that the core institutions had achieved
their basic shapes in the six-year period between 1898 and 1904.

Ernest Mandel and late capitalism. Surprisingly, Lenin's influence on the
theory of stages has been less pervasive within European Marxism....

An important exception to this neglect of Lenin in Europe is the
work of Ernest Mandel....

In his monumental *Late Capitalism* Mandel develops a theory of long
waves of capitalist development. These long waves form the basis for
periodizing capitalism into stages:

> The long waves...do not simply represent statistical averages for given
> time spans....They represent historical realities, segments of the
> overall history of the capitalist mode *of* production that have defi-
> nitely distinguishable features. For that very same reason they are of
> irregular duration. The Marxist explanation of these long waves, with
> its peculiar interweaving of internal economic factors, exogenous
> "environmental" changes, and their mediation through sociopolitical
> developments (i.e., periodic changes in the overall balance of class
> forces and intercapitalist relationship of forces, the outcomes of
> momentous class struggles and of wars) gives this historical reality of
> the long wave an integrated "total" character. (Mandel, 1970, p. 97)

Mandel identifies three successive stages in capitalist history—competitive capitalism, classical imperialism, and late capitalism. As indicated by the choice of appellation, Mandel is indebted to Lenin's analysis as the basis for his second stage of classical imperialism "as described by Lenin." In the introduction to the English language edition, Mandel establishes the relationship between his analysis of the late capitalist era and Lenin's discussion of imperialism as directly analogous to the relationship between Lenin's analysis and that of Marx:

> The term "late capitalism" in no way suggests that imperialism has changed in essence, rendering the analytic findings of Marx's *Capital* and Lenin's *Imperialism* out of date. Just as Lenin was only able to develop his account of imperialism on the basis of *Capital*, as confirmation of the general laws governing the whole course of the capitalist mode of production discovered by Marx, so today we can only attempt to provide a Marxist analysis of late capitalism on the basis of Lenin's study of *Imperialism*. The era of late capitalism is not a new epoch of capitalist development. It is merely a further development of the imperialist, monopoly-capitalist epoch. By implication, the characteristics of the imperialist epoch enumerated by Lenin thus remain fully valid for late capitalism. (Mandel, 1970, p. 9)

The Uno School. This survey of Lenin's influence on the development of stage theories of capitalism would not be complete without a brief consideration of the work of Kozo Uno in Japan. The Uno School in Japan developed in the postwar period based on a series of writings that appeared between 1947 and 1954 (Sekine, 1980, p. xv). Uno developed an interpretation of Marx's *Capital* resting on a distinction among three levels of abstraction, "with the pure theory of capitalism at the most abstract level, the empirical analysis of the current state of the capitalist economy at the least abstract level, and the stages-theory of capitalist development mediating them" (Uno, 1980, p. xxiii)....

Uno finds, however, that acceptance of the validity of the Hilferding-Lenin doctrine of imperialism poses the problem of its relationship to Marx. Uno contends that the doctrine of imperialism cannot be considered as a mere extension of the argument in *Capital*. The elaboration of a stage theory by Lenin makes it clear according to Uno that in the course of writing *Capital* Marx was operating at all three of the above-mentioned levels of abstraction. He was developing a "pure theory of capital," an analysis of the liberal stage of capital that preceded the stage of imperialism, and a concrete history of nineteenth-century Britain. Uno contends that *Capital* can only be understood if these three levels of argument are untangled, a job Marx was unable to do in advance of Lenin's discovery of stages theory. In this sense Uno's reading of Lenin's *Imperialism* forms the core of Uno's political economy:

> If...the relationship of the doctrine of imperialism to *Capital* is correctly interpreted, then the doctrine cannot remain as a mere economic history of capitalism in the Imperialist age. It must define the stage of imperialism characterized by the chrematistics of finance-capital in contrast to the earlier stages of mercantilism and liberalism shaped respectively by the activities of merchant and industrial capital....The method of the stages theory is therefore clearly different from that of the pure theory. (Uno, 1980, pp. xxvi—xxvii)

Sekine's summary of Uno's concept of stages places him squarely in the multifactoral, extraeconomic institutional tradition pioneered by Hilferding, Bukharin, and Lenin and carried forward in the work of Mandel, and Gordon, Edwards, and Reich:

> Stage-characteristic economic policies cannot be studied without regard for such concrete economic institutions as the financial system, foreign trade, public finance, etc., which directly involve political, juridical and sociological considerations. The fact that these concrete economic institutions form different types in the three stages of capitalist development suggests that the political, juridical, and sociological processes reflecting themselves in those economic institutions are also stage-typical. (Sekine, 1980, p. 157)

CONCLUSION

...It has been the contention of this article that *Imperialism* can...be considered as a pivotal contribution to stage theories of capitalist accumulation....The legacies of *Imperialism* from this perspective are the modern stage theories of capitalism, including the monopoly capital school,

Mandel's long wave-theory, the Uno School in Japan and the social structure of accumulation approach.

The motivation for writing *Imperialism* was not alone an attempt to understand the nature of imperialism in the capitalist world. *Imperialism, the Highest Stage of Capitalism* was rather a contribution to the extremely pressing problem of explaining the advent of capitalist recovery in the place of revolution. The credibility of Marxism as a guide to the working-class movement hung in the balance. In this context *Imperialism* must be seen as one of Lenin's most consequential achievements. If Lenin had made no other contribution, his role in the resolution of the first crisis of Marxism and in the development of the stages theory of capitalist history would assure him a central place in Marxism.

REFERENCES

Bukharin, Nikolai. 1915. *Imperialism and World Economy*. New York: Monthly Review Press, 1973.

Cohen, Stephen F. 1971. *Bukharin and the Bolshevik Revolution: A Political Biography 1888–1938*. Oxford: Oxford University Press, 1980.

Gordon, David M. 1978. "Up and Down the Long Roller Coaster." In *Capitalism in Crisis*. Edited by the Union for Radical Political Economics. New York: Union for Radical Political Economics.

———. 1980. "Stages of Accumulation and Long Economic Cycles." In *Process of the World System*. Edited by Terence Hopkins and Immanuel Wallerstein. Beverly Hills, Calif.: Sage Publications.

Hilferding, Rudolf. 1910. *Finance Capital*. London: Routledge and Kegan Paul, 1980.

Lenin, V. I. 1917. *Imperialism, the Highest Stage of Capitalism*. Moscow: Progress Publishers, 1968.

Mandel, Ernest. 1970. *Marxist Economic Theory*. New York: Monthly Review Press.

McDonough, Terence. 1994. "The Construction of Social Structures of Accumulation in US History." In *Social Structures of Accumulation: The Political Economy of Growth and Crisis*. Edited by David M. Kotz, Terence McDonough, and Michael Reich. Cambridge: Cambridge University Press.

Sekine, Thomas T. 1975. "Uno-Riron: A Japanese Contribution to Marxian Political Economy." *Journal of Economic Literature*, 13:3.

Uno, Kozo. 1964. *Principles of Political Economy*. Brighton: Harvester.

Van Duijn, J. J. 1983. *The Long Wave Wave in Economic Life*. London: Allen and Unwin.

16

EXPLORING THE ROOTS OF DEVELOPMENT THEORY IN LENIN

Gabriel Palma

In one of the few serious efforts to trace the roots of underdevelopment and depen-
dency to the thinking of Lenin, Gabriel Palma delves into Lenin's analysis of the
slowness of Russian development compared to other capitalist nations prior to the
Russian Revolution. He notes that obstacles to the growth of capitalism in Russia
might be characterized by some writers as the development of Russian underde-
velopment. He also observes that Lenin was sensitive to the uneven path to capi-
talist development and that various modes of production, precapitalist and capi-
talist, are linked in the transition to capitalism.

WITHIN THE MARXIST TRADITION IT is Lenin's work that we find the first
systematic attempt to provide a concrete analysis of the development of
capitalism in a backward nation. In his analysis he

> formulated with simplicity what would be the core of the depen-
> dency analyses: the forms of articulation between the two parts of a
> single mode of production, and the subordination of one mode of pro-
> duction to another. (Cardoso, 1974a, p. 325)

In this work then, we find a detailed and profound study of the
forms in which developing capitalism in Russia is articulated both to the

From Gabriel Palma, "Dependency: A Formal Theory of Underdevelopment or a Methodology for the Analysis of Concrete Situations of Underdevelopment?" *World Development*
6 (1978): 890–96. Reprinted with permission from Elsevier Science.

economies of Western Europe and to the other existing modes of production in Russia itself. That is to say, the way in which Russia—its classes, state and economy—is articulated to the corresponding elements in the countries of Western Europe. The essay was written as part of a profound controversy in Russia itself regarding the necessity and the feasibility of capitalist development there. Discussion of this controversy is particularly relevant, as it was in the context of an identical controversy in Latin America in the 1950s and 1960s that the contribution of the dependency studies was made.

Given that Russia was the first backward country in which Marxism developed, it is not surprising that it should have been the setting for the first Marxist debates regarding the feasibility of capitalist development, and as I have stated, Lenin's *Development of Capitalism in Russia* was part of this debate and of his constant polemic with the Narodniks.

The central argument of the Narodniks was that capitalist development was not necessary for the attainment of socialism in Russia, and that from an economic point of view it was by no means clear that capitalism was a viable system for a backward country such as Russia. They laid great stress upon the problems created by "late" entry into the process of capitalist industrialization.

Regarding the necessity for capitalist development in Russia, the Narodniks were convinced that the Russian peasant commune with its system of communal ownership was essentially socialist, and capable of forming the basis of a future socialist order; hence Russia might indeed lead the rest of Europe on the road to socialism.

From what Marx and Engels had written before they became interested in the Russian case it is possible to deduce a priori their disagreement with the Narodniks. It was a central point of their analysis that the peasantry, fundamentally on account of its feudal origins, was a backward element in European society, in relation to the capitalist bourgeoisie and, a fortiori, in relation to the proletariat. Wherever capitalism was advanced, the peasantry was a decadent class. On this account it is placed in the *Communist Manifesto* alongside a number of petty bourgeois groups, as Marx and Engels speak of "the small manufacturers, the shopkeepers, the artisan and the peasant...."

Only when the bourgeoisie and the proletariat, together or apart, are incapable of carrying out the bourgeois revolution and the overthrow of feudalism would it be permissible to support the peasantry and its political organizations, let alone to fight for its interest in individual ownership of the land.

At the end of the 1860s, attracted by the development of the left in Russia, Marx and Engels learned Russian and threw themselves into the current debates there. In 1875 Engels was stressing the necessity for capitalist development, though less as a necessity of an absolute nature than as a result of the fact that the Russian system of communal property was already decadent. For this reason it was impossible to "leap over" the capitalist stage through the transformation of the communal institutions of the feudal past into the fundamental bases of the socialist future. On the other hand, he argued, the triumph of the socialist revolution in the advanced capitalist countries would help Russia itself to advance rapidly towards socialism (see Carr, vol. 2, 1966, p. 385).

Two years later Marx entered the debate with the letter I have already discussed. In it he expresses a position similar to that of Engels, arguing that the possibility that a different transition to socialism might take place in Russia no longer appeared to exist:

> If Russia continues on the path which she has been following since 1861 [the emancipation of the serfs] she will be deprived of the finest chance ever offered by history to a nation of avoiding all the ups and downs of the capitalist order.

In the following year a group of young Narodniks led by Plekhanov broke with the rest and headed for Switzerland; their differences were both political and theoretical, in that they opposed the use of terrorism and embraced the spirit and letter of the *Communist Manifesto*. Nevertheless, they came to adopt positions more Marxist than those of Marx himself, and in 1881 Vera Sassoulitch wrote to Marx seeking a clarification of his views regarding the peasant commune. After composing three long drafts which are among his papers he contented himself with a brief response. His analysis of *Capital*, he stated, was based upon conditions in Western Europe, where communal property had long since disappeared; this analysis was by no means mechanically applicable to Russia, where such forms of property still survived in the peasant communes. Nevertheless, for these to serve as a starting-point for a "socialist regeneration of Russia" they would require a series of conditions which allowed them to develop freely. Nowhere in his reply does Marx express any doubt that capitalist development is possible in Russia; his argument is that perhaps—given the specificity of the Russian situation—the price of capitalist development in human terms would be too high for it to be counted as progressive development.

Regarding the other facet of the controversy with the Narodniks, that of the possibility of capitalist development in Russia, it is in the writings of the Narodniks that it is first suggested that capitalism may not be viable in a backward nation. Thus the Narodnik writer Vorontsov argued that

> The more belated is the process of industrialization, the more difficult it is to carry it on along the capitalist lines. (quoted in Walicki, 1969, p. 121)

For the Narodniks, furthermore,

> backwardness provided an advantage in that the technological benefits of modern capitalism could be used while its structure rejected. (Sutcliffe, 1974a, p 182)

For these reasons, then, for the Narodniks it as not only possible but economically imperative to escape from the capitalist stage and move directly toward socialism. This same position will be found, as we shall see, in the 1960s in Latin America in the writings of one group of dependency writers.

In the last decade of the nineteenth century, along with the first industrial strikes in Russia, there appeared a number of Marxist groups, while the Narodniks, caught in the blind alley of terrorism, were beginning to lose influence. One of these was the "League of Struggle for the Liberation of the Working Class," which appeared in Petrograd in 1895; among its members was a disciple of Plekhanov, who note successively under the pseudonyms of "Petrov," "Frei," and "Lenin," the latter after 1902. The young Lenin entered vigorously into the debate with the Narodniks, writing his major contribution toward it, the *Development of Capitalism in Russia* between 1896 and 1899.

Lenin agreed with the Narodniks only in one respect—that capitalism was a brutalizing and degrading economic system. Nevertheless, like Marx, he distinguished clearly between this respect of capitalism and the historical role which it played in Russia:

> Recognition of the progressiveness of capitalism is quite compatible...
> with the full recognition of its negative and dark sides..., with the
> full recognition of the profound and all around social contradictions
> which are inevitably inherent in capitalism, and which reveal the historically transient nature of this economic regime. *It is the Narodniks who
> exert every effort to show that an admission of the historically progressive nature of capitalism means an apology for capitalism....* The progressive historical role of
> capitalism may be summed up in two brief propositions: increase in
> the productive forces of social labor, and the socialization of that labor.
> (1899, pp. 602–603, emphasis added)

Their differences were not only at a theoretical level, however; for Lenin the Narodniks were in error over basic matters of fact. Lenin shows, after a long and detailed study of the labor market in Russia, that capitalism was already developing rapidly, and that it should already be considered as essentially a capitalist country, although "very backward as compared with other capitalist countries in her economic development" (1899, p. 507).

Furthermore, regarding the "obstacles" to the development of capitalism in Russia identified by the Narodniks, such as unemployment and underemployment, he states that these are the *characteristics* of capitalist development, and that the Narodniks are guilty of transforming "the basic conditions for the development of capitalism into proof that capitalism is impossible" (1899, pp. 589–90).

For Lenin what was indispensable was the profound study of why the development of capitalism in Russia, while rapid in relation to development in the precapitalist period, was slow in comparison to the development of other capitalist nations. It is in his approach to this question that, in my opinion, we find his most important contribution to the study of the development of capitalism in backward nations.

His analysis of the slowness of capitalist development in Russia (which some dependency writers would still insist on describing as "the development of Russian underdevelopment") has three interrelated themes:

(i)   the weakness of the Russian bourgeoisie as an agent for the furthering of capitalist development;

(ii) the effect of competition from Western Europe in slowing the growth of modern industry in Russia; and

(iii) the great and unexpected capacity for survival of the traditional structures of Russian society.

Regarding the weakness of the Russian bourgeoisie, Lenin was taking up a theme already discussed by the Russian left. The interesting feature of his analysis is that he relates this weakness to the ambiguous role played by foreign capital (from Western Europe) in the development of Russian capitalism. On the one hand it accelerates the process of industrialization, while on the other it lies behind the weak and dependent nature of the small Russian bourgeoisie.

In what he says in relation to the second factor which explains the slower pace of Russian capitalist development, Lenin stresses that as Russia was industrializing "late," the development of its modern industry had to compete not only with the production of traditional artesanal industry (as the first countries to industrialize had had to do) but also with the far more efficient industrial production of advanced countries within the capitalist system.

Finally, Lenin places great emphasis and explanatory value upon the great capacity for survival of traditional structures in Russia:

> In no single capitalist country has there been such an abundant survival of ancient institutions that are incompatible with capitalism, producer who [quoting Marx] "suffer not only from the development of capitalist production, but also from the incompleteness of that development." (1899, p. 607)

An important aspect of Lenin's analysis of the survival of traditional structures (and one that is particularly relevant to the present situation in Latin America) is his treatment of the interconnections which develop between the different modes of production which existed in Russia:

The facts utterly refute the view widespread here in Russia that "factory" and "handicraft" industry are isolated from one another. On the contrary, such a division is purely artificial. (1899, p. 547)

Lenin's view of capitalist development in Russia can be summarized as follows:

(i) in conformity with the central tradition of classical Marxist analysis he sees it as politically necessary and economically feasible;

(ii) through a concrete analysis he shows that its development is fully underway;

(iii) the development of capitalism in backward nations is seen for the first time not simply as a process of destruction and replacement of precapitalist structures, but as a more complex process of interplay between internal and external structures; in this interplay, the traditional structures play an important role, and their replacement will be slower and more difficult than previously supposed; and

(iv) despite the complexity of Russian capitalist development, both it and the bourgeois revolution which would accompany it would eventually develop and become relatively similar to that of Western Europe. (The development of capitalism in Russia would therefore be a kind of "slow-motion replay" of the same development in Western Europe.)

I shall now go on to examine the relationship between this analysis of Russian capitalism and Lenin's theory of imperialism.

THE LATER DEVELOPMENT OF LENIN'S THOUGHT REGARDING THE DEVELOPMENT OF CAPITALISM IN BACKWARD NATIONS

The two historical events which had a profound influence upon the future development of Lenin's thought in all its aspects were the revolution of 1905 and the collapse of the Second International. If the second of these showed that it was by no means clear that the development of capitalism led necessarily and "inevitably" to socialism, the first had shown the concrete possibility of interrupting capitalist development, avoiding its potential risks, and transferring to the proletariat the task of completing the democratic-bourgeois revolution.

The collapse of the Second International showed that as it developed, capitalism also created an unforeseen capacity to assimilate important sectors of the proletariat, and that therefore the development of its internal contradictions would take a more complex path than had hitherto been realized.

Marx had emphasized that capitalist development was condemned by its own nature to resolve its difficulties and contradictions through transformations which would necessarily lead to the creation of others even greater. Nevertheless, there seemed to be one aspect of capitalist development which at least in the medium term was acting in the opposite direction: rising real wages. These, essentially a result of the organization and struggle of the working class, played a crucial role in the development of capitalism, both from the point of view of its political stability, and of the increase in effective demand, so essential for the realization of surplus value.

In explaining both this capacity of capitalism to increase real wages much more than had been foreseen, and the political effect which it had upon the working class in the advanced capitalist countries, Lenin placed great emphasis upon the "superprofits of imperialist exploitation" (1916, p. 9). Not long afterwards, Henry Ford, following the analysis already proposed by Hobson (1902, 1911), stated:

> If we can distribute high wages, then that money is going to be spent and it will serve to make storekeepers and distributors and manufacturers in other lines more prosperous and this prosperity will be reflected in our sales. Country-wide high wages spell country wide prosperity. (1922, p. 124)

Kalecki (1933, 1934, 1935) and Keynes (1936) would later incorporate this insight into a new theoretical conceptualization of the development of capitalism; two years later, Harold Macmillan would refer as follows to the enormous political importance of extending to the working class some of the material benefits of capitalist development:

Democracy can live only so long as it is able to cope satisfactorily with the problems of social life. While it is able to deal with these problems, and secure for its people the satisfaction of their reasonable demands, it will retain their reasonable support sufficient for its defense. (1938, p. 375; quoted in Kay, 1975, p. 174)

In this context it is important to recall that although Marx's expectations regarding the standard of living of the working class under capitalism are not entirely clear, it seems evident that he did not expect an increase of the magnitude which eventually occurred. It emerged later that capitalism was going to provide rising real wages at a rate relatively similar to the rhythm of its development but only after a considerable "time-lag" (see Hicks, 1969, pp. 148–59). In 1923, in what would be his last article, Lenin wrote:

But the Western European countries are not completing this development [toward socialism] as we previously expected they would. They are completing it not through a steady 'maturing' of socialism, but through the exploitation of some states by others. (quoted in Foster-Carter, 1974, p. 67).

The train of history was not going to drop its passengers off at the station of their choice, socialism, unless they took charge of it at an earlier stage. The contribution of the events of 1905 in Russia was precisely that it showed that it was possible, though by no means necessarily economically feasible.

From 1905 onward, first in Trotsky and Parvus and later in Lenin, there began a change of position regarding the necessity of continuing with capitalist development. As we saw earlier, Marx had stated that no social order would disappear before having developed all the productive forces it could contain, and that higher relationships of production would not appear until the old order had run its full course. The events of 1905 showed both the limitations of the development of capitalism in Russia and the concrete possibility of interrupting it, transferring to the proletariat the task of completing the democratic-bourgeois revolution. Nevertheless, Engels had argued that for this to happen there would have to be a revolution Western Europe. Russia could play the role of the weakest link in the capitalist chain, and with the help of more developed socialist societies could follow the path toward socialism more rapidly. Therefore the socialist revolution could begin in a country such as Russia but it could not be completed there.

However, the events of 1905 did not only show Lenin and the Bolsheviks the path to follow; they also showed Nicolas II and his brilliant Minister, Stolypin, the need to embark upon a rapid process of social, economic and political restructuring if revolution was to be avoided. Of the transformations which they initiated Lenin said:

> Our reactionaries are distinguished by the extreme clarity of their class consciousness. They know very well what they want, where they are going and on what forces they can count. (quoted in Conquest, 1972, p. 61)

By this time Lenin's attitude toward the necessity for capitalist development was different than it had been in 1899. Should the policies of Stolypin succeed, and Russia enter definitively onto the capitalist path, the revolution would have to be postponed for a long time. As early as 1908 Lenin saw the dangers of Stolypin's policies:

> The Stolypin constitution and the Stolypin agrarian policy mark a new phase in the breakdown of the old semipatriarchal and semifeudal system of Tsarism, a new movement towards its transformation into a middle-class monarchy....It would be empty and stupid democratic [sic] phrasemongering to say that the success of such a policy is "impossible" in Russia....It is possible! If Stolypin's policy continues, Russia's agrarian structure will become completely bourgeois. (quoted in Laclau, 1972, p. 69, my translation)

The events of the subsequent period, which ended with the assumption of power by the Bolsheviks in October 1917, are the subject of one of the great controversies of modern history. On the one hand the policies initiated by Stolypin showed clearly that Lenin's analysis of the potential of capitalist development was correct; during that period Russia enjoyed a considerable industrial boom; and by 1917 the peasants were owners of more than three-quarters of Russian farmland. Perhaps it was factors such as these which led Lenin to conclude a lecture given in Zurich on

9 January 1917, only months before he was to come to power, with the words "we of the old generation will perhaps not live to see the decisive battles of our own revolution" (1917, p. 158, my translation).

But on the other hand it was precisely that industrial boom which strengthened the left in general and the Bolsheviks in particular. As the Mensheviks exercised political control over the older proletariat, the Bolsheviks needed a new proletariat to strengthen them—the industrial boom supplied them with it.

This already lengthy analysis can be pursued no further here. I have tried to extract from it its most important contributions to the debate which would later develop concerning the development of capitalism in other backward nations.

Russia then had a series of characteristics in common with countries which would later attempt capitalist development, such as those related to "late" industrialization, and to the leading role played by foreign capitalism and technology, and those linked to the emergence of a social class structure somewhat different from that resulting from capitalist development in Western Europe, and more complex in its composition, with a relatively weak and dependent bourgeoisie, a small but strong proletariat, and a relatively large "subproletariat" which is its potential ally.

Equally however, there are also significant differences: Russia was never the colony of a Western European power; late industrialization is not always the same if it occurs at different stages of development of the world capitalist system; and as Lenin demonstrates brilliantly for the Russian case, the particular features of the development of capitalism in any backward region will depend significantly on the characteristics of the precapitalist mode of production. In the case of Latin America for example, if there were countries (such as Brazil, Mexico, Chile, and Argentina) which were attempting to industrialize in the same period as industrialization was taking place in Russia, the social formations of those countries, inherited from Portuguese and Spanish colonization, were very different to those of Russia itself. In any case, if it is clear that the analyses of Lenin and his contemporaries cannot be applied mechanically to the development of capitalism in other periods and in other backward regions of the world, it remains true that in Lenin's analysis especially we find the essential road to follow; this is the study of the concrete forms of articulation between the capitalist sectors of the backward nations and the advanced nations in the system, and of the concrete forms taken by the subordination of precapitalist forms of production to the former, and to the rest of the system. It is essentially the study of the dynamic of the backward nations as a synthesis of the general determinants of the capitalist system (external factors) and the specific determinants of each (internal factors). But if neither Lenin, Bukharin, nor Luxemburg studied the concrete development of capitalism in other backward regions of the world, it is possible to derive from their analyses of imperialism the "general determinants of the capitalist system" or the "external factors" as they are generally labeled, which those regions will confront in their attempts to pursue capitalist development. These are essentially the driving forces which impelled the advanced capitalist countries toward the domination and control of the backward regions of the world: the specific determinants, or "internal factors" as they are generally called, will depend upon the characteristics of the particular backward societies. The driving forces behind the economic expansion of the advanced capitalist countries are identified, with differences of emphasis in each analysis, in the financial and in the productive spheres. The two are intimately connected, and are the result of a single process of transformation in the advanced capitalist countries. The financial driving forces are related to the need to find new opportunities for investment, due to the fact that their own economies are incapable of generating them at the same rate as they generate capital; those of the productive sphere are related to the necessity of ensuring a supply of raw materials, and continued markets for manufactured products. Thus it is that Bukharin and Preobrazhensky define imperialism as

> the policy of conquest which financial capital pursues in the struggle
> for markets, for the sources of raw material, and for pieces in which
> capital can be invested. (1919, p. 155)

The result of this would be a tendency towards a greater integration of the world economy, a considerable degree of capital movement, and an international division of labor which would restrict the growth of backward economies to the production of mineral and agricultural primary products. For these primary products to be supplied cheaply, the labor force in the backward countries would have to be kept at subsistence level.

As a result of the effects of the expansion of the advanced capitalist economies as they enter the monopoly phase of their development, the economies of the backward countries will tend be characterized by increasing indebtedness and by a productive structure which leads them consume what they do not produce, and to produce what they do not consume....If these relationships were shaped within a colonial context, they would clearly be unequal, and therefore for the colonial nation the possibilities of development would be very restricted. If they were shaped within a postcolonial context, the possibilities of development would depend upon the capacity of the national bourgeoisies and other dominant groups to establish a more favorable relationship with the advanced countries in the system, or upon their capacity to transform the economic structure of their respective countries, in effort to develop through a different type of integration into the world economy.

We may summarize the classical writers' conception of what capitalist development in backward regions of the world would tend to be as follows: imperialism would tend to hinder industrial development, but once the colonial bonds had been broken the backward countries would be able to develop their economies in a different way, and eventually to industrialize. This industrialization, given its "late" start and probably with the presence of foreign capital and technology, would face problems and contradictions, but as in the Russian case, these would not be insuperable. In the words of Rosa Luxemburg:

> The imperialist phase of capital accumulation...comprises the industrialization, and capitalist emancipation of the hinterland...[bourgeois] revolution is an essential for the process of capitalist emancipation. The backward communities must shed their obsolete political organizations, and create a modern state machinery adapted to the purpose of capitalist production. (quoted in O'Brien, 1975, p. 16)

This description of the role of capitalism in the colonies clearly differs from that of Marx and Engels, as it refers to different stages of capitalist development in the advanced countries. Discussing their writings, I showed how for them the Asiatic mode of production was characterized by its lack of internal tensions, which bestowed upon it an unchanging nature. The penetration of capitalism from abroad would therefore perform the task of "awakening" them. It follows directly that the concrete forms which the process would adopt would necessarily depend upon the type of capitalism involved.

Marx expected that the process which began with the development of railways in India would necessarily end with the placing of that country on the path toward industrialization. For the classical writers on imperialism on the other hand, while capitalism continued to be progressive in the backward nations of the world, it was precisely its progressiveness which would create contradictions with the needs of monopoly capitalism in the advanced countries; within a colonial context the imperialist countries can and will hinder the industrialization of the colonies. Once the colonial bonds are broken the incipient national bourgeoisies can proceed with the development which was hindered by the colonial bonds, completing the bourgeois revolution and attempting to industrialize. These writers did not of course mean to suggest in any way that such attempts at postcolonial industrialization would be free of problems and contradictions; they felt that as in the Russian case such countries would be able to overcome such problems and industrialize. Should that prove to be the case, there would appear in the postcolonial period new capitalist societies relatively similar to those in Western Europe (as in the United States and the regions of European settlement).

Nevertheless, the political independence of the backward nations has not been followed by development, contrary to the expectations of the authors I have been discussing. Even more, *in the case of Latin America it is precisely in the postcolonial period* that the development of individual nations (with the due economic and political variations) has taken upon itself the articulations with the advanced capitalist countries which the classical writers on imperialism noted in the colonies—the growth of their productive sectors concentrated on primary products, whether mineral or agricultural; the degree of industrialization was limited; and their financial dependence grew enormously.

REFERENCES

Bukharin, N., and E. Preobrazhensky. 1917. *The ABC of Communism.* Harmondsworth: Penguin, 1969.

Cardoso, F. H. 1974. "Notas sobre el estado actual de loe estudios sobre la dependencia." In *Desarrollo Latinamericanos: Ensayos Criticos.* Edited by J. Serra. Mexico: F.C.E.

Carr, E. H. 1966. *The Bolshevik Revolution.* Harmondsworth: Penguin.

Conquest, R. 1972. *Lenin.* London: Fontana.

Ford, H. 1922. *My Life and Work.* London: William Heinemann.

Foster-Carter, A. 1976. "From Rostow to Gunder Frank: Conflicting Paradigms in the Analysis of Underdevelopment." *World Development* vol. 4 (3): 17—31.

Hicks, J. 1969. A *Theory of Economic History.* London: Oxford University Press.

Kay, G. 1975. *Development and Underdevelopment: A Marxist Analysis.* London: Macmillan.

Laclau, E. 1969. "Modos de producción, sistemas económicos y población excedente: aproximación histórica a los casos argentinos y chilenos." *Revista Latinoamericana do Sociologia* vol. 2 (2): pp. 776—816.

Lenin, V. I. 1899, *The Development of Capitalism in Russia.* Moscow: Progress Publishers.

———. 1916. *Imperialism, the Highest Stage of Capitalism.* Peking: Foreign Languages Press, 1970.

———. 1917. 1905—*Jornadas Revolucionarias.* Santiago: B.E.P., 1970.

O'Brien, P. 1975. "A Critique of Latin American Theories of Dependency." In *Beyond the Sociology of Development.* Edited by I. Oxaal, T. Barnet, and D. Booth. London: Routledge and Kegan Paul.

Sutcliffe, B. 1972. "Conclusions." In *Studies in the Theory of Imperialism.* Edited by R. Owen and B. Sutcliffe. London: Longman.

Walicki, A. 1969. *The Controversy over Capitalism.* London: Oxford University Press.

PART THREE

IMPERIALISM AND DEVELOPMENT- UNDERDEVELOPMENT THEORY

OVERVIEW

17

MARXIST THEORY AND IMPERIALISM

Anthony Brewer

Imperialism usually is examined in light of its economic and political conse-
quences, but these, too, relate to cultural and ecological considerations. Anthony
Brewer, who has examined various theoretical understandings of imperialism and
development, elaborates on the breadth and depth of intellectual thinking on these
themes, identifies theoretical lines, and shows how theoretical advances have
emerged in the less developed regions. The selection below places into context most
of the ensuing Third World perspectives.

UNTIL RECENTLY, MOST MARXISTS THOUGHT of modes of production as successive stages in the evolution of human society, following each other in
a predestined order. In a transitional period, the old mode decays, while
the new mode first emerges within the previous system, and then
replaces it. The development of new forms of organization actively
undermines the old and accelerates their decay. At some stage, a revolution reconstructs the political and legal superstructures to fit the needs
of the new mode of production. The relation between the two modes
is therefore one of contradiction, and the new ruling class establishes
itself through class struggles in which it is irreconcilably opposed to the
old order. Each nation must go through the sequence of stages, though
external influences may accelerate or slow the process, or even allow a

From Anthony Brewer, *Marxist Theories of Imperialism: A Critical Survey*, 2d ed. (London and
New York: Routledge, 1990), pp. 226–29, 230–31, 232–36. Reprinted with permission of
Routledge.

stage to be skipped. This brief summary is, of course, a caricature, but I think it brings out the key ideas that underlie more sophisticated accounts. There is some warrant for it in Marx's own writings (especially the *Preface to the Critique of Political Economy*).

Trotsky had a somewhat different view. Although his thinking remained in essence bounded by a "stages" perspective, he stressed the importance of (relative) backwardness, and argued that the structure of societies that started to develop late was not the same as those that had led the way. This thesis, as applied to Russia, is scattered through his works. Russia, he argued, came under pressure, military and economic, from the more advanced West, and the Russian state, reacting to this pressure, took the initiative in promoting both industrial development and (limited) measures of social and administrative modernization designed to increase the military efficiency of the state. The state machine had a larger, and the bourgeoisie a smaller, relative weight than in the countries of Western Europe, and there were massive disparities between the industrial cities and the impoverished and backward countryside. This is summarized in the phrase "uneven and combined development," meaning that nations, sectors, and areas develop at different rates, but do not do so in isolation from each other. What is distinctive about Trotsky's view is his emphasis on the role of the state. As it stands it is difficult to think of many areas except Russia, Japan, and parts of southeast Europe to which it is relevant; in other areas national states went under when confronted with western pressure. Ex-colonial territories frequently exhibit a rather similar enlarged state apparatus, though they have reached this condition by a different route.

The classic account of a transition from feudalism to capitalism is Lenin's *The Development of Capitalism in Russia* (1974, first published 1899). Russia was in the middle of the transition, and Lenin, grappling with the problems of political strategy in a relatively backward country, looked in detail at the process of transition and at the transitional forms created. The issues he focused on are substantially those that concern Marxists in the underdeveloped world today: the prospects for capitalist development and the class struggles and possible class alliances inherent in the situation.

Lenin identified four main processes at work in the countryside. First, commodity production and exchange were emerging through the progressive separation of successive "industrial" activities from agriculture. These activities formed distinct industries, perhaps organized on a craft basis but rapidly penetrated by capitalist relations of production, linked to each other and to agriculture by exchange (recall Marx's similar analysis). Second, there was a progressive differentiation of the peasantry, as the "middle peasantry" of relatively self-sufficient family units broke down into a rural bourgeoisie (the *kulaks*) and a rural proletariat. Third, the role of the landlord was transformed as the (feudal) *corvee* or labor-service system was supplanted by capitalist agriculture based on the employment of wage-labor. Capitalist agriculture emerged by two routes: the rise of a rural bourgeoisie from the peasantry, and the conversion of the Landlords' economy into capitalist estates. Finally, there was a developing pattern of specialization within agriculture itself, and thus a development of commodity exchange within agriculture as well as between agriculture and industry.

In this process a great variety of transitional forms were created; "the systems mentioned are actually interwoven in the most varied and fantastic fashion" (Lenin, 1974, p. 197). Lenin was able to make sense of them only by setting them in the context of a process of transition from one fairly well-defined system (feudalism) to another (capitalism). I suspect that at least part of the debate about contemporary underdeveloped countries is bedeviled by a desire to link immediately observable features of society (the "fantastic form" that Lenin described) directly to the defining features of various modes of production without setting them adequately in the context of a historical process.

The classical Marxist analysis has had considerable success in analyzing European history, when applied in a creative and undogmatic way. Whether it can be used with the same success in dealing with non-European societies is a matter of dispute. In a "stages" perspective, one must either say that underdeveloped countries are precapitalist, that they are capitalist, or that they are in transition (thus implying that they are becoming capitalist). In the orthodox Marxist view, the capitalist stage has three main characteristics: first, commodity production, second, the relation between wage-labor and capital, and third, the pressure to accumulate and to introduce new methods of production. In underdeveloped countries the penetration of commodity production went ahead rapidly but, for a long time, wage-labor and best practice levels of productivity were confined to small sectors. Either these countries are not becoming capitalist (in which case what are they?) or capitalism has quite different laws of motion in underdeveloped areas (in which case, what use is the concept of capitalism?). Some attempts to solve these problems have already been discussed.

Frank and Wallerstein took the most drastic line. Capitalism, they argued, is a world system, defined in terms of production for the world market, whether wage-labor is employed or not. This is a fundamental shift of definition. Its laws of motion, too, are quite unlike those analyzed by Marx. Capitalism does not promote general development; it promotes the development of some areas at the expense of others. I have criticized Frank and Wallerstein for the lack of any well-worked-out theoretical analysis to back up their sloganistic generalizations. Amin's analysis is an advance, using more traditional concepts of modes of production in an overall framework derived from dependency theory; it is open to criticism, but on other grounds.

An alternative to Frank and Wallerstein, more faithful to Marx, is to treat the wage relation as the defining feature of capitalism, as Laclau suggested, and argue that different modes of production can coexist within a single society, either permanently (abandoning the "stages" perspective) or over a very long-drawn-out transition. Various phrases have been used in this context; one can talk of a "conservation-dissolution" relation (between capitalism and the subordinated mode), of a "blocked" transition (preserving a "stages" view, at least verbally) or, as Bettelheim does in another context, of a transition "between" two stages without implying movement in one direction or another. All these devices seem to be essentially semantic; what matters is the substance of the analysis.

The case for focusing on the relation between the direct producers and their exploiters, and thus on the wage relation as the defining characteristic of capitalism, was put most forcefully by Brenner (1977), in work on the origins of capitalism in Europe. He argued that the production of relative surplus value and the tendency to increase productivity differentiates capitalism from all previous modes of production....

The existence of free wage-labor matters for two reasons. First, because only in a system of free labor can labor be reallocated from one task to another and gathered into ever larger and more complex productive organizations. Capital can only be genuinely mobile where it can gather labor and means of production freely in the market. Second, and perhaps more important, in a wage-labor system all the needs of reproduction have to be bought in the market and competition then acquires coercive force. Any enterprise that fails to keep up with socially established levels of productivity is driven out of business; the process of concentration and centralization, an essential part of the development of capitalism, thus depends on the wage relation. Labor-saving innovation allows costs to be cut by making workers redundant, an option not open in feudal systems in which peasants are tied to a particular estate. Competition forces capitalists to minimize costs, constantly recreating a mobile reserve army of labor.

In a feudal system, the needs of reproduction are met by peasant plots, so the *demesne* product, which may be sold on the market, is all surplus product. A feudal lord, maximizing short-run profit, will attempt to restrict peasants' mobility (to keep them under his control) and to reduce the land and labor time devoted to the peasants' plots, not by increasing productivity, but by increasing absolute surplus value, even to the point where the long-run reproduction of the system is threatened. An extension of market opportunities can even intensify feudal exploitation and promote regression in the forces of production. Brenner had a telling example; in the Poland of the "second serfdom" (one of Wallerstein's favorite examples), "despite the orientation of the entire economy to exports, it could send out at best 5 percent to 7 percent of its total grain produce" (Brenner 1977, pp. 69–70). Peasant plots were more productive than *demesnes*, and could generate a larger marketable surplus per acre, but they were ruthlessly cut down to expand the lord's profits. Here profitability (for the rulers) generated regression. A switch to wage-labor would only be profitable for the lords in the very long run, if at all. Wage-labor was only used where serfdom had decayed beyond possibility of restoration.

An alternative system in agriculture is small peasant proprietorship. Here again the market lacks coercive force if peasants can produce their own subsistence (cf. Luxemburg), and here again the attachment of producers to the means of production inhibits flexibility and thus technological advance. England was the one place in Europe where serfdom had been eliminated without small peasant proprietorship taking its place. There are also cases in which the producers are wholly dependent on the market for their subsistence without labor-power, as such, becoming a commodity. Peasant producers of industrial raw materials are an example. In these cases fully capitalist production can penetrate relatively easily.

The mode of production, defined by the relation between the direct producers and the owners of the means of production, is thus not a purely formal characteristic of the social system, nor does it define classes opposed to each other in purely distributive terms. It is of crucial importance in determining the evolution of the forces of production, and in determining development and underdevelopment. Brenner displayed the mechanisms linking structural features of the mode of production to its dynamics, and thus demonstrated their relevance rather than merely asserting it. Development and underdevelopment are the product of class structures which are themselves the outcome of a historical process of development that cannot be analyzed in the abstract.

Perhaps the most important and sophisticated discussion of the role of modes of production is by P. P. Rey....

What is most relevant in understanding Rey's work is the idea that a social formation (like Laclau's "economic system") may contain more than one mode of production. Althusser and Balibar insisted that one mode of production dominates, defining a dominant or ruling class, except during brief periods of transition. Rey's concept of the *articulation of modes of production* is firmly set in a classical Marxist analysis of transition, analyzed in Althusserian style. As noted above, the classical Marxists conceived of modes of production as stages of development which succeed each other in turn. Since one mode cannot replace another overnight, there must be a long process of transition in which the old mode dominates at first, while allowing the new to grow up, then the new mode comes to dominate, while the old persists for a further period. Rey's originality is in insisting that this process takes so long that transition is the normal state of affairs, and analyzing the process with the rigor usual in the study of "pure" modes.

In a transitional social formation the two modes of production are not independent of each other, just sitting side by side. There is an interaction, in which each affects the workings of the other, so the evolution of a transitional social formation cannot be understood by analyzing the logic of one mode of production in isolation. The two modes are in contradiction, in the sense that one will replace the other but, during the transition, each must be reproduced, so the conditions of their reproduction must be compatible. This Rey called the "articulation" of two modes.

In all the cases Rey dealt with, the expanding mode is capitalism. Like Luxemburg he insisted that capitalism has an inherent tendency to expand at the expense of the precapitalist societies it finds around itself. This insistence on what Foster-Carter (1978) called the "homofience" of capitalism (literally, "having the same effect") put him firmly in the classical Marxist tradition and led him to reject any explanation of underdevelopment in terms of restrictive behavior by capitalists, as proposed by Baran and Frank:

> Let us cease to reproach capitalism with the one crime that it has not committed, that it could not think of committing, constrained as it is by its own laws always to enlarge the scale of production. Let us keep firmly in mind that all the bourgeoisies of the world burn with desire to develop the "underdeveloped" countries. (Alliances, p. 16)

Why, then, have some areas advanced while others have not? If capitalism by itself has the same effect everywhere, the difference must be in the other half of the articulation, in the precapitalist modes that are the "medium and soil" (in Luxemburg's words) of capitalist development. Rey criticized Luxemburg for not taking the internal workings of these modes seriously. Capitalism prospered where it succeeded feudalism, while "generally speaking, non-Western countries, apart from Japan, have shown themselves and still show themselves to be wretched environments for the development of capitalist relations of production" (Alliances, p. 11).

Rey proceeded by considering the conditions required for the expanded reproduction of capital. The first is a class of free wage-laborers, so the articulation with the precapitalist mode must be such as to exclude a growing section of the population from precapitalist production (or at least to ensure that they have to spend a part of their time or a stage in their lives working for a wage). Capitalism is relatively slow to establish itself in agriculture, especially in the production of basic foods. The capitalist sector must, therefore, obtain means of subsistence for its workers by trading with precapitalist agricultural producers. In the heartlands of capitalism, where it succeeded feudalism as the dominant mode, these needs were met by the expulsion of peasants and the sale of a surplus product extracted as rent, as Marx showed in his account of primitive accumulation.

In the rest of the world, however, precapitalist modes did not evolve naturally to meet the needs of capitalism, so capitalist relations of production could not arise from within. These areas could (and did) engage in exchange, and were drawn into the world market, but exchange reinforced the hold of precapitalist ruling classes and strengthened resistance to the implantation of capitalist relations of production. This is really the most crucial part of Rey's argument; he argued it in detail only for a particular area in Congo-Brazzaville, and it is not at all clear that the argument generalizes to other areas.

Since the preconditions for capitalist production did not arise naturally in most parts of the world, they were imposed by external force. To open up these areas for capital, it was necessary to displace the existing ruling class and reorganize indigenous societies. Direct military and administrative coercion was used to recruit workers and to compel villagers to sell cash crops (especially food crops). Rey called this system of administrative coercion the *colonial mode of production*. Once the precapitalist framework has been transformed to fit the needs of capital, it can be left to itself. Capitalist reproduction and growth can be assured by economic means and by the local state: the "neo-colonial" pattern of the underdeveloped world today. Formal decolonization is no threat to the economic interests of capital. The expansion of capitalist relations of production is, however, hindered by the persistence, in a modified form, of preexisting modes, since capitalist mechanisms cannot, for a long time, provide for reproduction on their own.

Rey deduced his central political conclusions from this account. Capitalism and the restructured precapitalist modes of production need each other and sustain each other. It is therefore impossible to try to abolish precapitalist forms of oppression without at the same time seeking to overthrow capitalism, while anticapitalist revolutions (Russia, China) have been able to abolish these archaic restrictions in a very short space of time.

On a world scale, the development of capitalism went ahead in previously feudal areas, but was blocked elsewhere. Capitalist and noncapitalist areas were linked by exchange, but precapitalist societies did not respond well to market signals, since exchange does not alter the basic relations of production and does not provide any strong stimulus to a more rational organization of production. There were thus good reasons for capitalist expansion into noncapitalist areas, but the means were lacking. The blockage was broken when central capitalism reached the stage of finance capital, according to Rey, because it was only at this stage that capital could impose capitalist relations of production from the outside. This part of the argument is not very clear. European states did, in fact, reorganize the mode of production in colonial territories much earlier (e.g., Latin America from the sixteenth century), but they imposed precapitalist, not capitalist, modes of production. Rey's whole chronology is geared to Africa. The epoch of finance capital is thus also the age of imperialism and colonial conquest, but for reasons rather different from those proposed by Lenin.

Gathering the story together, it goes as follows. Capitalism emerged in previously feudal areas, and went through a whole process of development there (the capitalism feudalism articulation), with a corresponding, massive, development of the forces of production; the rest of the world was drawn into relations of exchange without the transformation of relations or forces of production. The rise of finance capital was the signal for forcible conquest and transformation of "underdeveloped" areas, followed (in the end) by decolonization, leaving capitalist relations of production dominant, but with development still retarded by the persistence of precapitalist modes alongside capitalism.

Rey drew heavily on the classical Marxists. Like Rosa Luxemburg, he emphasized the role of coercion in the expansion of capitalist relations of production, but he distinguished between the transition from feudalism to capitalism (coercion by the feudal ruling class itself) and other transitions (coercion from outside), and also between the transformation of a "natural economy" into a commodity producing system (which need not involve coercion) and the transformation of relations of production by the creation of a proletariat. His argument has obvious (and acknowledged) roots in Marx's treatment of primitive accumulation, of the Asiatic mode of production, and of merchant capital. The aspects of Marx's work that Rey built on had been substantially neglected in the intervening period, so to point to these roots in Marx is not to decry

Rey's contribution. More important, he provided an explanation for a "neocolonial" stage following colonialism, connecting the present stage of development to its predecessors and to a coherent account of the history of capitalism.

REFERENCES

Brenner, R. 1977. "The Origins of Development: A Critique of Neo-Smithian Marxism." New Left Review 104 (July—August): 25—93.

Foster-Carter, A. 1978. "The Modes of Production Controversy." New Left Review 107 (January—February): 47—77.

Lenin, V. I. 1899. The Development of Capitalism in Russia. Moscow: Progress Publishers, 1974.

CONTRASTING
THIRD
WORLD
PERSPECTIVES

18

BACKWARDNESS

Paul Baran

During the late fifties, Paul Baran, an economist at Stanford University, published his best-selling (especially in the Third World) analysis of underdevelopment, with attention to the question of surplus and to backwardness. Three chapters of the book focus on backwardness and serve as a foundation for later theory on underdevelopment and dependency. They also link to earlier ideas on imperialism. The excerpts below give a glimpse of his presentation.

IT IS OBVIOUSLY IMPOSSIBLE EVEN to conjecture on the speed with which the now backward countries would have gone the way of Japan and would have autonomously generated a process of capitalist development and economic growth, in the absence of Western invasion and exploitation. Indeed, the rapidity of Japan's transformation into a capitalist, industrialized country was due to a large extent to the military and economic threat from the West. Yet whatever might have been the tempo and the specific circumstances of the forward movement, there is ample evidence in the history of all the countries in question to indicate the nature of its general trend. Regardless of their national peculiarities, the precapitalist orders in Western Europe and in Japan, in Russia and in Asia were reaching at different times and in different ways their common historical destiny. By the eighteenth and nineteenth centuries they were

From Paul A. Baran, *The Political Economy of Growth* (New York: Monthly Review Press, 1957).

universally in a state of disintegration and decay. Peasants' revolts and the rise of the bourgeoisie shattered everywhere their very foundations. Depending on specific historical conditions, on the internal strength of their precapitalist social orders and on the intensity of the antifeudal pressures, bourgeois revolutions and the development of capitalism were more or less effectively resisted and retarded. Nowhere would they have been indefinitely prevented. Indeed, if the most advanced countries' contact with the backward world had been different from what it was, if it had consisted of genuine cooperation and assistance rather than of oppression and exploitation, then the progressive development of the now underdeveloped countries would have proceeded with incomparably less delay, less friction, less human sacrifice and suffering. A peaceful transplantation of Western culture, science, and technology to the less advanced countries would have served everywhere as a powerful catalyst of economic progress. The violent, destructive, and predatory opening up of the weaker countries by Western capitalism immeasurably distorted their development. A comparison of the role played by British science and British technology in the development of the United States with the role played by British opium in the development of China fully epitomizes this difference....

This is the really important "indirect influence" of foreign enterprise on the evolution of the underdeveloped countries. It flows through a multitude of channels, permeates all of their economic, social, political, and cultural life, and decisively determines its entire course. There is first of all the emergence of a group of merchants expanding and thriving within the orbit of foreign capital. Whether they act as wholesalers—assembling, sorting, and standardizing commodities that they purchase from small producers and sell to representatives of foreign concerns—or as suppliers of local materials to foreign enterprises, or as caterers to various other needs of foreign firms and their staffs, many of them manage to assemble vast fortunes and to move up to the very top of the underdeveloped countries' capitalist class. Deriving their profits from the operations of foreign business, vitally interested in its expansion and prosperity, this comprador element of the native bourgeoisie uses its considerable influence to fortify and to perpetuate the *status quo*.

There are secondly the native industrial monopolists, in most cases interlocked and interwoven with domestic merchant capital and with foreign enterprise, who entirely depend on the maintenance of the existing economic structure, and whose monopolistic status would be swept away by the rise of industrial capitalism. Concerned with preventing the emergence of competitors in their markets, they look with favor upon absorption of capital in the sphere of circulation, and have nothing to fear from foreign export-oriented enterprise. They, too, are stalwart defenders of the established order.

The interests of these two groups run entirely parallel with those of the feudal landowners powerfully entrenched in the societies of the backward areas. Indeed, these have no reason for complaints about the activities of foreign enterprise in their countries. In fact, these activities yield them considerable profits. Frequently they provide outlets for the produce of landed estates, in many places they raise the value of land, often they offer lucrative employment opportunities to members of the landed gentry.

What results is a political and social coalition of wealthy compradors, powerful monopolists, and large landowners dedicated to the defense of the existing feudal-mercantile order. Ruling the realm by no matter what political means—as a monarchy, as a military-fascist dictatorship, or as a republic of the Kuomintang variety—this coalition has nothing to hope for from the rise of industrial capitalism which would dislodge it from its positions of privilege and power. Blocking all economic and social progress in its country, this regime has no real political basis in city or village, lives in continual fear of the starving and restive popular masses, and relies for its stability on Praetorian guards of relatively well-kept mercenaries.

In most underdeveloped countries social and political developments of the last few decades would have toppled regimes of that sort. That they have been able to stay in business—for business is, indeed, their sole concern—in most of Latin America and in the Near East, in several "free" countries of Southeast Asia and in some similarly "free" countries of Europe, is due mainly if not exclusively to the aid and support that was given to them "freely" by Western capital and by Western governments acting on its behalf. For the maintenance of these regimes and the operations of foreign enterprise in the underdeveloped countries have become mutually interdependent. It is the economic strangulation of the colonial and dependent countries by the imperialist

powers that stymied the development of indigenous industrial capitalism, thus preventing the overthrow of the feudal-mercantile order
and assuring the rule of the comprador administrations. It is the preservation of these subservient governments, stifling economic and social
development and suppressing all popular movements for social and
national liberation, that makes possible at the present time the continued foreign exploitation of underdeveloped countries and their
domination by the imperialist powers....

To be sure, neither imperialism itself nor its *modus operandi* and ideological trimmings are today what they were fifty or a hundred years ago.
Just as outright looting of the outside world has yielded to organized
trade with the underdeveloped countries, in which plunder has been
rationalized and routinized by a mechanism of impeccably "correct"
contractual relations, so has the rationality of smoothly functioning
commerce grown into the modern, still more advanced, still more
rational system of imperialist exploitation. Like all other historically
changing phenomena, the contemporary form of imperialism contains
and preserves all its earlier modalities, but raises them to a new level.
Its central feature is that it is now directed not solely toward the rapid
extraction of large sporadic gains from the objects of its domination, it
is no longer content with merely assuring a more or less steady flow of
those gains over a somewhat extended period. Propelled by well-orga-
nized, rationally conducted monopolistic enterprise, it seeks today to
rationalize the flow of these receipts so as to be able to count on it in
perpetuity. And this points to the main task of imperialism in our time:
to prevent, or, if that is impossible, to slow down and to control the economic development of underdeveloped countries.

That such development is profoundly inimical to the interests of
foreign corporations producing raw materials for export can be readily
seen. There is of course the mortal threat of nationalization of raw
materials producing enterprises that is associated with the ascent to
power of governments in backward countries that are determined to
move their nations off dead center; but, even in the absence of nationalization, economic development in the source countries bodes nothing
but evil to Western capital. For whichever aspect of economic development we may consider, it is manifestly detrimental to the prosperity of
the raw materials producing corporations. As under conditions of eco-

nomic growth employment opportunities and productivity expand in other parts of the economy, and the class consciousness and bar gaining power of labor increase, wages tend to rise in the raw materials producing sector. While in some lines of output—on plantations primarily—those increased costs can be offset by the adoption of improved techniques, such mechanization involves capital outlays that are obviously repugnant to the corporations involved. And in mining and petroleum operations even this solution is hardly possible. These in general employ the same methods of production that are in use in the advanced countries, so that the technological gap that could be filled is accordingly very small. With the prices of their products in the world markets representing a fixed datum to the individual companies—at least in the short run—increased labor costs combined with various fringe benefits resulting from growing unionization, as well as rising costs of other local supplies, must lead necessarily to a reduction of profits. If thus the longer-run effects of economic development cannot but be damaging to the raw materials exporting corporations, the immediate concomitants of economic development are apt to be even more disturbing. They will be, as a rule, higher taxes and royalties imposed on the foreign enterprises by the local government seeking revenue to finance its developmental ventures, foreign exchange controls designed to curtail the removal of profits abroad, tariffs rendering the importation of foreign-made equipment more expensive or raising the prices of imported wage goods, and others—all inevitably interfering with the freedom of action of foreign enterprise and encroaching upon its profitability.

Small wonder that under such circumstances Western big business heavily engaged in raw materials exploitation leaves no stone unturned to obstruct the evolution of social and political conditions in underdeveloped countries that might be conducive to their economic development. It uses its tremendous power to prop up the backward areas' comprador administrations, to disrupt and corrupt the social and political movements that oppose them, and to overthrow whatever progressive governments may rise to power and refuse to do the bidding of their imperialist overlords. Where and when its own impressive resources do not suffice to keep matters under control, or where and when the costs of the operations involved can be shifted to their home countries' national governments—or nowadays to international agencies such as the International Bank for Reconstruction and Development—the diplomatic, financial, and, if need be, military facilities of the imperialist power are rapidly and efficiently mobilized to help private enterprise in distress to do the required job.

19

CAPITALIST DEVELOPMENT OF UNDERDEVELOPMENT
André Gunder Frank

The notion that capitalism promotes underdevelopment challenged prevailing assumptions about the diffusionist potential of capitalism and the possibility of emulating in backward countries the developmental examples of Western Europe and the United States. Frank explained this idea by drawing on the metropole-satellite dichotomy reflected in past writings on colonialism and imperialism. This essay served as the basis for his influential Capitalism and Underdevelopment in Latin America *(1967).*

WE CANNOT HOPE TO FORMULATE adequate development theory and policy for the majority of the world's population who suffer from underdevelopment without first learning how their past economic and social history gave rise to their present underdevelopment. Yet most historians study only the developed metropolitan countries and pay scant attention to the colonial underdeveloped lands. For this reason most of our theoretical categories and guides to development policy have been distilled exclusively from the historical experience of the European and North American advanced capitalist nations.

Since the historical experience of the colonial and underdeveloped countries has demonstrably been quite different, available theory there-

From André Gunder Frank, "The Development of Underdevelopment," *Monthly Review* (September 1966): 17—31 Also published in Robert I. Rhodes, *Imperialism and Underdevelopment: A Reader* (New York: Monthly Review Press, 1970), pp. 4—17. Copyright © 1966 by Monthly Review Press. Reprinted with permission from Monthly Review Foundation.

fore fails to reflect the past of the underdeveloped part of the world entirely, and reflects the past of the world as a whole only in part. More important, our ignorance of the underdeveloped countries' history leads us to assume that their past and indeed their present resembles earlier stages of the history of the now developed countries. This ignorance and this misconception lead us into serious misconceptions about contemporary underdevelopment and development. Further, most studies of development and underdevelopment fail to take account of the economic and other relations between the metropolis and its economic colonies throughout the history the worldwide expansion and development of the mercantilist and capitalist system. Consequently, most of our theory fails to explain the structure and development of the capitalist system as a whole and to account for its simultaneous generation of underdevelopment in others.

It is generally held that economic development occurs in a succession of capitalist stages and that today's underdeveloped countries are still in a stage, sometimes depicted as an original stage of history, through which the now developed countries passed long ago. Yet even a modest acquaintance with history shows that underdevelopment is not original or traditional and that neither the past nor the present of the underdeveloped countries resembles in any important respect the past of the now developed countries. The now developed countries were never *under*developed though they may have been *un*developed. It is also widely believed that the contemporary underdevelopment of a country can be understood as the product or reflection solely of its own economic, political, social, and cultural characteristics or structure. Yet historical research demonstrates that contemporary underdevelopment is in large part the historical product of past and continuing economic and other relations between the satellite underdeveloped and the now developed metropolitan countries. Furthermore, these relations are an essential part of the structure and development of the capitalist system on world scale as a whole. A related and also largely erroneous view is that the development of these underdeveloped countries and within them of their most underdeveloped domestic areas, must and will be generated or stimulated by diffusing capital, institutions, values, etc., to them from the international and national capitalist metropoles. Historical perspective based on the underdeveloped countries' past experience suggests that on the contrary in the underdeveloped countries economic development can now occur only independently of most of these relations of diffusion.

Evident inequalities of income and differences in culture have led many observers to see "dual" societies and economies in the underdeveloped countries. Each of the two parts is supposed to have a history of its own, a structure, and a contemporary dynamic largely independent of the other. Supposedly, only one part of the economy and society has been importantly affected by intimate economic relations with the "outside" capitalist world; and that part, it is held, became modern capitalist, and relatively developed precisely because of this contact. The other part is widely regarded as variously isolated, subsistence-based, feudal, or precapitalist, and therefore more underdeveloped.

I believe on the contrary that the entire "dual society" thesis is false and that the policy recommendations to which it leads will, if acted upon serve only to intensify and perpetuate the very conditions of underdevelopment they are supposedly designed to remedy.

A mounting body of evidence suggests, and I am confident that future historical research will confirm, that the expansion of the capitalist system over the past centuries effectively and entirely penetrated even the apparently most isolated sector of the underdeveloped world. Therefore, the economic, political, social, and cultural institutions and relations we now observe there are the products of the historical development of the capitalist system no less than are the seemingly more modern or capitalist features of the national metropoles of these underdeveloped countries. Analogously to the relations between development and underdevelopment on the international level, the contemporary underdeveloped institutions of the so-called backward or feudal domestic areas of an underdeveloped country are no less the product of the single historical process of capitalist development than are the so called capitalist institutions of the supposedly more progressive areas. In this paper I should like to sketch the kinds of evidence which support this thesis and at the same time indicate lines along which further study and research could fruitfully proceed.

The Secretary General of the Latin American Center for Research in the Social Sciences writes in that Center's journal: "The privileged position of the city has its origin in the colonial period. It was founded by the Con-

queror to serve the same ends that it still serves today; to incorporate the
indigenous population into the economy brought and developed by that
conqueror and his descendants. The regional city was an instrument of
conquest and is still today an instrument of domination." The Instituto
Nacional Indigenista (National Indian Institute) of Mexico confirms this
observation when it notes that "the mestizo population, in fact, always
lives in a city, a center of an intercultural region, which acts as the metropolis of a zone of indigenous population and which maintains with the
underdeveloped communities an intimate relation which links the
center with the satellite communities" (Instituto Nacional Indigenista,
1962, p. 34). The Institute goes on to point out that "between the mestizos
who live in the nuclear city of the region and the Indians who live in the
peasant hinterland there is in reality a closer economic and social inter-
dependence than might at first glance appear" and that the provincial
metropoles "by being centers of intercourse are also centers of exploitation" (Instituto Nacional Indigenista, 1962, pp. 33–34, 88).

     Thus these metropolis-satellite relations are not limited to the impe-
rial or international level but penetrate and structure the very economic, political, and social life of the Latin American colonies and countries. Just as the colonial and national capital and its export sector
become the satellite of the Iberian (and later of other) metropoles of the
world economic system, this satellite immediately becomes a colonial
and then a national metropolis with respect to the productive sectors
and population of the interior. Furthermore, the provincial capitals,
which thus are themselves satellites of the national metropolis and
through the latter of the world metropolis—are in turn provincial centers around which their own local satellites orbit. Thus, a whole chain
of constellations of metropoles and satellites relates all parts of the
whole system from its metropolitan center in Europe or the United
States to the farthest outpost in the Latin American countryside.

     When we examine this metropolis satellite structure, we find that
each of the satellites, including now-underdeveloped Spain and Portugal, serves as an instrument to suck capital or economic surplus out of
its own satellites and to channel part of this surplus to the world
metropolis of which all are satellites. Moreover, each national and local
metropolis serves to impose and maintain the monopolistic structure
and exploitative relationship of this system (as the Instituto Nacional

Indigenista of Mexico calls it) as long as it serves the interests of the metropoles, which take advantage of this global, national, and local structure to promote their own development and the enrichment of their ruling classes.

These are the principal and still surviving structural characteristics which were implanted in Latin America by the Conquest. Beyond examining the establishment of this colonial structure in its historical context, the proposed approach calls for the study of the development—and underdevelopment—of these metropoles and satellites of Latin America throughout the following and still continuing historical process. In this way we can understand why there were and still are tendencies in the Latin American and world capitalist structure which seem to lead to the development of the metropolis and the underdevelopment of the satellite and why, particularly, the satellized national, regional, and local metropoles in Latin America find that their economic development is at best a limited or underdeveloped development.

That present underdevelopment of Latin America is the result of its centuries-long participation in the process of world capitalist development, I believe I have shown in my case studies of the economic and social histories of Chile and Brazil. My study of Chilean history suggests that the conquest not only incorporated this country fully into the expansion and development of the world mercantile and later industrial capitalist system but that it also introduced the monopolistic metropolis-satellite structure and development of capitalism into the Chilean domestic economy and society itself. This structure then penetrated and permeated all of Chile very quickly. Since that time and in the course of world and Chilean history during the epochs of colonialism, free trade, imperialism, and the present, Chile has become increasingly marked by the economic, social, and political structure of satellite underdevelopment. This development of underdevelopment continues today, both in Chile's still increasing satellization by the world metropolis and through the ever more acute polarization of Chile's domestic economy.

The history of Brazil is perhaps the clearest case of both national and regional development of underdevelopment. The expansion of the world economy since the beginning of the sixteenth century successively converted the Northeast, the Minas Gerais interior, the North, and the Center-South (Rio de Janeiro, São Paulo, and Parana) into export economies and incorporated them into the structure and development of the world capitalist system. Each of these regions experienced what may have appeared as economic development during the period of its respective golden age. But it was a satellite development which was neither self-generating nor self-perpetuating. As the market or the productivity of the first three regions declined, foreign and domestic economic interest in them waned; and they were left to develop the underdevelopment they live today. In the fourth region, the coffee economy experienced a similar though not yet quite as serious fate (though the development of a synthetic coffee substitute promises to deal it a mortal blow in the not too distant future). All of this historical evidence contradicts the generally accepted theses that Latin America suffers from a dual society or from the survival of feudal institutions and that these are important obstacles to its economic development.

During the First World War, however, and even more during the Great Depression and the Second World War, São Paulo began to build up an industrial establishment which is the largest in Latin America today. The question arises whether this industrial development did or can break Brazil out of the cycle of satellite development and underdevelopment which characterized its other regions and national history within the capitalist system so far. I believe that the answer is no. Domestically the evidence so far is fairly clear. The development of industry in São Paulo has not brought greater riches to the other regions of Brazil. Instead, it converted them into internal colonial satellites, decapitalized them further, and consolidated or even deepened their underdevelopment. There is little evidence to suggest that this process is likely to be reversed in foreseeable future except insofar as the provincial poor migrate and become the poor of the metropolitan cities. Externally, the evidence is that although the initial development of São Paulo's industry was relatively autonomous it is being increasingly satellized by the world capitalist metropolis and its future development possibilities are increasingly restricted. This development, my studies lead me to believe, also appears destined to limited or underdeveloped development as long as it takes place in the present economic, political, and social framework.

We must conclude, in short, that underdevelopment is not due to the survival of archaic institutions and the existence of capital shortage in regions that have remained isolated from the stream of world history. On the contrary, underdevelopment was and still is generated by the very same historical process which also generated economic development: the development of capitalism itself. This view, I am glad to say, is gaining adherents among students of Latin America and is proving its worth in shedding new light on the problems of the area and in affording a better perspective for the formulation of theory and policy.

The same historical and structural approach can also lead to better development theory and policy by generating a series hypotheses about development and underdevelopment such as those I am testing in my current research. The hypotheses are derived from the empirical observation and theoretical assumption that within this world-embracing metropolis-satellite structure the metropoles tend to develop and the satellites to underdevelop. The first hypothesis has already been mentioned above: that in contrast to the development of the world metropolis which is no one's satellite, the development of the national and other subordinate metropoles is limited by their satellite status. It is perhaps more difficult to test this hypothesis than the following ones because part of its confirmation depends on the test of the other hypotheses. Nonetheless, this hypothesis appears to be generally confirmed by the nonautonomous and unsatisfactory economic and especially industrial development of Latin America's national metropoles, as documented in the studies already cited. The most important and at the same time most confirmatory examples are the metropolitan regions of Buenos Aires and São Paulo whose growth only began in the nineteenth century, was therefore largely untrammeled by any colonial heritage, but was and remains a satellite development largely dependent on the outside metropolis, first of Britain and then of the United States.

A second hypothesis is that the satellites experience their greatest economic development and especially their most classically capitalist industrial development if and when their ties to their metropolis are weakest. This hypothesis is almost diametrically opposed to the generally accepted thesis that development in the underdeveloped countries follows from the greatest degree of contact with and diffusion from the metropolitan developed countries. This hypothesis seems to be confirmed by two kinds of relative isolation that Latin America has experienced in the course of its history. One is the temporary isolation caused by the crises of war or depression in the world metropolis. Apart from minor ones, five periods of such major crises stand out and seem to confirm the hypothesis. These are: the European (and especially Spanish) Depression of the seventeenth century, the Napoleonic Wars, the First World War, the Depression of the 1930s, and the Second World War. It is clearly established and generally recognized that the most important recent industrial development—especially of Argentina, Brazil, and Mexico, but also of other countries such as Chile—has taken place precisely during the periods of the two World Wars and the intervening Depression. Thanks to the consequent loosening of trade and investment ties during these periods, the satellites initiated marked autonomous industrialization and growth. Historical research demonstrates that the same thing happened in Latin America during Europe's seventeenth-century depression. Manufacturing grew in the Latin American countries, and several of them such as Chile became exporters of manufactured goods. The Napoleonic Wars gave rise to independence movements in Latin America, and these should perhaps also be interpreted as confirming the development hypothesis in part.

The other kind of isolation which tends to confirm the second hypothesis is the geographic and economic isolation of regions which at one time were relatively weakly tied to and poorly integrated into the mercantilist and capitalist system. My preliminary research suggests that in Latin America these regions which initiated and experienced the most promising self-generating economic development of the classical industrial capitalist type. The most important regional cases probably are Tucuman and Asuncion, as well as other cities such as Mendoza sad Rosario, in the interior of Argentina and Paraguay during the end of the eighteenth and the beginning of the nineteenth centuries. Seventeenth- and eighteenth-century São Paulo, long before coffee was grown there, is another example. Perhaps Antioquia in Colombia and Puebla and Queretaro in Mexico are other examples. In its own way, Chile was also an example since, before the sea route around the Horn was opened, this country was relatively isolated at the end of the long voyage from Europe via Panama. All of these regions became manufacturing centers and even exporters, usually of textiles, during the periods preceding their effective incorporation as satellites into the colonial, national, and world capitalist system.

Internationally, of course, the classic case of industrialization through nonparticipation as a satellite in the capitalist world system is obviously that of Japan after the Meiji Restoration. Why, one may ask, was resource-poor but unsatellized Japan able to industrialize so quickly at the end of the century while resource-rich Latin American countries and Russia were not able to do so and the latter was easily beaten by Japan in the War of 1904 after the same forty years of development efforts? The second hypothesis suggests that the fundamental reason is that Japan was not satellized either during the Tokugawa or the Meiji period and therefore did not have its development structurally limited as did the countries which were so satellized.

A corollary of the second hypothesis is that when the metropolis recovers from its crisis and reestablishes the trade and investment ties which fully reincorporate the satellites into the system, or when the metropolis expands to incorporate previously isolated regions into the worldwide system, the previous development and industrialization of these regions is choked off or channeled into directions which are not self-perpetuating and promising. This happened after each of the five crisis cited above. The renewed expansion of trade and the spread of economic liberalism in the eighteenth and nineteenth centuries choked off and reversed the manufacturing development which Latin America had experienced during the seventeenth century, and in some places at the beginning of the nineteenth. After the First World War, the new national industry of Brazil suffered serious consequences from American economic invasion. The increase in the growth rate of Gross National Product and particularly of industrialization throughout Latin America was again reversed and industry became increasingly satellized after the Second World War and especially after the post-Korean War recovery and expansion of the metropolis. Far from having become more developed since then, industrial sectors of Brazil and most conspicuously of Argentina have become structurally more and more underdeveloped and less and less able to generate continued industrialization and/or sustain development of the economy. This process, from which India also suffers, is reflected in a whole gamut of balance-of-payments, inflationary, and other economic and political difficulties, and promises to yield to no solution short of far-reaching structural change.

Our hypothesis suggests that fundamentally the same process

occurred even more dramatically with the incorporation into the system of previously unsatellized regions. The expansion of Buenos Aires as a satellite of Great Britain and the introduction of free trade in the interest of the ruling groups of both metropoles destroyed the manufacturing and much of the remainder of the economic base of the previously relatively prosperous interior almost entirely. Manufacturing was destroyed by foreign competition, lands were taken and concentrated into latifundia by the rapaciously growing export economy, intraregional distribution of income became much more unequal, and the previously developing regions became simple satellites of Buenos Aires and through it of London. The provincial census did not yield to satellization without a struggle. This metropolis-satellite conflict was much of the cause of the long political and armed struggle between the Unitarists in Buenos Aires and the Federalists in the provinces, and it may be said to have been the sole important cause of the War of the Triple Alliance in which Buenos Aires, Montevideo, and Rio de Janeiro, encouraged and helped by London, destroyed not only the autonomously developing economy of Paraguay but killed off nearly all of its population which was unwilling to give in. Though this is no doubt the most spectacular example which tends to confirm the hypothesis, I believe that historical research on satellization of previously relatively independent yeoman-farming and incipient manufacturing regions such as the Caribbean islands will confirm it further. These regions did not have a chance against the forces of expanding and developing capitalism, and their own development had to be sacrificed to that of others. The economy and industry of Argentina, Brazil, and other countries which have experienced the effects of metropolitan recovery since the Second World War are today suffering much the same fate, if fortunately still in lesser degree.

A third major hypothesis derived from the metropolis-satellite structure is that the regions which are the most underdeveloped and feudal-seeming today are the ones which had the closest ties to the metropolis in the past. They are the regions which were the greatest exporters of primary products to and the biggest sources of capital for the world metropolis and which were abandoned by the metropolis when for one reason or another business fell off. This hypothesis also contradicts the generally held thesis that the source of a region's underdevelopment is its isolation and its precapitalist institutions.

This hypothesis seems to be amply confirmed by the former super-satellite development and present ultra-underdevelopment of the once sugar-exporting West Indies, Northeastern Brazil, the ex-mining districts of Minas Gerais in Brazil, highland Peru, and Bolivia, and the central Mexican states of Guanajuato, Zacatecas, and others whose names were made world famous centuries ago by their silver. There surely are no major regions in Latin America which are today more cursed by under-development and poverty, yet all of these regions, like Bengal in India, once provided the lifeblood of mercantile and industrial capitalist devel-opment in the metropolis. These regions' participation in the develop-ment of the world capitalist system gave them, already in their golden age, the typical structure of underdevelopment of a capitalist export economy. When the market for their sugar or the wealth of their mines disappeared and the metropolis abandoned them to their own devices, the already existing economic, political, and social structure of these regions prohibited autonomous generation of economic development and left them no alternative but to turn in upon themselves and to degenerate into the ultra-underdevelopment we find there today.

These considerations suggest two further and related hypotheses. One is that the latifundium, irrespective of whether it appears as a plantation or a hacienda today, was typically born as a commercial enterprise which created for itself the institutions which permitted it to respond to increased demand in the world or national market by expanding the amount of its land, capital, and labor and to increase the supply of its products. The fifth hypothesis is that the latifundia which appear isolated, subsistence-based, and semifeudal today saw the demand for their prod-ucts or their productive capacity decline and that they are to be found principally in the above-named former agricultural and mining export regions whose economic activities declined in general. These two hypotheses run counter to the notions of most people, and even to the opinions of some historians and other students of the subject, according to whom the historical roots and socioeconomic causes of Latin America's latifundia and agrarian institutions are to be found in the transfer of feudal institutions from Europe and/or in economic depression.

The evidence to test these hypotheses is not open to easy general inspection and requires detailed analyses of many cases. Nonetheless, some important confirmatory evidence is available.

The growth of the latifundium in nineteenth-century Argentina and Cuba is a clear case in support of the fourth hypothesis and can in no way be attributed to the transfer of feudal institutions during colonial times. The same is evidently the case of the postrevolutionary and contemporary resurgence of latifundia particularly in the North of Mexico, which produce for the American market, and of similar ones on the coast of Peru and the new coffee regions of Brazil. The conversion of previously yeoman-farming Caribbean islands, such as Barbados, into sugar-exporting economies at various times between the seventeenth and twentieth centuries and the resulting rise of the latifundia in these islands would seem to confirm the fourth hypothesis as well. In Chile, the rise of the latifundium and the creation of the institutions of servitude which later came to be called feudal occurred in the eighteenth century and have been conclusively shown to be the result of and response to the opening of a market for Chilean wheat in Lima. Even the growth and consolidation of the latifundium in seventeenth-century Mexico—which most expert students have attributed to a depression of the economy caused by the decline of mining and a shortage of Indian labor and to a consequent turning in upon itself and ruralization of the economy—occurred at a time when urban population and demand were growing, food shortages became acute, food prices skyrocketed, and the profitability of other economic activities such as mining and foreign trade declined. All of these and other factors rendered hacienda agriculture more profitable. Thus even this case would seem to confirm the hypothesis that the growth of the latifundium and its feudal-seeming conditions of servitude in Latin America has always been and still is the commercial response to increased demand and that is does not represent the transfer or survival of alien institutions that have remained beyond the reach of capitalist development. The emergence of latifundia, which today really are more or less (though not entirely) isolated, might then be attributed to the causes advanced in the fifth hypothesis—i.e., the decline of previously profitable agricultural enterprises whose capital was, and whose currently produced economic surplus still is, transferred elsewhere by owners and merchants who frequently are the same persons or families. Testing this hypothesis requires still more detailed analysis, some of which I have undertaken in a study on Brazilian agriculture.

All of these hypotheses and studies suggest that the global extension and unity of the capitalist system, its monopoly structure and
uneven development throughout its history, and the resulting persistence of commercial rather than industrial capitalism in the underdeveloped world (including its most industrially advanced countries)
deserve much more attention in the study of economic development
and cultural change than they have hitherto received. Though science
and truth know no national boundaries, it is probably new generations
of scientists from the underdeveloped countries themselves who most
need to, and best can, devote the necessary attention to these problems
and clarify the process of underdevelopment and development. It is
their people who in the last analysis face the task of changing this no
longer acceptable process and eliminating this miserable reality.

They will not be able to accomplish these goals by importing sterile
stereotypes from the metropolis which do not correspond to their satellite economic reality and do not respond to their liberating political
needs. To change their reality they must understand it. For this reason,
I hope that better confirmation of these hypotheses and further pursuit
of the proposed historical, holistic, and structural approach may help the
peoples of the underdeveloped countries to understand the causes and
eliminate the reality of their development of underdevelopment and
their underdevelopment of development.

REFERENCES

Instituto Nacional Indigenista. 1962. *Los centros coordinadores indigenistas*. Mexico.

20

IMPERIALISM, COLONIALISM, AND NEOCOLONIALISM
Amílcar Cabral

One of the leading theorists and revolutionary practitioners in Africa, Amílcar Cabral analyzed the relationship of colonialism, neocolonialism, and imperialism. His work significantly emphasized cultural resistance alongside armed struggle as ways to struggle against these forces. In this essay he argues that national liberation implies the need for revolution in search of freedom from foreign dominance and imperialism. He distinguishes between colonial and neocolonial situations and analyzes class relations and struggle within foreign and indigenous segments of society.

NOW WE HAVE SEEN THAT the principal and permanent characteristic of imperialist domination, whatever its form, is the usurpation by violence of the freedom of the process of development of the dominated socioeconomic whole. We have also seen that this freedom, and it alone, can guarantee the normal course of the historical process of a people. We can therefore conclude that national liberation exists when, and only when, the national productive forces have been completely freed from all and any kind of foreign domination.

It is often said that national liberation is based on the right of all

From Amílcar Cabral, "The Weapon of Theory," in *Unity and Struggle: Speeches and Writings of Amílcar Cabral* (New York: Monthly Review Press, 1979), pp. 130–34. Copyright © 1979 by Monthly Review Press. Reprinted with permission of Monthly Review Foundation. See also Ronald H. Chilcote, *Amílcar Cabral's Revolutionary Theory and Practice* (Boulder: Lynne Rienner Publishers, 1991).

peoples to decide their destiny freely and that the aim of this liberation is to gain national independence. Although we might agree with this vague and subjective way of expressing a complex reality, we prefer to be objective. For us the basis of national liberation, whatever the formulas adopted in international law, is the inalienable right of every people to have their own history: and the aim of national liberation is to regain this right usurped by imperialism, that is, to free the process of development of the national productive forces.

For this reason, in our view any national liberation movement that does not take into consideration this basis and this aim may struggle against imperialism, but will certainly not be struggling for national liberation.

This means that, bearing in mind the essential characteristics of the present-day world economy, as well as experiences already gained in the field of anti-imperialist struggle, the principal aspect of national liberation struggle is the struggle against what is conventionally called neocolonialism. Furthermore, if we accept that national liberation demands a profound mutation in the process of development of the productive forces we see that the phenomenon of national liberation necessarily corresponds to a revolution. The important thing is to be aware of the objective and subjective conditions in which this revolution may occur, and to know the types or type of struggle most appropriate for its accomplishment.

We will not repeat here that these conditions are openly favorable in the present state of the history of mankind. We shall merely recall that unfavorable factors also exist, just as much on the international level as on the internal level of each nation struggling for its liberation.

On the international level, it seems to us that the following factors at least are unfavorable to the national liberation movement: the neocolonial situation of a great number of states which, having won political independence, are tending to join up with others already in that situation; the progress made by neocapitalism, notably in Europe, where imperialism is resorting to preferential investments to encourage the development of a privileged proletariat with a consequent lowering of the revolutionary level of the working classes; the open or concealed neocolonial situation of some European states which, like Portugal, still have colonies; the policy of so-called aid to underdeveloped countries, practiced by imperialism with the aim of creating or reinforcing native pseudobourgeoisies necessarily subjected to the international bourgeoisie, and thus obstructing the path to revolution; the claustrophobia and timidity about revolution which leads some recently independent states, whose internal economic and political conditions are favorable to revolution, to accept compromises with the enemy or with their agents: the growing contradictions between anti-imperialist states; and, finally, the threats to world peace, posed by the prospect of atomic war on the part of imperialism. All these factors combine to strengthen the action of imperialism against the national liberation movement.

If the repeated interventions and growing aggressiveness of imperialism against the peoples can be interpreted as a sign of desperation before the extent of the national liberation movement, they are to some extent explained by the weaknesses within the general front of anti-imperialist struggle created by these unfavorable factors.

On the internal level, it seems to us that the most significant weakness or unfavorable factors are inherent in the socioeconomic structure and in the trends of its evolution under imperialist pressure or, better still, in the little or no attention paid to the characteristics of this structure and these trends by the national liberation movements in drawing up their strategy for struggle.

By saying this we do not wish to minimize the significance of other internal factors which are unfavorable to national liberation, such as economic underdevelopment and the consequent social and cultural backwardness of the mass of the people, tribalism and some other minor contradictions. It should, however, be noted that the existence of tribes is only manifested as a significant contradiction as a function of opportunist attitudes (generally on the pad of detribalized individuals or groups) within the national liberation movement. Contradictions between classes. even when the latter are embryonic, are of far greater importance than the contradictions between tribes.

Although the colonial and neocolonial situations are identical in essence, and the main aspect of the struggle against imperialism might be the neocolonialist aspect, we feel it is vital to distinguish between these two situations in practice. In fact the horizontal structure of the native society, whether more or less differentiated, and the absence of a political power composed of national elements in the colonial situation, make possible the creation of a broad front of unity and struggle that is vital for the success of the national liberation movement. But this possibility does not remove the need for a rigorous analysis of the indigenous social structure and the trends of its evolution, and for the adoption in practice of appropriate measures for ensuring a genuine national liberation. While we admit that everyone knows best what to do in his own house, we feel that among these measures it is vital to create a firmly united vanguard, conscious of the true meaning and objective of the national liberation struggle which it must lead. This necessity is all the more acute because it is certain that, with rare exceptions, the colonial situation neither allows nor invites the meaningful existence of vanguard classes (an industrial working class and rural proletariat) which could ensure the vigilance of the mass of the people over the evolution of the liberation movement. On the contrary, the generally embryonic character of the working classes and the economic, social, and cultural situation of the major physical force in a national liberation struggle—the peasants—do not allow these two principal forces of that struggle to distinguish on their own genuine national independence from fictitious political independence. Only a revolutionary vanguard, generally an active minority, can have consciousness *ab initio* of this distinction and through the struggle bring it to the awareness of the mass of the people. This explains the fundamentally political nature of the national liberation struggle and to some extent provides the significance of the form of struggle in the final outcome of the phenomenon of national liberation.

In the neocolonial situation, the more or less accentuated structuring of the native society as a vertical one and the existence of a political power composed of native elements—national state—aggravate the contradictions within that society and make difficult, if not impossible, the creation of as broad a united front as in the colonial case. On the one hand, the material effects (mainly the nationalization of cadres and the rise in native economic initiative, particularly at the commercial level) and the psychological effects (pride in believing oneself ruled by one's fellow countrymen, exploitation of religious or tribal solidarity between some leaders and a fraction of the mass of the people) serve to demobilize a considerable part of the nationalist forces.

But on the other hand, the necessarily repressive nature of the neocolonial state against the national liberation forces, the aggravation of class contradictions, the objective continuance of agents and signs of foreign domination (settlers who retain their privileges, armed forces, racial discrimination), the growing impoverishment of the peasantry, and the more or less flagrant influence of external factors contribute toward keeping the flame of nationalism alight. They serve gradually to awaken the consciousness of broad popular strata and, precisely on the basis of awareness of neocolonialist frustration, to reunite the majority of the population around the ideal of national liberation.

In addition, while the native ruling class becomes increasingly "bourgeois" the development of a class of workers composed of urbanized industrial workers and agricultural proletarians—all exploited by the indirect domination of imperialism—opens renewed prospects for the evolution of national liberation. This class of workers, whatever the degree of development of its political consciousness (beyond a certain minimum that is *consciousness of its needs*), seems to constitute the true popular vanguard of the national liberation struggle in the neocolonial case. However, it will not be able completely to carry out its mission in the framework of this struggle (which does not end with the gaining of independence) unless it allies itself firmly with the other exploited strata: the peasants in general (farm laborers, tenants, sharecroppers, petty farm-owners) and the nationalist petty bourgeoisie. The achievement of this alliance demands the mobilization and organization of the nationalist forces within the framework (or by the action) of a strong and well-structured political organization.

Another important distinction to draw between the colonial and neocolonial situations lies in the prospects for struggle. The colonial case (in which the *nation class* fights the repressive forces of the bourgeoisie of the colonizing country) may lead, ostensibly at least, to a nationalist situation (national revolution): the nation gains its independence and theoretically adopts the economic structure it finds most attractive. The neocolonial case (in which the class of workers and its allies fight simultaneously the imperialist bourgeoisie and the native ruling class) is not resolved by a nationalist solution: it demands the destruction of the capitalist structure implanted in the national soil by imperialism and correctly postulates a socialist solution.

This distinction arises mainly from the different levels of the productive forces in the two cases and the consequent sharpening of the class struggle. It would not be difficult to show that in time this distinction becomes scarcely apparent. It is sufficient to recall that in the present historical circumstances—alienation of imperialism which lays its hands on every possible means to perpetuate its domination over our peoples, and consolidation of socialism over a considerable part of the globe—there are only two possible paths for an independent nation: to return to imperialist domination (neocolonialism, capitalism, state capitalism) or to take the socialist road. This option, on which depends the compensation for the efforts and sacrifices by the mass of the people during the struggle, is considerably influenced by the form of struggle and the degree of revolutionary consciousness of those who lead it.

The facts make it unnecessary for us to waste words proving that the essential instrument of imperialist domination is violence. If we accept the principle that *the national liberation struggle is a revolution*, and that it is not over at the moment when the flag is hoisted and the national anthem is played, we shall find that there is and there can be no national liberation without the use of liberating violence, on the part of the nationalist forces, in answer to the criminal violence of the agents of imperialism. Nobody can doubt that imperialist domination, whatever its local characteristics, implies a state of permanent violence against the nationalist forces. There is no people in the world which, after being subjected to the imperialist yoke (colonialist or neocolonialist), has gained independence (nominal or effective) without victims. The important thing is to decide what forms of violence have to be used by the national liberation forces, in order not only to answer the violence of imperialism but also to ensure, through the struggle, the final victory of their cause, that is true national independence.

21

IMPERIALISM AND UNDERDEVELOPMENT
Malcolm Caldwell

With particular attention to Asia, Malcolm Caldwell has analyzed capitalist underdevelopment in terms of its imperialist legacy. In the following selection, he identifies some of the trends that have characterized this historical experience in the Third World. He shows how imperialism is accompanied by the growing efficiency of production and that capital reaches out worldwide to change historical conditions and ensure hegemony over colonial and neocolonial countries. He identifies stages in this process and concludes with analysis of dependent development.

SINCE THE EIGHTEENTH CENTURY, THERE have been distinct phases in the development of underdevelopment. From the beginnings of the industrial revolution proper, in the second half of the eighteenth century, until the last third of the nineteenth century, there is a first stage. During this period, industrial production proper is restricted to the pioneering countries of western Europe (and to their offspring in North America). In this sphere, surplus value is extracted from wage labor employed in increasingly large-scale manufacturing industry. The peripheral countries of eastern Europe, Asia, Africa, and South America continue to contribute to the coffers of the industrializing countries; "primitive accumulation" goes on in innumerable forms, the proceeds largely accruing to nationals of the imperialist powers and, to a much lesser extent, to their "native" agents. Manufactured exports pouring

From Malcolm Caldwell, *The Wealth of Some Nations* (London: Zed Press, 1977), pp. 55–60. Reprinted with permission of Zed Press.

out of the industrialized countries of the northern hemisphere flood the more accessible parts of the Third World and hasten the disappearance of local preindustrial manufactures and handicrafts. But capital is still—measured against the magnitude of the task of transforming the countries of western Europe and North America into recognizably modern industrial powers—comparatively scarce, and therefore is devoted almost exclusively to metropolitan purposes. Moreover, the relatively underdeveloped modes of long-distance transport and communications effectively restrict the opening up of vast areas of hinterland to exposure to the cascade of cheap new manufactured goods. For both reasons, *some* semiperipheral countries succeed in taking the first hesitant steps toward autonomous industrialization (for instance, Russia, Japan, Spain, and Italy). In others, attempts to do the same are thwarted because the accumulation of capital is already controlled by local agencies of the imperialist powers.

By the last third of the nineteenth century the picture is being fundamentally changed in a host of ways. Technical innovations in transport and communications (the steamship, the electric telegraph, the opening of the Suez Canal) combine with the growing release of capital, expertise, and productive capacity from the tasks of completing the domestic transport networks of the industrial countries to make possible a real revolution in international communications. A genuine world market, coextensive with all populated parts of the globe (minus a few isolated pockets), now exists. The products of Western industry can reach everywhere—and everywhere assault the remaining bastions of handicraft and preindustrial manufacturing production.

The enormously expanded capacity of the industrial countries to generate capital permits of its export on an unprecedented scale. This, too, dooms such efforts as have been made elsewhere in the world autonomously to follow the example of the pioneering capitalist countries (except where—as in Japan—it proves possible to take effective steps to prevent foreign investment pushing in from the leading industrial countries). The export of Western capital all over the world aborts, thwarts and distorts Third World development in many ways.

In the first place, the fact that industrially experienced Westerners, possessed of (or with access to and disposal of) immeasurably greater resources than any available locally, now dominate the nonagricultural sector means petrification of local elites in the precapitalist rural economy, or—to the extent that they have already developed outside it, or are felt useful outside it—their cooptation to the economic and political needs and requirements of the imperialists. The actual forms of such arrangements and accommodations varied widely in detail from one Afro-Asian-Latin American country to another, but the outcome in every case is quite clear and unequivocal: every economic activity in the colonial or semicolonial country is now subordinated to the overriding interests of the metropolitan powers. Only activities compatible with or complementary to these interests are permitted to survive or to develop. These include the distribution of Western imported goods into the interior in petty trading and peddling; the purchasing and delivery to Western warehouses and to exit ports of smallholder cash crop produce; clerical work in Western offices, banks, insurance houses, and the like; all kinds of comprador functions for Western trading and agency houses; all kinds of services, ranging from domestic service to hotel-keeping, and the running of bars, casinos, and brothels, etc.; interpreting and catering to the tourist trade; some construction work; dealing in land; repairing machinery in small workshops; and so on.

Another aspect of the matter is that production of raw materials is now rapidly modernized. The enormous growth of industry has, of course, increased demand for raw materials many times over. But the growing *efficiency* of production exacerbates the problem, for—as each unit of capital and labor turns out a greater number of units of output—the significance of the raw material cost in each unit of output must rise. Capital, therefore, impatiently reaches out worldwide to replace older organizations of production of raw materials by new ones; slavery in the southern states of the USA gives way to capitalist planting, farming, and processing; the Culture System in Indonesia gives way to the organization of production by big capitalist corporations ("the Corporation System"); Britain moves directly into Southern Africa, the Malay states; and so on. The price of raw materials embarks upon that century-long secular slide downward (1873–1973). (Many oscillations make the actual course of prices exhibit a wave pattern, though.)

But the "modernization" of raw material production is relative, for such "modernization" in no way urges the economies of the Third World forward toward independent and balanced economic development. On the contrary, it freezes them into an unbalanced and dependent pattern, characterized by primary sector predominance, and by secondary and tertiary sectors specifically fashioned to facilitate imperialist exploitation of their resources and labor. Moreover, the failure of Third World economies to move ahead, in conjunction with the surge of their populations, ensures that the labor remains cheap. This is attractive in itself to the Western investor, but it also means that there is little incentive to replace labor by machinery, further defining the nature and trajectory of the now rapidly underdeveloping countries. In turn, the existence of attractive labor-intensive investment opportunities in the Third World eases the problems of overaccumulation of capital in the metropolitan countries—a phenomenon already apparent by the end of the nineteenth century. But perpetuation of a low-wage economy (and of a precapitalist subsistence agriculture sector) makes the domestic Third World market unattractive to the domestic Third World would-be manufacturer and investor, whose entrepreneurial and investment choices therefore harden, on the one hand, into those avenues left open by the imperialists and on the other into traditional outlets (land, jewelry, usury) or into Western-owned and managed enterprises.

A third stage emerges out of the prolonged interwar depression and the interlude between Britain's relinquishing the reins of overall responsibility for maintaining the rules and momentum of the international capitalist economy and America's picking them up. As suggested earlier, there has to be accommodation to the phased termination of the older forms of colonialism and neocolonialism associated with the middle era of "classical" imperialism. Besides, the pace of technological change and innovation is accelerating, producing complex international economic repercussions. There is also a much more conscious attempt at international economic management and at international economic integration for the benefit of the bourgeoisie of the imperialist countries and of their compradors, political gauleiters, mercenaries, and the like in the now postcolonial (or neocolonial) Third World.

But even the comparatively brief postwar period cannot adequately be characterized as if it is a single stage of development evincing uniform features throughout. In particular, the 1970s have witnessed a sea change in international economic circumstances the long-term significance of which cannot be exaggerated....However, we can risk a number of generalizations about the quarter of a century following the end of the Second World War.

The first thing to notice is that capital investment to the countries of the Third World, though of continuing importance, is of relatively less weight compared with inter investment by the imperialist powers among themselves. There are many reasons for this, among them greater political instability in the now independent countries and consequently enhanced risk attaching to investment; the threat of nationalization and expropriation by incoming radical regimes; the transfer of *some* raw material production to the imperialist metropoles themselves (a leading example of which is the substitution of a host of petro-chemical products for formerly imported natural inputs—e.g., synthetic rubber for natural rubber); and the increasingly common practice on the part of imperialist enterprises of financing their Third World activities out of profits made on the spot.

A second aspect is that the postwar years have seen a rapid spread of industrialization in at least some of the countries of Asia, Africa, and Latin America. It is, needless to say, industrialization of a particular type. Much of it is undertaken by Western and Japanese and multinational corporations in order to derive the benefits of a cheap and plentiful labor force, savagely repressive labor legislation that is inconceivable today in the richer countries (except the Soviet bloc ones), generous investment incentives offered by right-wing Third World governments, official and unofficial corruption, and other such advantages. Another major section consists of joint ventures in which, by the nature of things, the economically stronger rich country partners tend to dominate. Yet another category consists of entirely local enterprises which spring up to provide services for the others—picking up any opportunity left open by them. Then there are the Third World state-run industries covering an enormous span of processes and products.

Two things must be stressed, though. In the first place, such industrialization as has taken place has been to the gain of the imperialist powers, directly or indirectly: directly, by supplying a market for machinery (the manufacture and export of which have grown steadily in relative importance in the overdeveloped countries); indirectly, by enabling imperialist interests to reduce and partly evade the consequences of the squeeze on their profits consequent upon postwar policies of full employment, provision of social welfare, and greater cooptation of social democratic parties and the trade unions into the management of metropolitan capitalism. In the second place, in none of the Third World countries which have experienced a considerable industrialization is the resulting pattern of enterprises remotely similar to, or even comparable with, the pattern typical of the countries which much earlier achieved fully autonomous national economic development. On the contrary, what we have is a highly specific pattern of *dependent* development.

This basic dependency has a number of features. Not all of them occur in all cases, but at least some of them occur in all. Nor are all of them peculiar to underdeveloped countries of the Third World, for some occur in poorer developed countries. But the bunching of them in all underdeveloped countries produces a quite distinctive, qualitatively different, economic pattern from that evinced by developed countries. Let us review some of these features.

One is the dependence upon foreign aid, a dependence that tends to grow with the passage of time and that inevitably puts a great deal of power in the hands of those providing the aid. And those able to provide aid are, naturally, the rich and the powerful heavyweights of the international economy, notably the United States, Japan, the EEC countries, and, to a lesser extent, Russia and some of her stronger East European satellites (such as East Germany). Conditions attached to aid are seldom, if ever, beneficial to the recipient country's short- and long-term economic prospects. But that is not the point: they are beneficial to the favored local elites and most certainly to the aid-giving countries. Some aid simply buys political support in the international community and perhaps also military advantage in the way of bases and the like. But most has a hard economic purpose: construction of infrastructure vital for modern sophisticated investment projects; restriction of local credit to reduce local competition and to preclude local state activity in areas deemed profitable terrain for "market forces" (namely, foreign investors) to operate in; dictation and imposition of legislation granting favorable conditions to foreign investors; and the like.

Another is the scale of that segment of the economy effectively in foreign hands. This inevitably cramps the scope of local initiative (except to the extent favored by the ruling elites and their foreign advisers for their joint and several reasons). In some cases, as in Kenya or Malaysia, foreign-owned plantations take a lion's share of the cultivable land, exacerbating the problems and poverty of land-hungry poor peasants. Whatever example we take there is the threat of sudden withdrawal of the foreign operators if they feel that a switch of their investments elsewhere would be more profitable. This in itself can create very serious problems for the deserted host economy, but it is also an extremely powerful instrument to be held in reserve to deal with undesirable "radical" tendencies appearing locally in the neocolony. It is true that even the poorest of countries can, with correct political leadership, embark on the road of autarky, as the Cambodian experience shows, but where radical leadership is hesitant, is partly dependent upon liberal middle class support, and is pledged to "peaceful transition to socialism," foreign investor non-cooperation and sabotage can be fatal (as in the Chilean case).

22

CAPITALIST UNDERDEVELOPMENT OF BLACK AMERICA
Manning Marable

Influenced by the work of Walter Rodney, Manning Marable delves into the negative impact of capitalism in Black America. His analysis shows how Third World conditions of oppression, poverty, and backwardness exist in the midst of advanced capitalism in the United States. The comparative implications are strong and provocative and suggest the need to integrate understanding of imperialism and underdevelopment in the developed world. The road to Black liberation can be through socialism.

LIKE RODNEY'S SEMINAL WORK, I have attempted to delve "into the past only because otherwise it would be impossible to understand how the present came into being and what the trends are for the near future." As we have seen, the basic social division within the Black community, the Black worker majority versus the Black elite, was an essential by-product of primitive capital accumulation in slave societies. This class division became more pronounced in the twentieth century, and represented a tendency among many "middle class" Blacks in electoral politics, the church, small business and education to articulate a "capitalist road" to Black liberation. With Rodney, I have argued the thesis that Black economic, political, and social development is possible "only on the basis of a radical break with...the capitalist system, which has been the principal agency of underdevelopment." The data and historical

From Manning Marable, *How Capitalism Underdeveloped Black America* (New York: South End Press, 1983), pp. 255–62. Reprinted with permission of South End Press.

examples I have collected, in my judgment, more than justify the thesis. What remains to be developed, however, is the "formulation of a strategy and tactics" implied within the historical evaluation, which will uproot the hegemony of American capitalism. By necessity, such a strategy cannot be limited to Black Americans and their conditions, because the symbiotic processes of institutional racism and capital accumulation affect all American working and poor people.

The road to Black liberation must also be a road to socialist revolution. But what strategy is required, keeping in mind the special history of American society, and the convergence of racism, sexism, and economic exploitation which comprises the material terrain of this nation? I would suggest ten points of departure, programmatically and theoretically, which may provide some tentative suggestions for social transformation and the end to the "underdevelopment" of Black America:

1. Any authentic social revolution in the United States must be both democratic and popular in character and composition. A majority of Americans, Black, Latino, and white, must endorse socialism. By this statement, I do not imply that a majority of Americans will become socialists or Marxists. I mean that a clear majority of American people, with a large base in the working class, will support the general program of socialist construction. That expression of support may be electoral, but it should *not* be interpreted narrowly by social democrats to mean a constitutional majority within the electoral apparatus as it now exists. Visions of a revolutionary Black, radical feminist, or "Marxist President of the United States" are illusions fostered by the implicit acquisition of the logic of the bourgeois "democratic" process among some American progressives.

2. The American state apparatus is capitalist and racist in its operations and social trajectory, yet it also manifests the class contradictions and struggles which are always present within bourgeois civil society as a whole. U.S. bourgeois "democracy" is oppressive and under Reagan is even moving toward unambiguous authoritarianism, yet is not specifically fascist in the classical sense. Progressives can have a direct impact upon public policies and the behavior of the state in certain respects, via electoral participation, lobbying, civil disobedience, mass demonstrations, etc. The state bureaucracy under a bourgeois "democracy" often accommodates the demands of the left into its own public policies. Progressives can gain positions within the state, especially at municipal and

state levels, which can help fund and support grassroots interests and indirectly assist in the development of a socialist majority.

Critical support for progressive and anticapitalist politicians (e.g., Ronald Dellums) who run for office within the Democratic Party *at the present time*, may be a necessary and constructive activity in building an anti-corporate consensus within the working class. Yet to view either major capitalist party as the *primary* or fundamental terrain for building socialism would be to court disaster. The Democratic Party will never be transformed into an appropriate vehicle for achieving the political hegemony of Blacks, Latinos, feminists, and the working class. This requires the creation of an antiracist and antisexist political formation which is distinctly anticapitalist, and represents the interests of working and poor people.

3. Direct confrontations with the coercive agencies of state order are inevitable in the future. Yet any socialist strategy which deliberately provokes the repressive powers of the capitalist/racist state against working and poor people cannot win in the United States. A series of urban rebellions can shake the perception of the American working class in capitalism as an inherently "fair" and "democratic" system, but these will not topple the powers of the state. The U.S. government cannot be directly equated, in short, with czarist Russia or Somoza's Nicaragua. A putschist strategy by the left will not only fail in overthrowing the racist/capitalist state, but will create the chaotic political conditions essential for the installation of U.S. fascism. From Gracchus Babeuf to Auguste Blanqui, ultraleftists have confused social revolution with conspiratorial coups which implicitly express an unstated distrust and even hatred for the people. "When most Americans think about a revolution, all they can think of is a *coup d'état*," write James and Grace Lee Boggs. "But people do not make anything as serious as a revolution to rub out a government or system. The only justification for a revolution is the fact that social, political, and economic contradictions have accumulated to the point that the existing government and the existing institutions obviously cannot resolve them. Therefore it is not so much that the revolution overthrows the government and the system as that the government and the system, by their failure and their misdeeds, drive the people to rescind their mandate to rule" (Boggs and Boggs, 1974, p. 260).

4. A long and painful ideological struggle must be mounted by progressives to create a "counter-hegemony" essential for socialism. Every

aspect of the capitalist civil society—educational institutions, the church, the media, social and cultural organizations—must be undermined. This "war of position," to use Antonio Gramsci's concept, must be viewed as the development of a popular "historic bloc" or "revolutionary social bloc" which is comprised of all progressive forces of divergent class and racial groups: women, Blacks, Hispanics, trade unions, Native Americans, antinuclear energy groups, environmentalists, anticorporate "populists," socialists, Communists, community and neighborhood associations, etc. A common program among these divergent forces would not be an informal alliance or a temporary convergence of formations as in a classical popular front. It would become the crystallization of a mass revolutionary bloc which would explicitly call for the transformation of the system as it now exists. It would wage a "war of position" for state legitimacy, for the majoritarian mandate to overturn the state. Within its structured forms, the embryonic models of what a socialist society would look like would be developed.

5. The immediate and preliminary goal of this historic bloc would be the achievement of "nonreformist reforms" which can be won within the present capitalist state. These would include, for instance, the passage of: the Equal Rights Amendment, abortion rights, antidiscriminatory legislation against gays and lesbians, strict restrictions to halt plant closings, affirmative action, massive job training programs, universal health care, the abandonment of nuclear power plant construction, and so forth. The successful achievement of these legislative socioeconomic reforms does *not* create a socialist society or state. But combined with legislation which restricts the legal prerogatives of private capital, and a mass mobilization of popular forces in the streets as well as in the legislatures, it will create the social and material foundations for a logical "alternative" to the bourgeois authority and hegemony. Throughout this initial process, a transitional program must be devised to divide and "win over" proletarian sections of the coercive apparatuses of the state, such as working class volunteers within the armed forces. The essential base of the historic bloc, however, must be the working class—not the petty bourgeoisie.

6. Progressives can only succeed in constructing this historic bloc if they articulate their demands in a popular and historical discourse, in a language readily accessible to the majority of American workers and

nonwhite people. This is not an issue of "public relations." The symbols of the American tradition of struggle from past generations must be planted deeply in the socialist praxis of the future. Thomas Paine's moving essays which denounced British tyranny must become our contemporary anti-imperialist vision. Frederick Douglas's belief in the humanity of Blacks and women must become our own worldview. Ida B. Wells's courage in the face of the Memphis lynch mob must become our inner strength. Osceola's fierce determination to fight for the preservation of the Seminole nation must become our will.

The "Other America" of Nat Turner, Malcolm X, Fannie Lou Hamer, Eugene V. Debs, Sojourner Truth, and Harry Bridges must be the historical starting point for our fresh efforts to build a genuine peoples' democracy, and a socialist economic system. We cannot create a revolution in the United States if we mistakenly view the enemy as Reagan alone, or all males, or all white people, rather than the *State*. In the midst of another social revolution, Amílcar Cabral observed that the people of Guinea-Bissau "criticise Salazar and say bad things about him. He is a man like any other....But we are not fighting against Salazar, we are fighting against the Portuguese colonial system. We don't dream that when Salazar disappears Portuguese colonialism will disappear" (Cabral, 1969, p. 79). The Boggs make the same observation somewhat differently. "A revolutionist does not hate the country in which the illegitimate and oppressive system and government continues to rule. Far less does the revolutionist hate the people of the country. On the contrary, a revolutionist loves the country and the people, but hates what some people are doing to the country and to the people (Boggs and Boggs, 1974, pp. 260–61).

7. Any Common Program or set of "transitional demands" developed by the anticapitalist bloc must be based from the beginning on the basic contradictions which have dominated American political and civil societies throughout the twentieth century. This program must be (a) uncompromisingly antiracist, (b) antisexist, (c) anticorporate—that is, it must call for fundamental and powerful restrictions on the rights of private capital, and (d) it must promote the necessity for world peace, and advocate an end to the escalating conventional and nuclear arms race with the Soviet Union. Support must be given to all legitimate national liberation struggles, and opposition to any wars of imperialist aggression

waged by Western capitalist nations and their clients against the Third World (e.g., the El Salvadorian junta's bloody suppression of that nation's peasantry and working class); the South African reich's terror against the peoples of Angola, Namibia, and Azania. In short, the bloc must commit itself in theory and practice to struggle against racism, sexism, U.S. imperialism, and capitalism. The principal force for oppression in the world is not the Soviet Union: it is the racist/capitalist state, best represented by the United States and South Africa.

8. Racism and patriarchy are both *precapitalist* in their social and ideological origin. The successful seizure of state power by the U.S. working class and the creation of workers' democracy within the economic sphere would destroy the *modern* foundations for racial prejudice and sexism; however, it would not obliterate the massive ideological burden of either form of oppression in the practices of millions of whites and males. Separate and even autonomous apparatuses must be created after the revolution to effectively uproot racism and patriarchy. In practice, this means that the historic bloc in the presocialist period, the war of position, must build antiracist and antisexist structures within their own organizations. Organizations comprised solely of Blacks, Hispanics, and/or women must be an essential part of the struggle to build a new society.

9. Every decisive gain achieved by the anticapitalist forces will be countered by the state against the working class. This repression will be significantly greater against Blacks and other national minorities than experienced by other sectors of the working class. Socialists must come to the conclusion at the outset that there will be no peaceful culmination in the achievement of state power. If every Congressional district elected a socialist, and if the executive and judicial branches of government were dominated by Marxists, capital would not sit by benignly and watch its power erode or be destroyed through legal measures. Chile illustrated this feature of capitalist "democracy" decisively. Major corporations will not turn over the keys to their factories willingly to the workers.

The final question of power will be determined in a "war of maneuver," at a point in history wherein the capitalist ruling class will find no alternatives left except raw coercion. C. L. R. James makes his point in his brief discussion of the past European revolutions. "Why did not Charles I and his followers behave reasonably to Cromwell? As late as 1646, two years after Marston Moor, Mrs. Cromwell and Mrs. Ireton had tea with Charles at Hampton Court. Cromwell, great revolutionary but great bourgeois, was willing to come to terms. Why did not Louis and Marie Antoinette and the court behave reasonably to the moderate revolutionaries?" James asked. "Why indeed? The monarchy in France had to be torn up by the roots" (James, 1967, p. 127). The racist/capitalist ruling elite in this country will do *whatever is necessary to stay in power.* Today it uses racist ideology to divide Blacks and whites, relies upon patriarchy to perpetuate males' suppression of women, and urges white workers to literally destroy a half century of labor reforms in the workplace through unionization by the relocation of factories and by pressuring the rank-and-file to accept contractual "give-backs" to corporate directors and owners. Tomorrow it may cloak itself in the flag and the Constitution while negating the civil liberties of millions of nonwhite, poor, and working people.

There can be no long term "Historic Compromise" with capitalism. The choice for Blacks is either socialism or some selective form of genocide; for the U.S. proletariat, workers' democracy or some form of authoritarianism or fascism.

10. We must always remind ourselves that history is an organic process, the evolution of the forces of production as they affect and in turn are influenced by the civil and political institutions, ideologies, and the cultures of human beings. Nothing in Black history, American history, or world history has ever been predetermined by any single factor or force. "Underdevelopment" and "socialism," when reduced to bare economic categories, outside of a particular history become meaningless abstractions. The socialism we construct will have to encounter racial, sexual, and class components which do not exist anywhere else in the world, exactly as they appear here. If we apply some rigid "iron laws" of revolution gleaned from the dusty textbooks of other revolutionaries, in the name of Marxism, we will not only succumb to a left form of economic determinism but will fail to build an alternative to the oppressive state which we seek to overturn. "Men make their own history," Marx observed in *The Eighteenth Brumaire of Louis Bonaparte,* "but they do not make it just as they please; they do not make it under circumstances chosen by themselves, but under circumstances directly encountered, given and transmitted from the past." I have devoted a great deal of space in these

pages toward analyzing Black history, therefore, because the transition to socialism and an end to Black underdevelopment did not begin in the 1980s, but in the racial and class struggles of past generations.

Our challenge is to interpret society in order to change it. But we must grasp that the particular manifestations of the American war of maneuver, the transition to socialism, will not be fixed or predetermined. C. L. R. James emphasized this point in his discussion of the Russian revolution. "The thing that we have to remember" about the development of the Petrograd's Soviet or workers' council of 1905, James noted, "is that nobody invented it. Nobody organized it. Nobody taught it to the workers. It was formed spontaneously...." A workers' democracy in America will not look precisely like anything we can ever imagine at this moment. A revolutionary rupture with the petty bourgeoisie's tendencies toward accommodation within Black America will generate new Black social organizations, new Black political institutions and workers' councils which many Marxists and revolutionary Black nationalists will not comprehend, and may at some point even oppose as "deviations" from their "master plan." We must consciously learn from other peoples' revolutionary experiences without reifying them into a pseudo-revolutionary catechism.

REFERENCES

Boggs, James, Grace Lee Boggs. 1974. *Revolution and Evolution in the Twentieth Century.* New York: Monthly Review Press.

Cabral, Amílcar. 1969. *Revolution in Guinea.* London: Stage 1.

James, C. L. R. 1963. *The Black Jacobins: Toussaint L'Ouverture and the San Domingo Revolution.* 2d ed., rev. New York: Vintage Books.

THEORETICAL
DIRECTIONS

23

THE NEW DEPENDENCY

Theotônio dos Santos

Two contributions emerge in this excerpt from the seminal article by Dos Santos, the Brazilian political economist. First, a definition and conceptualization of dependence, and, second, the identification of three historical forms of dependency. Dos Santos developed these ideas in Chile and Mexico where he was in exile for many years after the Brazilian military coup of 1964 and the Chilean coup of 1973.

THIS PAPER ATTEMPTS TO DEMONSTRATE that the dependence of Latin American countries on other countries cannot be overcome without a qualitative change in their internal structures and external relations. We shall attempt to show that the relations of dependence to which these countries are subjected conform to a type of international and internal structure which leads them to underdevelopment or more precisely to a dependent structure that deepens and aggravates the fundamental problems of their peoples.

WHAT IS DEPENDENCE?

By dependence we mean a situation in which the economy of certain countries is conditioned by the development and expansion of another economy to which the former is subjected. The relation of interdepen-

From Theotônio dos Santos, "The Structure of Dependence," *American Economic Review* 60 (May 1970): 231–36. Reprinted with permission of the American Economic Association.

dence between two or more economies, and between these and world trade, assumes the form of dependence when some countries (the dominant ones) can expand and can be self-sustaining, while other countries (the dependent ones) can do this only as a reflection of that expansion, which can have either a positive or negative effect on their immediate development.

The concept of dependence permits us to see the internal situation of these countries as part of world economy. In the Marxian tradition, the theory of imperialism has been developed as a study of the process of expansion of the imperialist centers and of their world domination. In the epoch of the revolutionary movement of the Third World, we have to develop the theory of laws of internal development in those countries that are the object of such expansion and are governed by them. This theoretical step transcends the theory of development which seeks to explain the situation of the underdeveloped countries as a product of their slowness or failure to adopt the patterns of efficiency characteristic of developed countries (or to "modernize" or "develop" themselves). Although capitalist development theory admits the existence of an "external" dependence, it is unable to perceive underdevelopment in the way our present theory perceives it, as a consequence and part of the process of the world expansion of capitalism—a part that is necessary to and integrally linked with it.

In analyzing the process of constituting a world economy that integrates the so-called national economies in a world market of commodities, capital, and even of labor power, we see that the relations produced by this market are unequal and combined—unequal because development of parts of the system occurs at the expense of other parts. Trade relations are based on monopolistic control of the market, which leads to the transfer of surplus generated in the dependent countries to the dominant countries; financial relations are, from the viewpoint of the dominant power, based on loans and the export of capital, which permit them to receive interest and profits, thus increasing their domestic surplus and strengthening their control over the economies of the other countries. For the dependent countries these relations represent an export of profits and interest which carries off part of the surplus generated domestically and leads to a loss of control over their productive resources. In order to permit these disadvantageous relations, the dependent countries must generate large surpluses, not in such a way as to create higher levels of technology but rather superexploited manpower. The result is to limit the development of their internal market and their technical and cultural capacity, as well as the moral and physical health of their people. We call this combined development because it is the combination of these inequalities and the transfer of resources from the most backward and dependent sectors to the most advanced and dominant ones which explains the inequality, deepens it, and transforms it into a necessary and structural element of the world economy.

HISTORIC FORMS OF DEPENDENCE

Historic forms of dependence are conditioned by: (1) the basic forms of this world economy which has its own laws of development, (2) the type of economic relations dominant in the capitalist centers and the ways in which the latter expand outward, and (3) the types of economic relations existing inside the peripheral countries which are incorporated into the situation of dependence within the network of international economic relations generated by capitalist expansion. It is not within the purview of this paper to study these forms in detail but only to distinguish broad characteristics of development.

Drawing on an earlier study, we may distinguish: (1) Colonial dependence, trade export in nature, in which commercial and *financial capital* in alliance with the colonialist state dominated the economic relations of the Europeans and the colonies, by means of a trade monopoly complemented by a colonial monopoly of land, mines, and manpower (serf or slave) in the colonized countries. (2) Financial-industrial dependence which consolidated itself at the end of the nineteenth century, characterized by the domination of big capital in the hegemonic centers and its expansion abroad through investment in the production of raw materials and agricultural products for consumption in the hegemonic centers. A productive structure grew up in the dependent countries devoted to the export of these products (which Levin labeled export economies; other analysis in other regions, producing what ECLA has entitled "foreign-oriented development" (*desarolloe hacia afuera*). In the postwar period a new type of dependence has been consolidated, based on multinational corporations which began to invest in industries geared to the internal market of underdeveloped countries. This form of dependence is basically technological-industrial dependence.

Each of these forms of dependence corresponds to a situation which conditioned not only the international relations of these countries but also their internal structures: the orientation of production, the forms of capital accumulation, the reproduction of the economy, and, simultaneously, their social and political structure.

24

SUBIMPERIALISM

Ruy Mauro Marini

The concept of subimperialism evolved in the thinking of Ruy Mauro Marini, a Brazilian economist who spent most of his time in exile after the Brazilian military coup of 1964. Marini believed that capitalism creates deformation and underdevelopment in the periphery and that dependent capitalism is unable to reproduce itself through accumulation. Given the impossibility of autonomous capitalism, he observed that the military dictatorship, together with domestic and foreign capital, had successfully reached outside Brazil to exploit its neighbors in a process he called subimperialism.

SUBIMPERIALISM [MAY BE DEFINED] AS a form which the dependent economy assumes in order to arrive at the stage of monopoly and finance capital. Subimperialism implies two basic components: on the one hand, a medium organic composition on the world scale of national productive apparatus, and, on the other, the exercise of a relatively autonomous expansionist policy, which is not only accompanied by a greater integration in the imperialist production system, but also is maintained under the hegemony exercised by imperialism on an international scale. Posed in these terms, it seems to us that independently of the efforts of Argentina and other countries to accede to the subimperialist rank only Brazil expresses fully, in Latin America, a phenomenon of this nature.

From Ruy Mauro Marini, "World Capitalist Accumulation and Sub-Imperialism," *Two Thirds* 1 (fall 1978): 34–36.

For the lack of more precise data, the organic composition of the capital of a nation can be inferred from the share of its manufactured products in its GNP.

The figures of UNCTAD, for the middle of the last decade, point out that the ninety-two underdeveloped countries, excluding Yugoslavia, of course, (which is also, the only socialist country looked at) and the Philippines (given the predominance here of the industry of Maquila) show a share equal or superior to 25 percent. Among them, the three Latin American countries of relatively greater development, from the strictly economic point of view, featured subimperialist traits: Brazil, Argentina, and Mexico. Iran constitutes, together with Brazil, a typical case of subimperialism; although something similar could be said of Israel. Spain, because of historical factors and its geographical position, is a very particular case and cannot be compared with the rest.

Brazilian subimperialism is not only the expression of an economic phenomenon. It results, in good measure, from the process of class struggle in the country and from the political project defined by the technocratic-military team which assumed power in 1964, combined with the conjunctural conditions in the world economy and in world politics. The political conditions are related to the recovery of imperialism, to the passage from monopolization to the hierarchical integration we have already mentioned, and more specifically, to the reaction, in the face of the Cuban revolution and the rising of the masses which occurred in Latin America in the past decade; we are not going to stop now to analyze these questions. The economic conditions on the other hand, are elated to the expansion of the world capitalism in the 1970s and to its particular expression: the financial *boom*.

We have indicated that the *boom* began in the middle of he past decade, but, in the beginning, this affected few underdeveloped countries. It is in 1970 that private capital, particularly euro-money, begins to flow to them.

In order to attract the flow of capital, the Brazilian institutional and juridical structure had begun to arm itself from the time the military regime assumed power. In 1965, the rules on foreign capital were expanded, through the modification of Law No. 4131 of 1962, which already furnished enough advantageous conditions and opened the door to the trading of currency loans between foreign and local enterprises. Beginning in 1967, new measures made it easier for commercial banks and investment banks to get and to pass on to enterprises in the country credits to finance fixed and circulating capital. Then a true capital market sprang up in the country.

While banking credit was extended to the private sector, as credit, assured by finance and investment companies, foreign capital flowed into the country in mass. Though they increased in volume, governmental credits and those of international institutions lost importance relative to private capital. Between 1966 and 1970, their share in external financing had been 26.3 percent, but this dropped to 15.6 percent in 1971 and 9.2 percent in 1972. Meanwhile, medium- and long-term foreign investment which added up to 1,028 million dollars in 1966–1970, grew in a geometric progression: 2,319 million in 1971 and 4,788 million dollars in 1972; the item which presented the most spectacular increase was loans and money financing, which rose from 479 to 1379 and to 3,485 million dollars in the periods indicated. While official external credits were channeled toward investment in infrastructure and basic industries, almost all (82.3 percent) of the private capital was directed to the manufacturing industry particularly to machinery, electric and communications materials, transportation, chemicals, rubber, pharmaceuticals, and metallurgy.

We understand, then, the necessity of assuring the full circulation of the capital thus invested, that is to say, of opening a path for its realization. We have already pointed out that the state actually intervened in this sense, creating or substituting demand (internal and external) for production. It occupied itself as well, with assuring investment areas abroad through the operations of state enterprise and intergovernmental credits or guarantees to private operations in Latin America and Africa. Thrown into the orbit of international finance capital, Brazilian capitalism did everything to attract the monetary flow, and since it did not have the capacity to assimilate and integrate so much productive capital, it then had to reintegrate it within the international movement of capital. With its dependent and subordinate state style, Brazil entered the capital export stage, as well as the plundering of raw materials and energy sources in the exterior, like petroleum, iron, and natural gas.

It is natural that, over the base of that dynamic economy, Brazil put into practice policy of power. But reducing subimperialism to this dimension and trying to replace the very concept of subimperialism by that of subpower only impoverishes completely the complex reality which we have before our eyes and does not permit an understanding of the role played today by Brazil on an international plane. Brazilian subimperialism implies policy of being a subpower; but the subpower that Brazil practices does not give us the key to the subimperialist stage which it has entered.

Recourse to the international level of analysis refers us to a fact which is frequently lost from view in economic analysis: that the process of the internationalization of capital does not imply a loss of force nor much less does it lead to the progressive disappearances of national states. This is so, above all else, because the internationalization of capital—objectively based in the integration of productive systems—does not constitute a univocal and uniform process which is exempt from contradictions. The supposition that the contrary took place, in the past, was an erroneous thesis of superimperialism which Lenin and Bukharin vigorously fought against. Bukharin, in particular, emphasized the fact that the internationalization of capital cannot be considered independent of its *nationalization* precisely basing on that contradiction the structure of the first two parts of his classic study on the theme. The dialectical play of the process of internationalization-nationalization is made manifest, he writes:

> The process of organization [of the system of world production] tends to leave the national frame; but then many more serious difficulties appear. In the first place, it is easier to overcome competition on the national terrain than on the world one (international ententes are generally formed on the basis of national monopolies already constituted; secondly, the difference in the economic structure and, consequently, in outlay for production for these advanced national groups, *and thirdly, the agglomeration with the state and its borders constitutes, in itself, a greater monopoly each time, which assures supplementary benefits.*

For Bukharin, this process implied that the internationalization of economic life had as its counterpart "a tendency to form tightly cohesive groups, armed to the teeth and ready at every moment to leap one over the other," in virtue of the suppression or absorption of weaker or backward states by the imperialist centers, the period of world history which led to the war in 1939 confirmed the correctness of that forecast, just as the new stage, which the end of the conflict opened, reviewed briefly at the beginning of this work, showed how powerful the tendency toward integration of contemporary capitalism is. But, the integration which caused greater capitalist development in the subordinate zones, like Latin America, also manifested its counter tendencies in greater degree in these zones, in particular those countertendencies that worked in the sense of reinforcing the national state.

When speaking of countertendencies, we should clear what is meant. The re-inforcement of the national state in dependent countries, acts, in fact, as one of the elements which, in a contradictory manner, assures the integration of system of production. From the economic point of view, the capital exported by imperialist countries to the dependent zones demands from the national state a growing capacity in infrastructure, defense of the internal market, financial and commercial negotiations with other countries, internal financing and the creation of favorable political conditions for foreign investment (in particular in the labor field). If the export of capital from the imperialist country marks the moment when the tendency of capital to internationalize itself is expressed in a pure form, its conversion into productive capital, which is the mark of a determined national economy, represents its negation. The transferring of that capital depends on this economy—and therefore on the state which governs—in order to guarantee its reproduction. The exception (once production enclaves of raw materials cease, as in the case of petroleum, in which the role of the national dependent state in the reproduction of capital was accentuated) is the capital which operates in the maquila industry which is not effectively integrated in the national economy and which finds itself then incorporated into the capitalist matrix, with headquarters in the imperialist economy. The fact that capital invested in the maquila utilizes the manpower of the dependent economy has practically the same effect as if this manpower transferred physically to the imperialist economy, in order to be exploited there by the matrix of capital.

Furthermore, it is not only the interest of "nationalized" foreign capital which determine the reinforcement of the national dependent state. Other contradictory elements intervene here resulting from the conflict of interests between national and foreign capital. We are not attempting here a return to the old thesis of the antagonism between the national bourgeoisie and imperialism though one observes contradictions in this sense at the lower levels of the national bourgeoisie which are of a markedly secondary character. The basic problem is different: precisely by consciously assuming the decision to submit to the integrative tendency which the imperialist centers encourage the bourgeoisie of dependent countries needs to concentrate and organize its forces in order to make this of benefit to them. Its disadvantages before the imperialist bourgeoisie are too great to wish to negotiate directly with it. Because of this, they opt for the reinforcement of the national state as an intermediary instrument. This, in addition to the accentuation of the process of concentration and centralization of capital which occurs in independent countries, and to the "agglomeration" of capital with the national state, to which Bukharin alludes; this phenomenon is reproduced in these countries, entangling foreign and national capital.

We must avoid mechanistic reasoning here: the product of that agglomeration is not the pure and simple subjection the state to capital. Although, it is evident that the state is converted into what Bukharin calls the "the national capitalist trust," the very fact that it would be called upon to order and arbitrate national and economic life (to the point where its arbitration is compatible with subordination to imperialist states) encourages a situation in which its *relative autonomy* before distinct capitalist groups is accentuated. To a great degree, the phenomenon of the modern Latin American military state has its explanation therein (constituting the imperialist counterrevolution in the region in another level of the analysis).

It has been as a function of this, that the Brazilian state was able to launch the project, not of a subimperialist structure but of a subimperialist *policy* with a degree of rationality greatly superior to that which national and foreign capital operating in Brazil could impose. It also permits it to compel capitalist groups to implement that project, with respect to the economic interests of these same groups, as well as with respect to the political interests (or, if you please, the interests of power) that characterize the military-technocratic elite that has control of the state apparatus. To a degree much more profound than in Brazil, this phenomenon has already been noted in Czarist Russia, as Rosa Luxemburg pointed out.

More than just an analytical category, subimperialism is a historical phenomenon and, insofar as it is, its study demands the careful examination of its process of development. We do not intend to continue that study here; what we are presenting are the results of earlier works. It seems useful to us, however, to indicate that the new capitalist crisis, in whose lap we find ourselves, constitutes an obligatory point of reference. In this sense, we must pay particular attention to the global planning the United States has attempted when faced with the crisis: what is expressed through multipolarity, put into practice through the foreign policy which remains marked by the figure of ex-Secretary of State Henry Kissinger, and which establishes a return to monopolization such as one finds today with the Carter Administration. It is in that context that one is able to understand the subimperialist dynamic of Brazil in the last five years, and in particular, the room to maneuver which the Brazilian state counts on in order to move its project ahead.

In any case, any study about the manner in which the capitalist crisis affects a world reality that has been forged in the postwar years, demands the deepening of our knowledge of the same reality, that is of its nature and its tendencies. It is illusory to believe that the world capitalist economy could go back and reestablish the situation existing twenty-five years ago. The very development of the crisis, whose end even now is not yet in view, intensifies the action of the factors that work for the conformation of a new economy, whose results are already beginning to be paraded in front of our eyes. The more we are able to understand those results during the process of their gestation, and well before they crystallize, the more we will be in condition to furnish the means of active intervention in the crises to the social forces which are in struggle in our countries to overcome of backwardness and dependency, and therefore, for the suppression of capitalism.

Every profound capitalist crisis opens possibilities for this to be realized or, at the least, to be seriously posed. There is not any reason to suggest that, in the course of the present crisis, the peoples of Latin America should proceed in another manner.

25

ASSOCIATED DEPENDENT CAPITALIST DEVELOPMENT
Fernando Henrique Cardoso

The Brazilian sociologist, Fernando Henrique Cardoso, delved into Lenin's understanding of imperialism and concluded that while Leninist theory had been relevant in the early twentieth century, imperialism had reached a new stage after the Second World War in which multinational and big corporate capital, rather than bank control and finance capital, accounted for accumulation in the periphery. Countering the proposition that imperialist capitalism promotes only underdevelopment in the periphery, Cardoso elaborated on the possibility of "associated dependent development" based on the Brazilian experience.

THE MAIN POINTS OF LENIN'S characterization of imperialism that are essential to the present discussion can be summarized as follows:

a. The capitalist economy in its "advanced stages" involves a concentration of capital and production (points that were well established by Marx in *Capital*) in such a way that the competitive market is replaced in its basic branches by a monopolistic one.
b. This trend was historically accomplished through internal differentiation of capitalist functions, leading not only to the formation of a financial stratum among entrepreneurs but to the marked prominence of the banking system in the capitalist mode

From Fernando Henrique Cardoso, "Dependency and Development in Latin America," *New Left Review* 74 (July–August): 84–85, 87, 88–91. Reprinted with permission of New Left Review.

of production. Furthermore, the fusion of industrial capital with financial capital under the control of the latter turned out to be the decisive feature of the political and economic relations within capitalist classes, with all the practical consequences that such a system of relations has in terms of state organization, politics, and ideology.

c. Capitalism thus reached its "ultimate stage of development" both internally and externally. Internally, control of the productive system by financiers turned the productive forces and the capital accumulation process toward the search for new possibilities for investment. The problem of "capital realization" became in this way an imperative necessity to permit the continuing of capitalist expansion. In addition there were internal limits that impeded the continuous reinvestment of new capital (impoverishment of the masses, a faster rate of capital growth than that of the internal market, and so on). *External outlets* had to be found to ensure the continuity of capitalist advance and accumulation.

d. The increased and increasing speed of the development of productive forces under monopolistic control also pushed the advanced capitalist countries toward the political control of foreign lands. The search for control over *raw materials* is yet another reason why capitalism in its monopolistic stage becomes expansionist.

In short, Lenin's explanations of why advanced capitalist economies were impelled toward the control of backward lands, was based on two main factors. One stressed movements of capital, the other outlined the productive process. Both were not only linked to each other but also related to the global transformation of the capitalist system that had led to the control of the productive system by financiers. It is not difficult to see that such modifications deeply affected state organization and functions as well as the relationship among nations, since a main thrust of capitalist development in the stage of imperialism was toward the territorial division of the world among the leading capitalist countries. This process guaranteed capital flows from the overcapitalized economies to backward countries and assured provision of raw materials in return.

NEW PATTERNS OF CAPITAL ACCUMULATION

In spite of the accuracy of Lenin's insights as measured against historical events during the first half of the century in many parts of the world, some important recent changes have deeply affected the pattern of relationships between imperialist and dependent nations. These changes demand a reappraisal of emergent structures and their main tendencies. Even if these modifications are not so deep as the shift that enabled Lenin to characterize a new stage of capitalism during the period of imperialist expansion, they are marked enough to warrant a major modification of the established analyses of capitalism and imperialism. Nevertheless, contemporary international capitalist expansion and control of dependent economies undoubtedly prove that this new pattern of economic relationships among nations remains imperialist. However, the main points of Lenin's characterization of imperialism and capitalism are no longer fully adequate to describe and explain the present forms of capital accumulation and external expansion.

NEW FORMS OF ECONOMIC DEPENDENCY

Recent figures demonstrate that foreign investment in the new nations and in Latin America is moving rapidly away from oil, raw materials, and agriculture and in the direction of the industrial sectors. Even where the bulk of assets continues to remain in the traditional sectors of imperialist investment, the rate of expansion of the industrial sector is rapid. This is true not only for Latin America but also for Africa and Asia.

The point is not only that multinational corporations are investing in the industrial sectors of dominated economies, instead of in the traditional agricultural and mineral sectors. Beyond that, even when "traditional" sectors of dependent economies, they are operating in technically and organizationally advanced modes, sometimes accepting local participation in their enterprises. Of course, these transformations do not mean that previous types of imperialistic investment, i.e., in oil or metals, are disappearing, even in the cases of the most industrialized dependent economies, i.e., Argentina, Brazil, and Mexico in Latin America. However, the dominant traits of imperialism in those countries, as the process of industrialization continues, cannot be adequately described and interpreted on the basis of frames of reference that posit the exchange of raw material for industrialized goods as the main feature of trade, and suppose virtually complete external ownership of the dependent economies' means of production.

Even the mineral sector (such as in Brazil, copper in Chile during Frei's government, or petro-chemicals in various countries) is now being submitted to new patterns of economic ownership. The distinguishing feature of these new forms is the joint venture enterprise, comprising local state capital, private national capital, and monopoly international investment (under foreign control in the last analysis).

As a consequence, in some dependent economies—among these, the so-called developing countries of Latin America—foreign investment no longer remains a simple zero-sum game of exploitation as was the pattern in classical imperialism. Strictly speaking—if we consider the purely economic indicators—it is not difficult to show that *development* and *monopoly penetration* in the industrial sectors of dependent economies are not incompatible. The idea that there occurs as kind of development of underdevelopment, apart from the play on words, is not helpful. In fact, *dependency, monopoly capitalism,* and *development* are not contradictory terms: there occurs a kind of *dependent capitalist development* in the sectors of the Third World integrated into new forms of monopolistic expansion.

As a result in countries like Argentina, Brazil, Mexico, South Africa, India, and some others, there is an internal structural fragmentation, connecting the most "advanced" parts of their economies to the international capitalist system. Separate although subordinated to these advanced sectors, the backward economic and social sectors of the dependent countries then play the role of "internal colonies." The gap between both will probably increase, creating a new type of dualism, quite different from the imaginary one sustained by some non-Marxist authors. The new structural "duality" corresponds to a kind of internal differentiation of the same unity. It results directly, of course, from capitalist expansion and is functional to that expansion, in so far as it helps to keep wages at a low level and diminishes political pressures inside the "modern" sector, since the social and economic position of those who belong to the latter is always better in comparative terms.

If this is true, to what extent is it possible to sustain the idea of *devel-*

opment in tandem with dependence? The answer cannot be immediate. First of all, I am suggesting that the present trend of imperialist investment allows some degree of local participation in the process of economic production. Let us indicate a crucial feature in which present and past forms of capitalism differ. During the previous type of imperialism, the market for goods produced in dependent economies by foreign enterprise was mostly, if not fully, the market of the advanced economies: oil, copper, coffee, iron bauxite, manganese, etc., were produced to be sold and consumed in the advanced capitalist countries. This explains why the internal market of dependent economies was irrelevant for the imperialist economies, excepting the modest portion of import goods consumed by the upper class in the dominated society....

On the other hand, and in spite of internal economic development, countries tied to the international capitalism by that type of linkage remain economically dependent, insofar as the production of the means of production (technology) are concentrated in advanced capitalist economies (mainly in the United States).

In terms of the Marxist scheme of capital reproduction, this means that sector I (the production of means of production)—the strategic part of the reproductive scheme—is virtually nonexistent in dependent economies. Thus, from a broad perspective, the realization of capital accumulation *demands* a productive complementarity which does not exist within the country. In Lenin's interpretation the imperialist economies needed external expansion for the realization of capital accumulation. Conversely, within the dependent economies capital returns to the metropole in order to complete the cycle of capitalist reproduction. This is the reason why "technology" is so important. Its "material" aspect is less impressive than its significance as a form of maintenance of control and as a necessary step in the process of capital accumulation. Through technological advance, corporations make secure their key roles in the global system of capital accumulation. Some degree of local prosperity is possible insofar as consumption goods locally produced by foreign investments can induce some dynamic effects in the dependent economies. But at the same time, the global process of capitalist development determines an interconnection between the sector of production of consumption goods and the capital goods sector, reproducing in this way the links of dependency.

One of the main factors which explained imperialist expansion in Lenin's theory was the search for capitalist investment. Now since foreign capital goes to the industrial sector of dependent economies in search of external markets, some considerable changes have occurred. First, in comparison with expanding assets of foreign corporations, the net amount of foreign capital actually invested in the dependent economies is decreasing: local savings and the reinvestment of profits realized in local markets provides resources for the growth of foreign assets with limited external flows of new capital. This is intimately related to the previously discussed process of expansion of the local market and it is also related to the mounting of "joint ventures" linking local capitalists and foreign enterprise.

Secondly, but no less important, statistics demonstrate that dependent economies during the period of monopolistic imperialist expansion are *exporting* capital to the dominant economies.

As a reaction against that process, some dependent countries have tried to limit exportable profits. Nevertheless, international corporations had the foresight to sense that the principal way was to send returns abroad is through the payment of licenses, patents, royalties, and related items. These institutional devices, together with the increasing indebtedness of the exploited nations vis-à-vis international agencies and banks (in fact controlled by the big imperialist countries), have altered the main forms of exploitation.

It is not the purpose of this presentation to discuss all the consequences of this for a monopoly capitalist economy. However, some repercussions of the new pattern of imperialism on the United States and other central economies are obvious. If a real problem of capital realization exists under monopoly capitalism, the new form of dependency will increase the necessity to find new fields of application for the capital accumulated in the metropolitan economies. Witness the push toward more "technical obsolescence" administered by corporations. Military expenditures are another means of finding new outlets for capital.

26

IMPERIALISM AND UNEQUAL EXCHANGE
Arghiri Emmanuel

The contribution of Arghiri Emmanuel draws on the analysis in the third volume of Marx's Capital *and an examination of the "imperialism of trade" in the exploitation of poor nations. He attacked David Ricardo's thesis on comparative costs and natural advantages by showing the disadvantages faced by poorer nations. In this selection, he argues that unequal exchange is an elementary transfer mechanism that facilitates development in the advanced countries and leads to exploitation in the less developed countries.*

...THINGS HAVE NOT IMPROVED MUCH since [1920], especially in the Marxist camp, which one might have expected to be the first to get down to the task of forging the theoretical weapon needed by the "proletarian nations," in the way that Marx did last century on behalf of the proletarians within each nation.

As far as the underdeveloped countries are concerned, however, awareness is advancing inexorably. Already these have ceased to think of themselves merely as countries that happen to be relatively poor, and instead see themselves as *the poor of the world*, which means that they expect the world to take responsibility for them. International aid has ceased to be regarded as a one-sided and gratuitous act on the part of

From Arghiri Emmanuel, *Unequal Exchange: A Study of the Imperialism of Trade* (New York: Monthly Review Press, 1972), pp 264–69. Copyright © 1972 by Monthly Review Press. Reprinted with permission of Monthly Review Foundation.

the rich countries and is seen as an obligation that corresponds to a certain right of compensation.

Compensation for what? That is indeed the question, and this is
what I have tried to answer. To do it I had to discover and take to pieces
the mechanism whereby one nation exploits another (what has been
called "exploitation at a distance"), the task that Marx set aside for the
end of his work but did not have time to complete. I do not claim that
unequal exchange explains by itself the entire difference between the
standards of living of the rich countries and the poor ones, even though,
if we base ourselves on certain statistical data that are available, however fragmentary and arguable these may be, we arrive at a loss in
double factoral terms (if not in terms of trade) that is enormous in relation to the poverty of the underdeveloped countries while being far
from negligible in relation to the wealth of the advanced countries.
Even if we arrive that unequal exchange is only of the mechanisms
whereby value is transferred from one group of countries to another,
and that its *direct* effects account for only part of the difference in standards of living. I think it is possible to state that unequal exchange is the
elementary transfer mechanism, and that, as such, it enables the advanced
countries to begin and regularly to give new impetus to that *unevenness of
development* that sets in motion all the other mechanisms of exploitation
and fully explains the way that wealth is distributed.

Now, established economic science takes no note of the exchange of
nonequivalents, except where this occurs as a momentary accident of
market-price fluctuations, or as the effect of imperfect competition due
either to economic monopoly or to political domination. Since Condillac
said that, in exchange generally, equal value is not given for equal value,
but less for more, and for this was struck down by the thunderbolts of
Le Trosne, for whom things exchanged were equivalent, economists
have been divided into objectivists and subjectivists, but unequal
exchange is denied by both parties—by one party because for them
exchange is always equal in a situation of equilibrium, and by the other
because for them equal exchange does not exist and, equivalence being
an *ex post* market phenomenon, there is no such thing as either unequal
or equal exchange in itself. The worsening in the terms of trade over a
long period is either seen as a statistical illusion or is relegated to the
jungle of those structural tendencies of the elasticities of demand, as

improbable as they are ill defined, which concern one category of products to perpetual decline and another to perpetual rise.

As the worsening in factoral terms cannot be denied, the supporters of the first-mentioned position content themselves with repeating the basic argument of the theory of comparative costs, namely, that the gap between incomes is due to the difference in respective national averages of comparative productivity for the article exported and the article imported. If this determination were operating today, most of the underdeveloped countries ought to be able to reward their factors at a rate far superior to that of the industrial countries, since the inferiority of the advanced countries in the article imported (coffee, sugar, oil, exotic fruits) is generally much greater than their superior in the article exported (machinery, hardware, vehicles, etc.).

As for the second conception, which is blind to the very notion of productivity, knowing only the *profitability* of labor, and which afflicts a certain category of products with an inferiority allegedly inherent in their natural properties, Viner, though himself a convinced marginalist, has observed with some reason that all that has been accomplished on this basis is a dogmatic identification of agriculture with poverty and industry with wealth, to refute which one has only to mention Australia, New Zealand, and Denmark, on the one hand, and Spain, Italy, and Japan on the other. The supporters of this doctrine easily forget that what worsens is not the terms of trade of certain products but those of certain countries, regardless of the kind of products they may export or import.

It has therefore been necessary to go beyond world market relations, to study world *production* relations. We have had to look at equivalence inside the nation first of all, that is, under conditions of mobility (or rather of competition) of the factors, and then outside the nation, that is, under condition on of immobility (or noncompetition) of one or more factors. Then we have had to go back to the classical and Marxist labor theory of value and study successively the case of a single factor where it is the quantities this factor that determine equilibrium prices, and the case of two or more factors, where it is still the quantities of the factors that determine equilibrium prices, but these are weighted by their respective rewards; We have thus succeeded in integrating unequal exchange and the theory of international value into the general the of value *tout court*, as propounded by the classical economists and by Marx, and proving that the former, far from being the weak spot in the latter, as the opponents of the labor theory of value have hitherto claimed, constitutes on the contrary an additional proof of its validity, since it succeeds precisely in explaining such phenomena as the long-term worsening of a certain category of prices, something that all the tricks played with the fundamental deficiencies of demand have proved unable to account for. In short, we have had to show that the formation of international value is a special case of the general theory of labor value in its developed form as the theory of price of production. This was done by using the assumption that seems to me the most realistic possible in the world of today, the assumption that the capital factor is mobile but the labor factor is immobile on the international plane.

Finally, after we had studied the relative disadvantages that the low-wage countries may suffer from free trade, it remained to refute the premise that a general and absolute advantage accrues automatically to the world as a whole from free trade and the international division of labor, by showing that under conditions of regional disparity in rewarding of the factors, and in particular the labor factor, nothing guarantees that specialization—in accordance with the rewarding of the factors shall correspond to specialization in accordance with the quantities of the factors and thereby result in the sought-for world optimum.

On the basis of the classical and Marxist doctrine of labor value, I reversed the fundamental assumption of Ricardo's theory of international trade. Instead of equal wages and unequal rates of profit, I adopted the assumption of unequal wages and of profits subject to standardization and tending to equalization. These premises led me to the opposite line on all points to the official theory of international trade. However provocative my conclusions may be, I do not think any different one can be drawn, once my assumptions are accepted.

What must the underdeveloped countries now do in face of the inequality of exchange and the continual worsening of their terms of trade? A sudden leveling up of their wage levels to those of the advanced countries being, of course, out of the question a priori, they can only seek means to keep for themselves and prevent from leaking abroad the excess surplus value that they extract from their own workers. Somebody has to benefit from these low wages. If the national capitalists cannot do this, owing to the standardization of profits, and if it is not desired that the foreign consumer shall be the beneficiary, then only two solutions are left: a tax on exports that will transfer this excess surplus value to the state; and diversification of production through transfer of factors from the traditional exporting branches to the branches that can replace imports, which will enable the national consumer to benefit from the low national wage level. Both of the methods described are suitable ways for channeling the excess surplus value into the hands of the national community, to be used for development purposes, the former through direct utilization of these additional items of revenue in order to finance investment projects, and the second through measures of redistribution that it is permissible to take since we accept the assumption that real wages, and thereby consumption, cannot he raised immediately

If, though, we consider that taxes on exports presuppose agreement between several producing countries, that consequently they are difficult to apply except where there is a natural monopoly, and that, also, they bear a more or less spectacularly aggressive character that entails the risk of provoking very sharp reactions and reprisals on the part of the consuming countries, then we are left with the second solution, that of diversification. This is a very effective weapon, for it strikes at the trading partner in two ways. On the one hand, the traditional exports diminish, while the world's needs continue unchanged for a certain period, which results in an upward pressure on prices; on the other, the traditional imports also diminish, and the partner who stays geared to an expansion of trade sees his sales fall off sharply, which compels him to reduce his prices.

In any event, the equilibrium of world transactions cannot be maintained or restored unless the diversification of the production of one country or group of countries is followed by a diversification on an equal scale in the rest of the world. Since diversification requires a certain time to be carried through properly, this gives a the finite advantage to the countries that take the initiative in it. When, however, "the rest of the world" is made up of highly developed countries whose existing specializations involve substantial investments; in which, moreover, any contraction of foreign trade brings dangerous repercussions on the level of internal activity; and in which, also, certain raw materials and certain products of the soil are absolutely lacking, regardless of any question of costs—then we can understand the ferocity with which the advanced countries and the international financial authorities...combat all the tendencies to protectionism and development directed toward the internal economy, wherever they appear, but especially in the countries of the Third World.

What then becomes of the international division of labor and the benefits, so highly praised, that it brings to mankind as a whole?

When we consider that most tropical products, among them those that today seem most traditional, result from transplants, which themselves were often the result of mere historical accidents; when we consider that the most formidable specialization ever known, that of England in cotton textile goods (Marx called his time the Age of Cotton), was an entirely voluntaristic operation, the weaving of cotton having flourished in other continents before Europe, and in several countries of Continental Europe before England; that nothing marked England out specifically for this particular specialization; that in the eighteenth century England possessed neither the relevant new material nor any experience of weaving expert from the weaving of wool; that that industry had itself been implanted just as artificially a century and a half earlier, by means of a draconic ban on the export of wool, with such sanctions as cutting off the arms of anyone who broke this ban, because the cloth industry of Flanders was so much more productive that it was able, despite transport costs, to offer a better price for English wool than could be offered by the English manufacturers themselves; that, subsequently, it was through tariffs and direct legislative coercion that England made India her supplier of cotton and Australia her storehouse of wool—something that, let it be said in passing, had the effect of ruining India but enriching Australia, which is a further proof that the "old colonial system" did not in itself imply impoverishment of the colonies unless it was associated with a low wage level in the countries concerned—when we consider all this, we can legitimately harbor a few doubts as to the intrinsic value of the international division of labor.

Even admitting that however this structure may have originated, a sudden smashing of the existing structure of specializations would entail losses for the world as a whole, it would, I think, be unwarranted to suggest to the poor countries that they sacrifice their national interests for the good of humanity.

27

UNEVEN DEVELOPMENT AND LATE CAPITALISM

Ernest Mandel

The Belgian economist Ernest Mandel contributed to two major ideas: first, an elaboration of the theory, inherent in the thought of Leon Trotsky, of combined and uneven development or the process in which various modes of production are combined and capitalist development evolves in uneven ways; and, second, the notion of late capitalism in which delayed capitalist development in the periphery is explained by unequal exchange leading to the juxtaposition of development in growth sectors and underdevelopment elsewhere. In elaborating on these ideas, Mandel shows that while monopoly capital and imperialism are pervasive, differences within nations are enhanced and socialist revolutions will eventually break out in the underdeveloped and backward nations and lead to socialist world revolution. In this way the imperialist chain and U.S. hegemony can be broken at its weakest links. He also looks at class differences within nations to understand the unevenness of development.

IT IS CLEAR THAT ONLY the most mechanistic and undialectical "marxists" would deny that the national liberation movements in colonial and semicolonial countries, their potential development into socialist revolutions (under adequate proletarian leadership), are part and parcel of the process of *world revolution* as it has unfolded for forty years, since the second Chinese revolution of 1925–27. This means that the interrelationship between the colonial revolution and the socialist revolution in the West (as well as the interrelationship between the colonial revolu-

From Ernest Mandel, "The Laws of Uneven Development," *New Left Review* 59 (January–February 1970): 20ff. Reprinted with permission from New Left Review.

tion and the political antibureaucratic revolution in the so-called socialist countries) is complex and manifold.

The difference between revolutionary Marxists and supporters of "Third Worldism" does not lie in the fact the first deny this interrelationship and the second uphold it. It lies in two basically distinct approaches to the nature of that interrelationship. Revolutionary Marxists do not believe in a fatal time-sequence, whereas "Third Worldists" do believe that imperialism has *first* to be overthrown in all, or the most important underdeveloped countries, before socialist revolution is on the agenda again in the West. Lin Piao's famous thesis that the "countryside" will have to "encircle the cities" is the most striking expression of this idea. Revolutionary Marxists do not believe that the loss of an important or even a decisive part of foreign colonial domains will *automatically* create a revolutionary situation inside the imperialist countries; they believe that these losses will only have revolutionary effects if they first trigger off internal material changes inside imperialist society itself. Between world politics and revolution in the West there is a *necessary mediation*: changes in the function of the economy, changes in the relationship of forces between classes, changes in the consciousness and militancy of different social groups....

The historical specificity of imperialism in this respect lies in the fact that although it unites the world *economy* into a single world market, it does not unify world *society* into a homogeneous capitalist milieu. Although monopoly capital succeeds in extracting super-profits, directly or indirectly, out of most of the people on earth, it does not transform most people in the world into industrial producers of surplus value. In short: although it submits all classes and all nations (except those which have broken out of its realm) to various forms of *common* exploitation, it maintains and strengthens to the utmost the *differences* between these societies. Although the United States and India are more closely interwoven today than at any time in the past, the distance which separates their technology, their life expectancy, their average culture, the way of living and of working of their inhabitants, is much wider today than it was a century ago, when there were hardly any relations at all between these two countries.

Only if we understand that imperialism brings to its widest possible application the universal *law of uneven and combined development*, can we understand [recent] world history....Only if we understand this law of uneven and combined development can we understand why, *because of* an integrated world market, the first victorious socialist revolutions could break out in three underdeveloped backward countries, Russia, Yugoslavia, and China. Only if we understand how this same law continues to operate today can we understand that the decisive battle for world socialism can only be fought by the German, British, Japanese, French, Italian, and American workers.

Lenin summarizes his position by stating that "imperialism is a superstructure of capitalism," and when it crumbles, the whole capitalist foundation still subsists. Imperialism, in other words, is a *combined* form of social development, locking together the most backward and the most modern forms of economic activity, exploitation and sociopolitical life, in variable forms, in different countries. For that reason, socialist world revolution, under imperialism, cannot be an instantaneous, simultaneous, synchronized event in all or most countries of the world. It can only be a process in which the imperialist chain is broken first in its weakest links. In order to determine what link is the weakest in each determinate phase of development, it is necessary precisely to study the economic, social, political, cultural, historical *differences* between various countries—in the last analysis: the different correlations of sociopolitical forces in these countries—which survive *in spite of* the "universal form of contradiction between labor and capital."...

THE LAWS OF MOTION OF CAPITALISM IN THIS CENTURY

There is only one basic driving force which compels capital in general to step up capital accumulation, extraction of surplus value and exploitation of labor, and feverishly to look for profits, over and above average profit: this is competition.

It is true that there is not only competition between capitalists, but also competition between capital and labor as well, i.e., the attempt of capitalists to replace living labor by "labor-saving" equipment, whenever there is full employment and the rate of exploitation (of surplus value) starts to decline as a result of a more favorable relationship of forces between wage-labor and employers. But capitalists' attempts to stop this decline in the rate of surplus value is again not caused by their fundamentally "evil" or "antilabor" character, but by the *compulsion* of competition. If they let labor get away with "excessive" wage increases, their own rate of capital accumulation will decline, they will fall behind in the competitive race and be unable to introduce the most modern technology and finally be destroyed by their competitors.

Today's world is no longer a "purely" capitalist world, and political-military considerations have played an important role in motivating some of the key decisions of us imperialism during the last decades. Imperialism feels threatened by the spread of social revolution and wants to stop it by all means, including open warfare as in Korea and Vietnam. On the other hand, a *purely* politico-military explanation of the world involvement of us imperialism misses two important economic points: first, that the very nature of capital accumulation, under monopoly capitalism even more than under "laissez-faire" capitalism, creates an *economic compulsion* to worldwide expansion for capital; second, that the emergence of a capital surplus, inevitably linked with monopoly capitalism itself in the leading imperialist nations, creates a strong economic compulsion for building up a powerful arms industry and military establishment. The existence of noncapitalist states and of a powerful revolutionary upsurge in the colonial world gave these processes a *specific* form; but in themselves, they existed before the Second World War, and before the October revolution at that.

Two questions related to our subject arise from this summary repetition of some of the basic origins and features of imperialism. What are the effects of international capital accumulation upon imperialist competition and rivalry, under the specific circumstances of present-day world developments? What are their effects on class relations inside the United States?

The answer to the first question can be read in all statistics relative to basic international capital movements since the end of the Second World War. For twenty years now, capital export has been larger and more powerful than ever before, but it has been flowing primarily *between* imperialist countries, and not from imperialist to underdeveloped countries. The worldwide upsurge of liberation movements in the colonial and semicolonial countries has created a risk of loss of capital, which apparently more than offsets the still higher rate of profit which foreign capital enjoys in these countries. Inasmuch as the world domain of imperialism has been shrinking and not expanding, such a powerful international flow of capital, and in general the stepping up of capital accumulation during the past two decades (or, what is the same thing under capitalism, the higher rate of economic growth) could only lead to an intensification of competition, as well as to its necessary corollary, an intensification of capital concentration. The emergence of the "multinational corporation," as the leading form of organization of monopoly capitalism today, testifies *both* to stronger national competition and greater international concentration of capital.

The answer to the second question is less obvious and more controversial but the inner logic of capitalism leads us to the inescapable conclusion that as long as competition clearly and unilaterally operates in favor of U.S. imperialism, it can neither threaten the standard of living of the working class, nor shatter the relative stability of employment....

Thus monopolists would much sooner conquer their competitors' markets and undermine employment there, than to have huge overproduction and unemployment inside the United States. If a point is reached where the United States is forced to intensify exploitation of American workers, it will only be because this alternative course of action is being increasingly closed to it. Yet this again can only be explained because the correlation of competitive forces has become such that "export" of intensified exploitation is increasingly impossible....

The relationship of forces between various imperialist powers can develop greatly to the advantage of one and at the expense of another. A massive relative superiority on the European continent was possessed by Germany, in the periods 1900–1916, and 1937–1944, and by France in the period 1919–1923. But that does not transform the competitors of the predominant power into *semicolonial nations*, which have lost control over the means of production of their country. Such semicolonial nations only arise when in fact the *key industries and banks in the country are owned or controlled by foreign capitalists*, and when *for that reason*, the state itself fundamentally protects the interests of the foreign imperialist class, as against those of the "native" bourgeoisie....

In fact, if one studies the evolution of the interrelationship of forces between U.S. imperialism and its main foreign competitors, one has to conclude that the United States reached the zenith of its power at the end of the Second World War, and that its hegemony has ever since been in decline. Of course, it still retains a great *relative* superiority. This relative superiority might even increase again, if there is no sufficient international interpenetration of capital on a European scale, if "European" multinational corporations are not established for systematic competition with U.S.-based "multinational corporations" on relatively equal terms. But independent ownership of capital, independent control of the "internal market" and independent use of state power, are still basic characteristics of European and Japanese imperialists.

As for new interimperialist wars, which the late Joseph Stalin predicted in his political testament, they are indeed extremely unlikely to break out, but not for reasons of U.S. supremacy, but because *all* imperialist powers are threatened by a much more deadly menace then interimperialist competition: the menace of the noncapitalist part of the world expanding through new victorious revolutions. Against the so-called socialist countries and new revolutions, imperialist powers indeed have an attitude of collective solidarity....

Imperialist competition continues, and will continue, including some very ruthless developments indeed; but it will unfurl *within the framework* of that collective solidarity towards the common enemy. Yet within that framework, the law of uneven development continues to operate inexorably, causing the relative decline of previously supreme powers and the emergence of newly strengthened imperialist forces. The fate of U.S. imperialism's supremacy will be decided neither on the battle-field nor in the "Third World"—at least in the coming years. It will be decided by the capacity of Western European imperialists (and Japanese imperialists) to set up colossal corporations, equivalent in financial power and industrial strength to that of their us competitors. I do not say that this development has already taken place on a sufficient scale or that it is inevitable. I have elsewhere made clear the obstacles and resistances toward that process. I only state that, if it takes place, it will force U.S. imperialism greatly to intensify the exploitation of the American working class, under the pressure of competition.

The discussion on "ultraimperialism" is, in fact, an old one. It was initiated by Kautsky after the outbreak of the First World War, and received at that time a scathing reply by Lenin. It was revived during the mid-twenties by various Social Democrats (Hilferding, Vandervelde and others), celebrating the constitution of the world steel cartel as a triumph of "ultraimperialism" and "peaceful development"; the rebuff which history inflicted a few years later to that illusion is still well known by everybody.

Lenin's answer to the fallacy of "ultraimperialism" can be summarized in one formula: the law of uneven development. "It is sufficient to pose the question clearly to see that the answer can only be negative. For one couldn't conceive, under capitalism, any other basis for the division in zones of influence, of interests, of colonies, etc., than the *strength* of the participants of that partition, their economic, financial, military strength, etc. Now among these participants of partition, that strength changes in a different way, for under capitalism, *even* development of enterprises, of trusts, of industries, of countries, is impossible." Lenin adds: "But if one speaks about the 'purely economic' conditions of the epoch of finance capital, as about a concrete historical epoch situated in the beginning of the twentieth century, the best answer to the dead abstractions about 'ultraimperialism'...is to oppose to them the concrete economic reality of the present-day world economy. Kautsky's theory of ultraimperialism is completely void of meaning and can only, among other things, encourage the deeply mistaken idea...that the domination of finance capital *reduces* the inequalities and contradictions of the world economy, whereas in reality it *strengthens* them" (Lenin, 1946)....

The sapping of the dollar's strength by foreign military outlays has so changed the financial relationship of forces in favor of other major imperialist powers, that the U.S. government now undertakes systematic efforts to force them...to spend *more* on rearmament (i.e., to redivide and so the speak "internationalize" the common burden of defending the "borders of the capitalist world"). But this is inconceivable without a *military* strengthening of these powers...which again shifts the interimperialist relationship of forces at the expense of U.S. imperialism....

Our theory, at the contrary, does not lead to the subordination of any sector of the international working class to any sector of world capitalism. We stand for independent class struggle of the working class in all capitalist countries. We stand for independent organization of the working class, defending its own class interests and bent upon a socialist revolution. We do not preach to American workers that they should "ally" themselves with any sector of the ruling class, nor do we propose anything of the kind to European workers. To say that bourgeois ideas lie underneath such a clear strategy of independent working-class struggle is somewhat preposterous....

There is no doubt that we are living in an epoch of tremendous "socialization" end "internationalization" of productive forces, on a scale unexpected even by Lenin or in Lenin's time. There is no doubt that the *basic* contradiction in such an epoch is the contradiction between capital and labor, in the process of production itself, and that the direct road of the working class toward a socialist revolution in the industrialized imperialist countries will be not through a fight for wages, but through objective challenges against capitalist relations of production. We have been writing this for many years, and there is no reason to assume that this will not be true in the United States, too.

It is also evident that the very supremacy of U.S. imperialism at the end of the Second World War tended to involve the ruling class of the United States with all world contradictions of imperialism, and tended to introduce all these contradictions in some form into American society itself. In spite of all its accumulated wealth and reserves, even U.S. imperialism has proved itself unable in the long run to pay, at one and the same time, the costs of playing world gendarme, of introducing "reforms" into U.S. society in order to avoid an exacerbation of social tensions, and of financing a constant modernization of equipment to assure a rate of productive capital accumulation which would enable it to maintain its technological advance on all its competitors.

The growing crisis of American imperialism can only transform itself into a decisive crisis of American society through the mediation of a growing instability of the American economy. This is our key thesis. In this growing instability of the American economy, the loss of U.S. sovereignty over the whole imperialist world, the relative decline of U.S. economic superiority vis-à-vis its imperialist competitors, and the sharpening competition and redivision of the international capitalist market—of which the internal market of the United States is the most important single sector—will play an important role.

REFERENCES

Lenin, V.I. 1946. *Oeuvres Choisies*. Vol. I. Moscow: Editions en Langues Etrangeres.

28

IMPERIALISM IN THE DRIVE FOR CAPITALISM
Bill Warren

In juxtaposition to views about the negative impact of capitalism, Bill Warren, in his work Imperialism: Pioneer of Capitalism *returned to an emphasis on progressive aspects of capitalism and argued in favor of imperialism as a means for undermining precapitalist modes and promoting industrialization and growth. He criticized Lenin for emphasis on the possibility of capitalism in precapitalist societies which, he believed, led to "the underdevelopment fiction" of contemporary times. The following excerpt is from an article that is representative of his thinking at the time.*

IF the extension of capitalism into noncapitalist areas of the world created an international system of inequality and exploitation called imperialism, it simultaneously created the conditions for the destruction of this system by the spread of capitalist social relations and productive forces throughout the noncapitalist world. Such has been our thesis, as it was the thesis of Marx, Lenin, Luxemburg, and Bukharin. These names are cited, for the weight of their authority, but to restore historical perspective to the discussion. If the Comintern of 1928 and the Left generally came round to the opposite view, viz. that imperialism prevented indigenous capitalist industrialization, they did so not without reason. In certain dramatic cases, notably India, it appeared that imperialism, having initiated the process, was now using its political control to

From Bill Warren, "Imperialism and Capitalist Industrialization," *New Left Review* 81 (September–October, 1973) 41–43. Reprinted with permission of New Left Review.

hold back the forces it had set in motion. It can now be seen that the elements inhibiting capitalist industrialization, which operated in the period of political control, were comparatively short-lived and that the postwar period is witnessing the full reemergence of those elements of imperialism conducive to capitalist industrialization. This is partly an impersonal process and partly a matter of the deliberate policy of the imperialist countries; even when brought about in the first place through a defensive reaction. There are now more powerful forces at work than ever before which are spurring capitalist industrialization, and the various elements of imperialist control which exercised a retarding influence have largely disappeared.

No one can doubt that capitalist industrialization faces serious problems. But these are now rooted in the internal contradictions of underdeveloped countries, centered around agricultural stagnation, excessive urbanization, growing unemployment, and the "premature" spread of socialism prior to the development of industrial capitalism. An analysis of the internal contradictions in which these problems are rooted cannot be given here.

We have tried to stress the role of the social forces *compelling* industrialization rather than of the social forces *leading* industrialization. This is to break with much current Marxist thinking, which has consistently emphasized the importance to Third World capitalist development of a vigorous national bourgeoisie. As a corollary, the alleged lack of capitalist industrialization is regarded as a consequence of the effect of imperialism in stunting, distorting or otherwise preventing the healthy ("normal") development of a national bourgeoisie (Baran et al.). Once emphasis is placed on the many forces compelling industrialization, however, then we need no longer associate industrialization with any particular ruling class and specifically not with a national bourgeoisie conceived of as relatively well-developed within the interstices of imperialism (India). Significant capitalist industrialization may be initiated and directed by a variety of ruling classes and combinations of such classes of their representatives, ranging from semifeudal ruling groups (northern Nigeria) and including large landowners (Ethiopia, Brazil, Thailand), to bureaucratic-military elites, petty bourgeoisies, and professional and state functionaries (especially in Africa and the Middle East). These "industrializers" may themselves become industrial bourgeoisies or may be displaced by the industrial Frankensteins they have erected or they may become fused with them. In any event, the crucial point is this—that it is the characteristic of the postwar period throughout the underdeveloped world that the social forces compelling industrialization have developed with more massive impetus and greater rapidity than ever before in history and in many, if not most cases, clearly in advance of the development of a stabilized bourgeoisie. This partly explains the importance of the state in most underdeveloped countries where it often assumes the role of a bourgeois ruling class prior to the substantial development of that class.

PART FOUR

IMPACTS OF IMPERIALISM

RETROSPECT
AND
PROSPECT

29

WHATEVER HAPPENED TO IMPERIALISM?

Prabhat Patnaik

Patnaik reminds us that earlier concerns with imperialism during the 1960s and 1970s remain relevant in the face of new thinking, revisionism, and the contemporary silence about imperialism in Marxist debates. He believes that imperialism is as important today as in the past, yet the silence of Marxists, especially in the United States, is due to the very consolidation of imperialism. Any retreat from resisting imperialism, he argues, would lead to racist and fundamentalist reactions in the Third World.

AN OUTSIDER CANNOT HELP NOTICING a remarkable transformation that has taken place in the Marxist discourse in the United States over the last decade: hardly anybody talks about imperialism anymore. In 1974, I left Cambridge, England, where I was teaching economics, and have now returned to the West, this time to the United States, after fifteen years. When I left, imperialism occupied perhaps the most prominent place in any Marxist discussion, and nowhere was more being written about and talked about on this subject than in the United States—so much so that many European Marxists accused American Marxism of being tainted with "Third Worldism." Herbert Marcuse had written that advanced capitalism had manipulated its internal class contradictions to a point where the only effective challenge that could be launched

From Prabhat Patnaik, *Whatever Happened to Imperialism and Other Essays* (New Delhi: Tolika, 1995), pp. 102–104. Originally published in *Monthly Review* 42 (1990): 1–6. Reprinted with permission of Monthly Review Foundation.

against it (other than from students and marginal groups within) was in the "periphery." *Monthly Review* had a more or less similar position. And there was a veritable flood of books and articles written on the role of U.S. imperialism in the Third World. Many of these were no doubt somewhat naive, and some almost subscribed to a conspiracy theory; but they had vigor, and Marxists everywhere looked to the United States for literature on imperialism.

That is obviously not the case today. Younger Marxists look bemused when the term is mentioned. Burning issues of the day such as Eastern Europe *or perestroika* are discussed, but without any reference to imperialism. Radical indignation over the invasion of Panama or military intervention in Nicaragua and El Salvador does not jell into theoretical propositions about imperialism. And the topic has virtually disappeared from the pages of Marxist journals, especially those of a later vintage.

Curiously, this is not because any one has theorized against the concept. The silence over imperialism is not the aftermath of some intense debate where the scales tilted decisively in favor of one side; it is not a theoretically self-conscious silence. Nor can it be held that the world has so changed in the last decade and a half that to talk of imperialism has become an obvious anachronism. Of course, a decade and a half ago, half a million U.S. troops had only recently withdrawn from a bloody war in Vietnam, while nothing of the sort is happening now. But no Marxist ever derived the existence of imperialism from the fact of wars; on the contrary, the existence of wars was explained in terms of imperialism. Why a Vietnam has not happened since then is thus a separate matter; but the theoretical perspective in terms of which we saw Vietnam is after all a more basic question and can not be brushed aside just because no Vietnam has happened in the last fifteen years.

Moreover, while nothing on the scale of Vietnam has happened since then, plenty has happened and is happening to belie the proposition that the world today is in any way fundamentally different. There was the invasion of Grenada, and more recently the invasion of Panama, justified on the argument that the jurisdiction of a U.S. court extends to foreign countries as well. There has been the remarkable spectacle of the United States using its domestic social crisis, i.e., drug abuse among the youth, as an argument for violating the sovereignty of states across the entire Latin American continent, waging battles against peasants to alter their production decisions (even while demands for raising the prices of alternative crops to coca have met with a stubborn refusal). These are not stray incidents: the idea has been espoused quite openly that the United States can legitimately allow kidnappings or even assassinations of foreign nationals who may have been guilty of crimes according to U.S. laws. Just the other day, the U.S. Attorney General openly justified the kidnapping of a Mexican doctor accused of complicity in the assassination of a drug enforcement agent, on the grounds that for him American lives came first (imagine what would happen if India abducted the Board of Directors of Union Carbide, the multinational corporation whose gross negligence resulted in the loss of thousands of lives by methyl isocyanate poisoning in Bhopal). And above all, there have been the wars sponsored in Nicaragua and El Salvador, not to mention the perennial struggle with Cuba.

These to be sure are epiphenomena. International skullduggery is a symptom of imperialism, but not its essence. Imperialism, viewed as a fundamental set of economic relations characterizing the world, is also stronger today than ever before, at least in the postwar period. Some years ago, there was talk of a New International Economic Order. The underdeveloped countries, notwithstanding their profound differences, met at various forums and articulated demands for a change in international economic relations. The demands often did not amount to much, but today there has been a systematic "rolling back" (to use Dulles's phrase) of all such efforts. The Third-World Group of Seventy-Seven is in a shambles. Commodity prices continue to be at a disastrous low, forcing the underdeveloped countries to dissolve their united stand and appear before the Group of Seven advanced capitalist countries as individual supplicants. The low commodity prices have contributed much towards the "successful" control of inflation in advanced capitalist countries, just as they have contributed much toward an aggravation of malnutrition over large tracts of the Third World, most noticeably in Africa. (At a time when world food stocks were at a record high, Africa was experiencing acute food shortages; international agencies like the World Bank and much of the economics profession pontificated to the African Countries on their domestic policy "failures," which may, of course, have been there, but nobody talked of Africa's reduced purchasing power on account of the collapse of commodity prices.) And what is more, now a new offensive is on to force open Third World markets, not just for goods, as Rosa Luxemburg had noted, but for services as well. Underdeveloped countries which had taken the lead in opposing the inclusion of services in the GATT agenda have been singled out for pressure from the U.S. administration.

It is unnecessary to go on. The point is not, as is often made out, whether the persistence of underdevelopment is because of imperialism or because of internal contradictions in the Third World (which in any case represents an ill-formulated counterposing of the two); the point is not whether capitalism can survive without imperialism (a speculative question foreign to the Marxist method); the point is not even whether this or that theoretician of imperialism was correct (that is hagiography, not analysis). The point is the paradox that while the system of relations covered under the rubric of imperialism has hardly changed over the last decade and a half, fundamental questions are discussed today, even among Marxists, without any reference to it. Yesterday's Marxists in Eastern Europe may have stopped talking about imperialism today for a variety of reasons. Mr. Gorbachev may have written a whole book called *Perestroika* without a single reference to imperialism. But why should American Marxists, who are under no constraints to emulate their Soviet and Eastern European counterparts, fall into the same deafening silence on the question?

The reason, one is tempted to speculate, lies precisely in the very strengthening and consolidation of imperialism. Vietnam was a crisis for imperialism. The fact that the United States had to send half a million troops to attempt to subdue a tiny country was itself an expression of a failure to "manage" things there; the fact that it lost the war only underscored the failure. Since then, however, there has been no comparable crisis. Imperialism has learned to "manage" things better; the very price the people of Vietnam had to pay to win the war has perhaps had a subduing influence on other Third World countries. They have also learned that the odds are heavily against them in other ways as well. The emancipation of the Third World, as almost everybody, whether in the first or the Third World, now realizes, resembles an obstacle race where the horse must fall at one of the obstacles. First, the coming to power of a revolutionary government is itself blocked in several ways;

if perchance it does come to power, an economic blockade is imposed upon it; the disaffection generated by social reforms and economic hardships, which are inevitable, is then utilized to foment a civil war; even if the government succeeds in winning the civil war, unable to rebuild its shattered economy with the meager resources at its command, it must go abroad for loans, at which point agencies like the International Monetary Fund and the World Bank come in, demanding a reversal of the reforms. While some years ago, there were dreams all over the Third World of socialism of all kinds, not just Marxian socialism, but Nehruvian socialism, Nyerere's socialism, Jagan's socialism, and the like; today we find the drab grey of IMF conditionalities" painted all over the third world (and even in the erstwhile socialist world). Many, of course, would say that this is because of the "follies" of the post-liberation regimes in the Third World. This argument, to use our earlier analogy, amounts to saying that if the horse could not clear all the obstacles, then it is the horse's fault. Maybe, but I would like to believe that the horse, if it is well-trained and intelligent, can clear all these obstacles. The point is a different one: we should not, in our enthusiasm for blaming the horse, become blind to the obstacles. And the very fact that imperialism has been so successful in putting up obstacles, has been so adept at "managing" potential challenges to its hegemony, has made us indifferent to its ubiquitous presence. Imperialism has learned that half a million troops do not have to be dispatched everywhere; and unless there are half a million troops dispatched somewhere, moral indignation is not widespread, and the reality of imperialism goes unrecognized. It is an irony of history that coercion which is so effective that it can afford to be silent is scarcely recognized as such; it is only on occasions when its effectiveness is diminished to a point where it has to come out in the ugliest of colors that its reality becomes apparent. The deafening silence about imperialism in the current Marxist discourse, especially in this country, is thus a reflection of the extraordinary strength and vigor it is displaying at present.

As Louis Althusser once remarked, however, apropos the French Communist Party's abandonment of the concept of the "dictatorship of the proletariat," theoretical concepts are not like a pair of old shoes that you can discard when you like; they come back to haunt you. In this case, we are talking about a concept which would come back to haunt us in a particularly vicious manner. Thanks to the fact of imperialism, the possibility of revolutionary transformation within the metropolitan countries has greatly receded. The theoretical blow that downplaying the concept would strike against Third World revolutionary movements cannot but enforce a practical retreat on their part. If there is such a retreat, the reality of imperialism would only mean that the right-wing opposition to it within the Third World would get strengthened. In other words, a weakening of the revolutionary opposition to imperialism would spawn racist, fundamentalist, and xenophobic movements in the Third World.

30

CAPITALISM AND GLOBALIZATION
William K. Tabb

This essay argues that globalization and internationalization of the economy have always been at the center of capitalism, and this emphasis is evident in Marx and Engels, especially their Manifesto. *Tabb shows that the state remains strong in the face of attention to a growing international economy, and he offers a critique of the globalization thesis, arguing that capitalism has always been a global system.*

THE GLOBALIZATION HYPOTHESIS IS THAT there has been a rapid and recent change in the nature of economic relations among national economies which have lost much of their distinct claim to separate internally driven development, and that domestic economic management strategies have become ineffective to the point of irrelevance. Internationalization is, in this view, seen as a tide sweeping over borders in which technology and irresistible market forces transform the global system in ways beyond the power of anyone to do much to change. Transnational corporations (TNCs) and global governance organizations, such as the World Bank and the IMF, enforce conformity on all nations no matter their location or preferences....

There is a great deal of difference, however, between the strong version of the globalization thesis which requires a new view of the inter-

From William K. Tabb, "Globalization Is *an* Issue, the Power of Capital Is *the* Issue," *Monthly Review* 49 (June 1997): 20, 21–24, 26–27, 28–29. Copyright © 1997 by Monthly Review Press. Reprinted with permission of Monthly Review Foundation.

national economy as one that "subsumes and subordinates national-level processes," and a more nuanced view which gives a major role to national-level policies and actors, and the central position not to inexorable economic forces but to politics. In the second perspective, current changes are considered in a longer historical perspective and are seen as distinct but not unprecedented, and as not necessarily involving either the emergence of, or movement toward, a type of economic system which is basically different from what we have known.

It is important to see that the first version of the globalization thesis is based on a myth, has profound political implications which are defeatist, and is not based on a sound analysis of what is a more complex and contestable set of processes. Thus the discussion of globalization is best undertaken as a two-step process. The first need is to critique the strong version of globalization which has disempowered much of the left. That is the task of this essay. The second step is to look more carefully at what *is* new in the present conjuncture. Capitalism is an ever-changing system, and it is necessary to base political strategy on an awareness of the nature of developments in the present period. But first we must address the defeatist acceptance of inexorable global capital hegemony.

Much of the U.S. labor movement has embraced the strong version of globalization, placing almost exclusive emphasis on runaway shops and the threat of low wage production venues in the Third World to American workers. Capital will go anywhere in the world seeking the lowest possible wages. But this is at best an oversimplification. It misrepresents the actual investment patterns of transnationals. Three-fourths of foreign investment and production by U.S.-based multinationals is in Western Europe, Canada, and other high wage countries and this investment is overwhelmingly to service these markets from local production sites. As for capital leaving the United States, it is important to recognize that since 1990 the United States has been a net importer of foreign direct investment, as the TNCs of other nations have located production in this country and employed American workers. The huge American balance of payments deficit is largely a result of borrowing and the U.S. role as consumer of last resort, the market which absorbs imports paid for with borrowed money. The United States absorbs almost half of manufactured exports from what is anachronistically still called the Third World. U.S. corporations have benefited from such policies and from the popular confusion between national well-being and the competitiveness of U.S.-based companies.

Production by TNCs outside their country of origin is important, yet 85 percent of industrial output is produced by domestic corporations in a single geographic location. The multinationals account for about 15 percent of the world's industrial output. Moreover, while much of the Left focuses on runaway shops to low wage venues, transnational capital avoids really low wage production sites, and indeed avoids investing in most developing countries. Nearly two-thirds of the world's population is basically written off as far as foreign investment is concerned. Growing inequality is a result of the marginalization of most of the world's population. Between 70 and 100 countries are worse off now than they were in 1980, according to UN figures. Greater incorporation into the international economy even for the so-called miracle economies does not necessarily last. A decade ago the development journals all produced special issues on Korea, the most successful of the New Industrial Economies. Today they carry stories about the parlous state of the Korean economy and the growing bankruptcies of the over leveraged *chaebols*. The fragility engendered by uncontrolled competition produces uncertainty at best, and often disaster for workers everywhere.

In any event, direct labor costs are not a big part of the price of many products and low wages alone are rarely decisive for most producers (although they are important in particular industries, for examples, garment producers and electronics assembly.) The major factor in the loss of manufacturing jobs is technological change. Domestic U.S. manufacturing output today is five times what it was in 1950 even as fewer workers are needed by the manufacturing sector. This is overwhelmingly the result of labor displacing technology, not of runaway shops. The lack of unionization in the fast-growing high-tech industries weakens all workers. The importance of such growth has also contributed to growing inequality in the U.S. economy.

THE LONGER PERSPECTIVE

Capitalism has always been a global system even if the particular ways the world economy affects workers in particular places changes over time. Economic historians ask us to see the present in such a perspective. The world's political economy is not more globalized than it was a hundred or a hundred and fifty years ago. Rereading *The Communist Manifesto* makes the point.

> The bourgeoisie has through its exploitation of the world-market given a cosmopolitan character to production and consumption in every country....In place of the old local and national seclusion and self-sufficiency, we have intercourse in every direction, universal interdependence of nations....In a word, it creates a world after its own image.

Such integration was clear even before cross oceanic telegraph cables integrated world markets and steel hulled steamers replaced wooden sailing ships; and such innovations in historical perspective were certainly more important in reorienting global production than air freight and containerization a century later. From such a large historical perspective one can conclude that: "If the theorists of globalization mean that we have an economy in which each part of the world is linked by markets sharing close to real-time information, then that began not in the 1970s but in the 1870s" (Hirst and Thompson, 1966, pp. 9—10). As to the huge sums of money moving around the globe at the push of a computer terminal button, economic historians find greater openness to capital flows at the beginning of the twentieth century (before World War I) than in the present period at century's end. Researchers find no increase in openness between 1875 and 1975, but rather a relative decline in capital movements. Bob Zevin concludes after a review of the evidence: "All these measures of transnational-securities trading and ownership are substantially greater in the years before the First World War than they are at present. More generally, every available description of financial markets in the late nineteenth and early twentieth centuries suggests that they were more fully integrated than they were before or have been since" (Zevin, 1992, pp. 5—12). Nontradables have grown as a proportion of total output between the beginning and end of the present century with the ever growing importance of locally consumed services (including those produced by governments).

Multinational manufacturing firms appeared in the middle of the nineteenth century and were well established by the beginning of the twentieth century. Two world wars and a great depression created what Eric Hobsbawm in his work on the "short" twentieth century has described as an interlude of national economics between eras of internationalized economics. In this reading, once recovery from world war and global depression were complete, what took place was not some new departure but a return to trend. Capital flows do not today influence economic development to the extent they did in the nineteenth century, and the world, as we have seen, is not more globalized today than a century ago. It is, however, in basic ways different than it was a half century ago and it is this lived memory which is the general referent for much of the discussion today. It is useful to see the ways in which the national Keynesian Welfare State political economy which emerged out of the trauma of war and global depression has eroded, and the extent to which we are back to pre-Keynesian economics and the ideological hegemony of laissez faire.

THE TRIUMPHS OF LAISSEZ FAIRE IDEOLOGY AND POLICY

The current offensive of capitalist logic into all realms of social life undermine many of the legitimation functions of the state which have provided citizen loyalty for the accumulation patterns of the capitalist system. The demand that everything be done through the market (that college tuition not be subsidized by the state, that legal aid should be abolished, public housing discontinued, and health care provided through the market) all represent attacks on programs which have broad support. But the self confidence with which market ideologists attack any sense of public space, of solidaristic provision of services and shelter from the relentless individualistic values of the market, represents a measure of the defeat of democracy. Similarly, the devolution of service provision in the United States from the federal to the state to the local levels, and then to individual procurement based on ability to pay, undermines the limited solidarities which hold society together. These processes have little to do with globalization, and a great deal to do with the victories of capital over labor, and the resulting damage to the rights of citizenship.

After thirty years during which wages have lagged behind prices, for the head of the Federal Reserve to claim that job insecurity is easing and so it is time to slow the economy is one of the clearest indicators of the triumph of capital in our era. In point of fact, America's corporations, whose profits adjusted for inflation have gone up by 50 percent since 1991, continue to both lay off and hire new workers. The defeat of progressive social policies and the decline in union strength means U.S. capitalism can have lower unemployment without rising wages. Even though jobs are relatively plentiful, new jobs are mostly bad jobs. They pay less than old ones; on average workers who get laid off and find new jobs receive fourteen percent less pay in their new jobs.

IT'S CAPITALISM, NOT GLOBALIZATION

In this context the idea that the state is powerless to stop these trends is a powerful tool of capital. The idea that "globalization" has weakened the state ignores the continuous technical ability of the state to regulate capital. Money can flee to tax havens and to offshore banking centers only if the core countries allow it to do so. If the United States penalized banks (and depositors) in jurisdictions which do not allow regulators access to information necessary to tax capital transfers, most tax haven banks would shut down. There is no reason regulators cannot impose transfer taxes and other regulations. It is the governments of the advanced nations, especially the United States and Britain which have encouraged deregulation. This was a political choice, not a technical necessity.

By insisting on basic workers' rights, the United States (which has done so much to undermine those rights) has the power to raise wages and improve working conditions everywhere. It is a *political* choice that the United States, in the name of free trade, encourages a race to the bottom. A counter hegemonic outlook of solidarity and social justice points to a very different set of rules. It is the ideological and organizational weakness of the Left which has lent power to the claims of globalists. It is not that U.S. employers do not routinely threaten to close plants and move to Mexico and elsewhere. They do, and such threats are effective in the current climate of labor regulation in the United States. But it is not international trade per se that is the problem but the political conditions under which that trade takes place.

Robin Blackburn in his new book, The Making of New World Slavery, informs us that by 1770 profits derived from slavery furnished a third of British capital formation. In what might be called a new international division of labor, slaves produced rice, coffee, sugar, and other products central to the living standard and personal fortunes of many Europeans. What is interesting is not how much globalization changes things but the continuities in capitalist mentality and practices. As Eric Foner has written: "Today's Chinatown sweatshops and Third World child labor factories are the functional equivalent of colonial slavery in that the demands of the consumer and the profit drive of the entrepreneur overwhelm the rights of those whose labor actually produces the saleable commodity" (Foner, 1997, p. 28). Working people have always resisted such demands. At the end of the twentieth century resistance will be stronger to the extent to which we do not allow the scarecrow of "globalization" to disempower us. The system is the same, its logic is the same, and the need for workers of the world to unite has never been greater. It is time for greater clarity in our critique of the basic workings of what are called "free markets" but are in reality class power. We need to counterpoise the need to control capital and to have the economy serve human needs rather than accept the continuous sacrifice of working people to such ideological constructions as competitiveness, free markets, and the alleged requirements of globalization.

REFERENCES

Foner, Eric. 1997. "Plantation Profiteering," The Nation (March 31).

Hirst, Paul, and Grahame Thompson. 1996. Globalization in Question: The International Economy and the Possibilities of Governance. Cambridge: Polity Press.

Zevin, Robert. 1992. "Our World Financial Market is More Open? If so, Why and with What Effect?" In Financial Openness and National Autonomy; Opportunity and Constraints. Edited by Tariq Banuri and Juliet B. Schor. New York: Oxford University Press.

BIBLIOGRAPHY

Amin, Samir. *Accumulation on a World Scale: A Critique of the Theory of Underdevelopment.* 2 vols. New York: Monthly Review Press, 1974.

———. *Unequal Development: An Essay on the Social Formations of Peripheral Capitalism.* New York: Monthly Review Press, 1976.

———. *Imperialism and Unequal Development.* New York: Monthly Review Press, 1977.

Arrighi, Giovanni. *The Geometry of Imperialism.* London: Verso, 1978.

———. *The Lone Twentieth Century: Money, Power, and the Origins of Our Times.* London: Verso, 1994.

Avineri, Shlomo. *Karl Marx on Colonialism and Modernisation.* New York: Anchor Books, 1969.

Bagchi, Amiya Kumar. *The Political Economy of Underdevelopment.* Cambridge, England: Cambridge University Press, 1982.

Baran, Paul A. *The Political Economy of Growth.* New York: Monthly Review Press, 1957.

Baran, Paul A., and Paul M. Sweezy. *Monopoly Capital.* New York: Monthly Review Press, 1966.

Barratt Brown, Michael. *The Economics of Imperialism.* Harmondsworth, England: Penguin, 1974.

Becker, David G., et al. *Postimperialism, International Capitalism, and Development in the Late Twentieth Century.* Boulder: Lynne Rienner, 1987.

Blaut, James. *The Colonizer's Model of the World: Geographical Diffusionism and Eurocentric History.* New York: Guilford, 1993.

Brenner, Robert. "The Origins of Capitalist Development: A Critique of Neo-Smithian Marxism," *New Left Review* 104 (July—August), 25—92.

Brewer, Anthony. *Marxist Theories of Imperialism.* London: Routledge and Kegan Paul, 1980, 1990.

Bukharin, Nikolai. *Imperialism and World Economy.* New York: Monthly Review Press, 1973.

Bukharin, Nikolai, and Rosa Luxemburg. *Imperialism and the Accumulation of Capital: An Anti-Critique.* New York: Monthly Review Press, 1972.

Caldwell, Malcolm. *The Wealth of Some Nations.* London: Zed Press, 1977.

Cardoso, Fernando Henrique. "Associated Dependent Development." In *Authoritarian Brazil.* Edited by Alfred Stepan. New Haven, Conn.: Yale University Press, 1973.

Cardoso, Fernando Henrique, and Enzo Faletto. *Dependency and Development.* Berkeley: University of California Press, 1979.

Chilcote, Ronald H. *Theories of Development and Underdevelopment.* Boulder: Westview Press, 1984.

Chilcote, Ronald H., ed. *The Political Economy of Imperialism: Critical Appraisals.* Boston: Kluwer Academic Publishers, 1999.

Cohen, Benjamin J. *The Question of Imperialism: The Political Economy of Dominance and Dependency.* New York: Basic Books, 1973.

Emmanuel, Arghiri. *Unequal Exchange: A Study of the Imperialism of Trade.* New York: Monthly Review Press, 1972.

Escobar, Arturo. *Encountering Development: The Making and Unmaking of the Third World.* Princeton: Princeton University Press, 1995.

Fann, K. T., and Donald C. Hodges, eds. *Readings in U.S. Imperialism.* Boston: Porter Sargent Publisher, 1971.

Fieldhouse, David K. *The Theory of Capitalist Imperialism.* London: Longman, 1967.

Foster-Carter, Aiden. "From Rostow to Gunder Frank: Conflicting Paradigms in the Analysis of Underdevelopment," *World Development* 4 (March 1976): 167–90.

Frank, André Gunder. *Capitalism and Underdevelopment in Latin America.* New York: Monthly Review Press, 1967.

Furedi, F. *The New Ideology of Imperialism: Renewing the Moral Imperative.* London: Pluto Press, 1994.

Furtado, Celso. *Development and Underdevelopment.* Berkeley: University of California Press, 1964.

Galtung, Johan. "A Structural Theory of Imperialism." *Journal of Peace Research* 7, no. 2 (1971): 81–117.

Gerschenkron, A. *Economic Backwardness in Historical Perspective.* Cambridge: Harvard University Press, 1966.

Gerstein, Ira. "Theories of World Economy and Imperialism." *Insurgent Sociologist* 7 (spring 1977): 9–22.

Griffin, Keith, and John Gurley. "Radical Analyses of Imperialism, the Third World, and the Transition to Socialism: A Survey Article." *Journal of Economic Literature* 23 (September 1985): 1089–1143.

Hayter, Teresa. *Aid as Imperialism*. Harmondsworth: Penguin Books, 1971.

Hilferding, Rudolf. *Finance Capital: A Study of the Last Phase of Capitalist Development*. London: Routledge and Kegan Paul, 1981.

Hobsbawm, Eric. *The Age of Empire*. New York: Pantheon, 1995.

Hobson, J. A. *Imperialism: A Study*. Ann Arbor: University of Michigan Press, 1965.

Hoxha, Enver. *Imperialism and Revolution*. Chicago: World View Publications, 1979.

Hunt, Diana. *Economic Theories of Development: An Analysis of Competing Paradigms*. Hemel Hemstead, England: Harvester Wheatsheaf, 1989.

Kay, Cristóbal. *Latin American Theories of Development and Underdevelopment*. London: Routledge, 1989.

Kay, Geoffrey. *Development and Underdevelopment: A Marxist Analysis*. London: Macmillan, 1975.

Kruijer, Gerald J. *Development through Liberation*. Atlantic Highlands, N.J.: Humanities Press International, 1971.

Landes, David. *The Wealth and Poverty of Nations: Why Some Are So Rich and Some So Poor*. New York: W.W. Norton, 1998.

Larraín, Jorge. *Theories of Development: Capitalism, Colonialism, and Dependency*. London: Polity Press, 1989.

Lenin, V. I. *Imperialism, the Highest Stage of Capitalism*. New York: International Publishers, 1937.

Lichtheim, George. *Imperialism*. New York: Praeger, 1971.

Löwy, Michael. *The Politics of Combined and Uneven Development: The Theory of Permanent Revolution*. London: Verso, 1981.

Luxemburg, Rosa. *The Accumulation of Capital*. London: Routledge and Kegan Paul, 1951.

Magdoff, Harry. *The Age of Imperialism: The Economics of U.S. Foreign Policy*. New York: Monthly Review Press, 1969.

———. *Imperialism: From the Colonial Age to the Present*. New York: Monthly Review Press, 1978.

Mandel, Ernest. *Late Capitalism*. London. New Left Books, 1975.

Miles, Gary B. "Roman and Modern Imperialism: A Reassessment." *Comparative Studies in Society and History* 32 (October 1990): 629–59.

Palloix, Christian. *L'Internalisation du Capital*. Paris: François Maspero, 1975.

Patnaik, Prabhat. *Whatever Happened to Imperialism and Other Essays*. New Delhi: Tolika, 1995.

Rhodes, Robert I., ed. *Imperialism and Underdevelopment: A Reader*. New York: Monthly Review Press, 1970.

Rodney, Walter. *How Europe Underdeveloped Africa.* London: Bogle L'Ouverture Publications and Dar es Salaam: Tanzania Publishing House, 1972.

Santos, Theotônio dos. *Imperialismo y dependencia.* Mexico City: Ediciones Era, 1978.

Schumpeter, Joseph. *Imperialism and Social Classes.* New York: World Publishing, 1955.

Smith, Tony. *The Pattern of Imperialism: The United States, Great Britain, and the Latin-Industrializing World Since 1815.* New York: Cambridge University Press, 1981.

Szymanski, Al. *The Logic of Imperialism.* New York: Praeger, 1981.

Taylor, John G. *From Modernization to Modes of Production: A Critique of the Sociologies of Development and Underdevelopment.* London: Macmillan, 1979.

Wallerstein, Immanuel. *The Modern World System.* 3 vols. New York: Academic Press, 1974–1979.

Warren, Bill. *Imperialism: Pioneer of Capitalism.* London: New Left Books, 1980.

CONTRIBUTORS

SHLOMO AVINERI is a theorist whose writing helps us understand how Marx's writing is relevant to primitive accumulation and imperialism in the third world.

PAUL BARAN (1910—1964), born in Russia, was a professor of economics at Stanford University and known for his writings on backwardness and surplus, including his popular *Political Economy of Growth* (1957).

ANTHONY BREWER is professor of the history of economics at the University of Bristol and author of several books, including *Marxist Theories of Imperialism* (1980 and 1990).

NIKOLAI BUKHARIN (1888—1938), a Russian Marxist theoretician and Bolshevik, wrote *Imperialism and World Economy* (1915).

AMÍLCAR CABRAL, a major African theorist and revolutionary, led the independence movement in Guinea Bissau and Cape Verde.

MALCOLM CALDWELL, a specialist on Asia, has published broadly on underdevelopment and imperialism.

FERNANDO HENRIQUE CARDOSO, a Brazilian sociologist and political econo-mist from São Paulo, wrote extensively on development questions, including imperialism and associated dependent capitalist development

ENRIQUE DUSSEL, a philosopher at the Universidad Autónoma de México, has systematically examined the original manuscripts and various edi-tions of Marx's work and is author of a multivolume guide to the *Grundrisse.*

ARGHIRI EMMANUEL elaborated on a theory of unequal exchange and extended Marx's theory of production prices to a study of the imperi-alism of trade in his seminal work, *Unequal Exchange* (1972).

ANDRÉ GUNDER FRANK is an economist and author of many books on underdevelopment and the world system. He is especially known for his thesis on the capitalist development of underdevelopment.

RUDOLF HILFERDING, an economist and Viennese Marxist, published his classic *Finance Capital* in 1910, a work that influenced Bukharin, Lenin, and others who elaborated a theory of imperialism.

JOHN ATKINSON HOBSON (1858—1940) published his classic *Imperialism: A Study* in 1902. His work influenced Lenin, Bukharin, Hilferding, and others who later wrote on imperialism. He appears to have been a socialist but was known as a liberal who was critical of capitalism and familiar with but critical of Marxist theory.

V. L LENIN (1870—1924), the Russian Marxist and Bolshevik revolutionary, led the Russian Revolution and was influenced by Marx. He wrote a political tract on imperialism and an analysis of capitalism in Russia.

ROSA LUXEMBURG (1871—1919), a German revolutionary and Marxist born in Russian Poland, wrote extensively on capitalist accumulation and engaged in debate with Bukharin over questions on imperialism.

KARL MARX (1818—1883), was a German thinker and author of *Capital* and coauthor with Freidrich Engels of *The Communist Manifesto.* He emphasized the labor theory of value, surplus value, and class struggle in an understanding that influenced thinkers of imperialism.

ERNEST MANDEL, a Belgian economist and Marxist, has written extensively on late capitalism and backwardness.

MANNING MARABLE, a professor of history and economics, extended Walter Rodney's thesis of underdevelopment in Africa to his study *How Capitalism Underdeveloped Black America* (1983).

RUY MAURO MARINI, a Brazilian political economist exiled for many years in Chile and Mexico, wrote on subimperialism and underdevelopment.

TERRENCE MCDONOUGH, a radical political economist, writes on structures of social accumulation and has published essays on the contributions of Lenin to an understanding of capitalist development.

KENZO MOHRI at the time of his writing on Marx and underdevelopment was a researcher at the Institute of Social Science, University of Tokyo.

GABRIEL PALMA, at the time of his writing on dependency, was associated with the Institute of Latin American Studies, University of London.

PRABHAT PATNAIK is a professor of economics at Jawaharial Nehru University, New Delhi, and writes on political economy and macroeconomic issues concerning developing countries.

THEOTÔNIO DOS SANTOS, a Brazilian political scientist and economist, has written broadly on underdevelopment and is especially known for his thesis on the new dependency.

JOSEPH SCHUMPETER (1883–1950), was an Austrian-American economist who focused on a theory of capitalist development and envisaged the end of imperialism.

PAUL SWEEZY is an economist and author of numerous books on capitalism and imperialism. He is founder and editor of the independent socialist journal *Monthly Review* in which he continues to update analysis of imperialism up to the new millennium.

WILLIAM K. TABB is a professor of economics at Queens College and of political science at the Graduate Center at the City University of New York.

BILL WARREN participated in debates on development by arguing that underdevelopment could be overcome through imperialism and capitalist development. Especially influential was his *Imperialism: Pioneer of Capitalism* (1980).

JOHN WILLOUGHBY is a professor of economics at American University in Washington, D.C., and has written extensively on the political economy of capitalist competition and the history of American imperialism.

ELLEN MEIKSINS WOOD is a professor of political theory at the University of Toronto and author of many books on capitalism and democracy. Recently she became an editor of the independent socialist journal, *Monthly Review*.

INDEX